AT THE PRESIDENT'S SIDE

AT THE PRESIDENT'S SIDE

The Vice Presidency in the Twentieth Century

EDITED BY TIMOTHY WALCH

UNIVERSITY OF MISSOURI PRESS

Columbia and London

Copyright © 1997 by
The Curators of the University of Missouri
University of Missouri Press, Columbia, Missouri 65201
Printed and bound in the United States of America
All rights reserved
5 4 3 2 1   01 00 99 98 97

Library of Congress Cataloging-in-Publication Data

At the President's side : the vice presidency in the twentieth century
/ edited by Timothy Walch.
    p. cm.
  Includes bibliographical references and index.
  ISBN 0-8262-1133-X (alk. paper)
    1. Vice-Presidents—United States—History—20th century.
  2. United States—Politics and government—20th century.   I. Walch,
  Timothy, 1947– .
  JK609.5.A7 1997
  973'.09'9—dc21   97-17515
                                                                CIP

∞ ™ This paper meets the requirements of the
American National Standard for Permanence of Paper
for Printed Library Materials, Z39.48, 1984.

Designer: Mindy Shouse
Typesetter: BOOKCOMP
Printer and Binder: Thomson-Shore, Inc.
Typeface: Palatino

IN MEMORY OF DONALD R. MCCOY
BELOVED PROFESSOR, PROLIFIC SCHOLAR, AND
DEVOTED PATRON OF PRESIDENTIAL LIBRARIES

Contents

Foreword   *John W. Carlin*   ix

Acknowledgments   xi

Introduction   *Timothy Walch*   1

I. The Fifth Wheel, 1905–1933

A Shadowed Office: The Vice Presidency and Its Occupants, 1900–1920
John Milton Cooper Jr.   9

The Republican Ascendancy: Calvin Coolidge, Charles Dawes, and Charles Curtis as Vice Presidents
Robert H. Ferrell   24

II. New Deal, Old Duties, 1933–1953

"Not Worth a Pitcher of Warm Piss": John Nance Garner as Vice President
Elliot A. Rosen   45

In the Shadow of FDR: Henry A. Wallace as Vice President
Richard S. Kirkendall   54

Seasoned Politicians: Harry S. Truman and Alben W. Barkley as Vice Presidents
Robert H. Ferrell   63

III. The Springboard, 1953–1963

"You Can Be President Someday": Richard M. Nixon as Vice President
Richard Norton Smith   79

Frustration and Pain: Lyndon B. Johnson as Vice President
Robert Dallek   88

IV. Tragedy and Crisis, 1965–1973

More Agony than Ecstasy: Hubert H. Humphrey as Vice President
Joel K. Goldstein   103

"I'll Continue to Speak Out": Spiro T. Agnew as Vice President
John Robert Greene 124

V. Recovery and Reflection, 1973–1981

Gerald R. Ford and Nelson A. Rockefeller: A Vice Presidential
Memoir
James Cannon 135

A New Framework: Walter Mondale as Vice President
Steven M. Gillon 144

VI. At the President's Side, 1981–1993

Looking Forward: George Bush as Vice President
Chase Untermeyer 157

Standing Firm: Personal Reflections on being Vice President
Dan Quayle 169

VII. Proximity and Power

Vice Presidents as National Leaders: Reflections Past, Present,
and Future
Richard E. Neustadt 183

Defining a Public Role for Vice Presidents: A Symposium
*Hugh Sidey, James Cannon, Robert H. Ferrell, Chase Untermeyer,
R. W. Apple Jr., and Richard E. Neustadt* 197

Guide to Further Reading
Timothy Walch 215

Notes on Sources 227

Notes on the Contributors 239

Index 243

Foreword

Presidents of the United States need little introduction. Even the more obscure presidents have their careers studied and reappraised or resurrected over the years. Vice presidents, on the other hand, often become nothing more than historical footnotes—unless they go on to become presidents.

In Kansas where I was raised, every child knew that Dwight D. Eisenhower of Abilene became president in 1953. But few among us had ever heard of Charles Curtis, the former Kansas senator who served as vice president of the United States from 1929 to 1933. Although Curtis had been only a heartbeat away from the presidency, he was lost to history and unknown to most Kansas schoolchildren and their parents.

Yet my government experience has taught me that, despite the relative obscurity of the position, few politicians turn down the opportunity to serve as vice president of the United States. Being elected vice president is often a stepping-stone to the presidency. Just since World War II, five vice presidents—Harry Truman, Richard Nixon, Lyndon Johnson, Gerald Ford, and George Bush—have gone on to become president. While it may not be glamorous, the vice presidency is an important training ground for national leadership.

I am pleased, therefore, to say a few words about this volume on the modern vice presidency. The essays that follow give historical context to the unusual individuals who served in the second highest office in the land during the twentieth century. Just as important, the book brings together in one volume information that is scattered across the country in dozens of libraries and archives.

This volume is the culmination of a conference held at the Herbert Hoover Presidential Library. One of the purposes of presidential libraries is to provide educational opportunities for scholars and citizens to gather to discuss civic issues of mutual interest. The broadcast of the conference by C-SPAN, the cable-satellite public affairs network, expanded this educational opportunity to millions more individuals.

I want to congratulate the staff of the Hoover Library and the scholars and journalists who contributed to the success of the conference. My thanks also goes to the Herbert Hoover Presidential Library Association and the University of Missouri Press for joining forces to bring the conference essays to a larger audience.

The presidential libraries, as part of the National Archives and Records Administration, ensure ready access to the essential evidence that documents the rights of American citizens, the actions of federal officials, and the national experience. The following essays draw upon those records to give direction and focus to our understanding of the vice presidency. As archivist of the United States, I am pleased that the National Archives and Records Administration could be a part of this enterprise.

—John W. Carlin
Archivist of the United States

Acknowledgments

A volume such as this one is the product of many hands. All but two of these essays were first prepared for a conference on the vice presidency held at the Hoover Library on October 25 and 26, 1995. "At the President's Side: Historical Perspectives on the Vice Presidency" brought together journalists, scholars, and former public officials to discuss the history of the vice presidency in this century and wrestle with the problems of choosing and using our vice presidents in the future. The quality of the essays that follow is a reflection of the success of this conference.

I also want to recognize the contributions of those who served as session chairmen during the conference: Lewis J. Bellardo, Deputy Archivist of the United States; Herbert A. Wilson, President of the Herbert Hoover Presidential Library Association; Ellis Hawley, Professor Emeritus of History at the University of Iowa; John H. Taylor, Director of the Richard M. Nixon Presidential Library and Birthplace; Frank H. Mackaman, Executive Director of the Everett McKinley Dirksen Congressional Leadership Research Center; and David Alsobrook, Director of the George Bush Presidential Materials Project. They did a superb job of asking penetrating questions and keeping the conference on schedule.

Many groups worked behind the scenes to make the conference run smoothly. I was particularly proud of the contributions made by the docents of the Hoover Presidential Library, who greatly eased the burden of planning and conducting a conference of this magnitude. Recognition goes to Donna Dean, John Brandt, Betty Burton, Marilyn Smith, John Langenhan, Phyllis Langenhan, Bill Oglesby, Sharon Oglesby, Cora Pedersen, Carolyn Huff, Eleanor Luckel, Gertrude Macqueen, Ruth Greenwald, Phyllis Knoche, Chet Doyle, Bob Holtzhammer, Shirley Sondergard, Charles Swisher, and JoAnn Torpey for all their fine work.

Above all, however, the conference succeeded due to the tireless efforts by the combined staffs of the Hoover Presidential Library Association, the Herbert Hoover National Historic Site, and the Hoover Presidential Library-Museum. Their willingness to work long, hard, and harmoniously was as commendable as it was predictable. Special plaudits go to Patricia Forsythe, Executive Director of the Library Association, who provided the conference funding and key advice and support; to Pat Hand, Cathy Grace, and Corinne James who handled registration for the conference and the arrangements for the vice presidential luncheon; and to Superintendent Carol Kohan for traffic control and logistical support. The continued support of the association and the historic site makes possible many vital library and museum activities.

Not enough can be said about the Hoover Library staff, the Public Building Service custodians, and the Hoover Library guard force. Each of these groups exhibited new talents and resiliency; each took on difficult assignments with enthusiasm. Would that I had the space to list all that they did during those two days; a list of their names will have to suffice: Rick Alderson, Don Barnhart, Jim Barnhart, Joan Cahill, Floyd Christianson, Jim Detlefsen, Mary Evans, Janlyn Ewald, Sylvia Ferguson, Joan Gibson, Maureen Harding, Pam Hinkhouse, Rosemary Hora, Roger MacDowell, Christine Mauw, Dale Mayer, Dwight Miller, Paul Mohr, Jennifer Pedersen, Kim Porter, David Quinlan, Dick Rex, Wade Slinde, Pat Wildenberg, and Cindy Worrell.

AT THE PRESIDENT'S SIDE

Introduction

TIMOTHY WALCH

Have pity on our poor vice presidents! This nation's first vice president, John Adams, called his job "the most insignificant office ever the invention of man contrived or his imagination conceived." And many of the forty-four men who succeeded him in the office have said much worse. Perhaps the humorist Finley Peter Dunne, in the guise of saloon keeper Martin J. Dooley, captured the office best when he said that the vice presidency was "not a crime exactly. You can't be sent to jail for it, but it's kind of a disgrace. It's like writing anonymous letters."

That is not much of a recommendation, even for an office that was an afterthought at the Constitutional Convention of 1787. Perhaps the biggest problem is that the job has a fancy title but few responsibilities. Other than presiding over the Senate, the vice president of the United States has no constitutional duties. In fact, it is not even clear whether the Founders of the Republic ever intended for the vice president to succeed to the presidency upon the death of an incumbent.

When the first Whig president, William Henry Harrison, died in 1841 after little more than a month in office, he was succeeded by his Democratic vice president, John Tyler. Had Whig Party leaders given any thought to the possibility of succession, they never would have put Tyler on the ticket.

And poor Tyler! Sure, he was president, but he was also the most despised man in Washington. The Democrats considered him a traitor to their party's cause, and Whigs thought of him as a turncoat Democrat who was not to be trusted. Worse still, the pundits lampooned Tyler by referring to him as "His Accidency." There is an old maxim that says "It is lonely at the top," but few men have had lonelier tenures as president than John Tyler.

The nature of the job and the quality of the men selected for the vice presidency did not change much throughout the nineteenth century. Vice presidents continued to be political afterthoughts: men selected to balance

1

national tickets in the hope of winning a few more electoral votes. Never were these men considered heirs apparent to the presidency.

Millard Fillmore, Andrew Johnson, and Chester Arthur suffered much the same fate as Tyler when they succeeded to the presidency. Fillmore followed Zachary Taylor and made a serious effort to master the job, but Fillmore was so despised by the Whigs that they refused to nominate him for a term of his own.

Johnson took office after the assassination of Abraham Lincoln and attempted to act with presidential authority. For his efforts, Johnson was impeached by the House of Representatives and came within one vote of being convicted in the Senate. Needless to say, Johnson's time in the White House was a bitter experience.

Few Americans remember Chester Alan Arthur these days. To be sure, Thomas Reeves has produced an exceptional biography of this largely forgotten president, but to little avail. A New York politico, Arthur was selected to run for the vice presidency to balance the presidential nomination of James A. Garfield of Ohio. At least Arthur did not disparage the job! In fact, he considered his election as vice president "a greater honor than I have ever dreamed of attaining." Had Garfield not been killed, it is unlikely that Arthur would have ever been considered for the presidency. "Chet Arthur, President of the United States!" one of his friends was heard muttering just after hearing the news of Garfield's death. "Good God!" As Reeves notes in his book, Arthur was a better president than had been expected. But that is hardly a ringing endorsement.

The first accidental president of the twentieth century was Theodore Roosevelt, and he broke the mold of vice presidential mediocrity. He had been nominated as William McKinley's vice president to "kick him upstairs." As governor of New York, Roosevelt had been a source of real irritation to the state's Republican Party leadership. The vice presidency was supposed to end Roosevelt's political career. "It is your duty to the country," McKinley was told by one party leader, "to live for four years."

But assassinations have a way of upsetting such political schemes. On September 6, 1901, at the Pan American Exposition in Buffalo, William McKinley was shot at point-blank range and died eight days later. What a tragedy! Worse still, the Republican Party leadership had inadvertently put Theodore Roosevelt in the White House! But unlike his predecessors, Roosevelt became a great president and won election to a term of his own.

The next man to succeed to the presidency as the result of another man's misfortune was Calvin Coolidge. Although he was well liked during his years in office, and won his own term as president, Coolidge has been given fairly low marks by historians. "Silent Cal" is often caricatured as a do-nothing president who allowed American business to lay the foundation for the Great Depression.

The men who followed Coolidge as vice president are all but lost to history. Who remembers Charles Gates Dawes or cares about Charles Curtis? Even Franklin Roosevelt's first two vice presidents, the colorful "Cactus Jack" Garner and the idealistic Henry A. Wallace, are not much remembered these days. Garner is best remembered for having compared the vice presidency unfavorably to "a pitcher of warm piss," and Wallace is remembered for being too liberal for the Democratic Party!

The man who succeeded Franklin Roosevelt on April 12, 1945, also was unknown to the American people. "Harry who?" many people asked. The fate of the free world had been put in the hands of a former Missouri senator named Harry S. Truman. The nation was shocked, and so was Truman. He told the press corps that he felt as if a bale of hay had just fallen on his head. He had been vice president for little more than ten weeks, and now he was the leader of the free world! But like Theodore Roosevelt, Harry Truman grew into his presidency. He surrounded himself with good advisers, he was not afraid to take tough stands against the steel industry and labor unions, and he stood up for minorities by integrating the armed forces. Most important, he convinced the American people to give him a term of his own.

Harry Truman made a difference in the presidency, not the least of which was his vice presidential experience. Even though it was well known in Democratic circles that FDR's health was failing, little thought was given to briefing Truman on the issues facing the nation. It was only after Roosevelt's death, for example, that Truman learned of the existence of an extraordinary new weapon called an atomic bomb.

What if Truman had been incapable of leading the nation? The governance of the United States is too important to be left to chance. More care was needed in selecting vice presidents and keeping them informed of the administration's actions and policies.

Ironically, no one wanted to be Truman's vice president when he ran for reelection in 1948. Most of the pundits were predicting that Tom Dewey was an almost certain winner in the election of 1948, and no one in the

Democratic Party with much of a political future wanted to be associated with Truman. "To err is Truman" was the quip of the election. Alben Barkley got the vice presidential nomination by calling Truman and asking for it! And as we all know, everybody underestimated Truman and the genial Senate majority leader. Barkley, therefore, was something of an accidental vice president.

Beginning with Richard Nixon, the vice presidency has received increasing measures of attention. Election as vice president of the United States no longer is seen as the end of a political career; in fact, it has become a springboard to the presidency. Four of the ten men who have served in that office over the past forty years have gone on to the presidency.

The essays in this book are an effort to trace the evolution of the vice presidency in the twentieth century from Theodore Roosevelt to Dan Quayle. The first five chapters tell the stories of a unusual collection of characters chosen for their native states or their political acumen, but not for their leadership abilities.

The next four chapters form a mosaic of tragedy. Richard Nixon and Lyndon Johnson rose from the vice presidency to the presidency only to be forced from office. Hubert Humphrey was humiliated as vice president by a man who should have known better. And Spiro Agnew was rousted from the office by petty greed.

The following four chapters tell the story of a new vice presidency. Nelson Rockefeller, Walter Mondale, George Bush, and Dan Quayle redefined the job that not many people wanted but that few could refuse. Quayle's essay is particularly useful because he reflects on the checkered past of his predecessors, gives credit to Walter Mondale for rehabilitating the vice presidency, and tells of his working relationship with George Bush. He offers readers a unique glimpse of an office that is quickly becoming the second most powerful in the nation.

But what of the future of this "insignificant office"? In an outstanding essay, Richard Neustadt provides a detailed analysis of the nucleus of vice presidential power: proximity to the president. To whit, we have Neustadt's maxim: The power and influence of a vice president are inversely proportional to the political distance between that vice president and his president. The greater the distance the less the power. A panel of experts heartily concurred.

I know that all of the individuals who contributed to the "At the President's Side: Historical Perspectives on the Vice Presidency" conference join me in hoping that this volume will stimulate more serious discussion of an important issue and generate an increased awareness of the role of vice presidents in American public life. Perhaps the pages that follow serve as something of a civics lesson, bringing readers in closer contact with the ideas of historians, journalists, political scientists, and a former vice president. At its core, however, we hope that this volume will encourage public appreciation of history as a pathway to understanding what has been and what may come to pass.

I

THE FIFTH WHEEL, 1905–1933

When the party conventions met in 1920, less than one year after the president's incapacity, the vice presidential selections betrayed no concern about the nominees' qualifications to fill the top office through succession or replacement. . . . It would take another half century—replete with three more presidents' deaths in office and several other, albeit lesser, brushes with incapacity—before real changes would occur.

—John Milton Cooper Jr.

In the business of choosing the vice presidents during the 1920s, choices were made as haphazardly as in the decades before and as in those to follow. The simple truth was that vice presidents were afterthoughts and received little attention either from their running mates or from party leaders.

—Robert H. Ferrell

A Shadowed Office: The Vice Presidency and Its Occupants, 1900–1920

JOHN MILTON COOPER JR.

Three facts overshadow almost everything else about the vice presidency of the United States and the four men who served in the office during the first two decades of the twentieth century. First, only one of these incumbents gained a great place in American history. Ironically, he was the one who served the shortest time in the office, only six months, before an assassin's bullet elevated him to the White House. This was Theodore Roosevelt. The second overshadowing fact about the four holders of the office is that they came from just two states. Roosevelt and James Schoolcraft Sherman, who served under William Howard Taft, hailed from New York. Charles W. Fairbanks, who was vice president during Roosevelt's second term, and Thomas Riley Marshall, who served during Woodrow Wilson's two terms, were both from Indiana. The final overshadowing fact about the vice presidency during this period is that the worst crisis of presidential "inability," as the Constitution defines the condition, occurred then and in a way that bared the dangers lurking within the traditional neglect of the nation's second highest office.

Exceptional in just about everything he did, Theodore Roosevelt offered a glaring contrast to other vice presidents even before he assumed the office. No one had ever gotten the nomination the way he did. It is true that, before and after his time, parties chose their vice presidential candidates to balance their tickets. Geographical balance was the main consideration, which led to the virtually unbroken pairing of northeasterners and midwesterners by both major parties from the Civil War through World War II. Beyond such regional sharing little else dictated the choice of running mates once a convention had filled the top spot. Even in 1900 this geographical rule seemed the paramount reason for Roosevelt's vice presidential selection; his New York birth, residency, and governorship complemented William McKinley's Ohio origins.

Such conventional considerations, however, masked a revolutionary departure. Given the Republican Party's dominance in the Northeast in

9

1900, a plethora of governors, senators, and representatives were available as ticket balancers. What gave Roosevelt the lock on the nomination and what departed from every previous convention's choice was the popular strength that he brought to the ticket. As is well known, Sen. Thomas C. Platt, the New York State Republican boss, had schemed to remove his obstreperous, uncontrollable governor by kicking him upstairs into the vice presidency. Even without those machinations, however, the demand for this glamorous war hero among rank-and-file Republicans throughout the country would probably have thrust the nomination upon him anyway. The only opposition sprang from Roosevelt himself, who preferred to stay on as governor, and from President McKinley's confidant, Sen. Mark Hanna, who snapped at fellow Republican leaders, "Don't any of you realize that there's only one life between this madman and the Presidency?" But no one else seemed to share Hanna's concern. Predictably, the vice presidential nominee stole the show in the 1900 campaign, as he matched the Democratic candidate, William Jennings Bryan, in dash and energy and color, if not oratorical prowess, on the campaign trail.

Once elected and inaugurated, Roosevelt suffered the vice president's usual fate of neglect and indifference from the White House. In 1901, this preternaturally active, intelligent, curious forty-two-year-old man faced the problem of how to occupy his time. Again predictably, Roosevelt hatched at least two novel plans. One was to resume the legal studies that he had abandoned twenty years earlier for the twin excitements of politics and ranching. Because it might have been awkward for the vice president to enroll in law school or study with a private attorney, Roosevelt arranged to become the sole pupil of the chief justice, who was arranging a course of reading to start in the fall of 1901. His other plan consisted of enlisting professors at leading universities to improve the study of politics and government and to make involvement in public affairs more attractive to their students. Several faculty members met with him during the summer of 1901, and he contemplated more organized activities during the following year. One of Roosevelt's enthusiastic recruits in this venture was a professor at Princeton named Woodrow Wilson. Both of these academic ventures fell by the wayside with his accession to the presidency in 1901.

Theodore Roosevelt's abbreviated vice presidency remains an intriguing might-have-been. The plans that he made for occupying himself and involving others betrayed not only chafing at his office's institutionalized inactivity but also resourceful thinking about how to expand

and overstep its limits. The artistic and cultural patronage that characterized his presidency might well have begun around the same time but under a different aegis, thereby transcending the near invisibility of his office. Most important, with his shrewd, restless pursuit of power, Roosevelt might have brought off the seeming miracle that finally came to pass only in the second half of this century: turning the vice presidency into a launching pad for nomination and election to the presidency. Theodore Roosevelt rarely failed to be ahead of his time, even in his vice presidency.

The other three holders of the office in these decades never achieved much visibility, mainly because of bad luck on their part and partly because of the second major fact about them: their states of political origin. Their bad luck sprang from having risen to the vice presidency at a time when a galaxy of stars emblazoned the political firmament. Sometimes dubbed a "second golden age of American politics," the first twenty years of this century witnessed the flourishing of a pair of presidential giants, Roosevelt and Wilson, together with the impact of such heavyweight contenders as Bryan, Taft, Robert La Follette, Henry Cabot Lodge, Elihu Root, and Charles Evans Hughes. In that kind of company, it was small wonder that these three vice presidents seldom made much of a stir.

The other factor that contributed to their obscurity was their political base in just two states, New York and Indiana. Unlike Roosevelt, none of his three vice presidential successors appeared to have much claim over other aspirants except residency in a ticket-balancing region. There was nothing the matter with these two states as breeders of political talent in those days, as attested by the rise of New Yorkers such as Roosevelt, Root, Hughes, Henry Stimson, and later Al Smith, and Hoosiers such as Albert J. Beveridge, John W. Kern, and Will Hays. But the vice presidential selection of these three men really told more about the distribution of votes in the electoral college than about their own appeal. With the South's nearly all-white electorate and leadership still stigmatized by the Civil War and unshakably Democratic, both parties shunned that section as a source of potential nominees for the top places. Rather, because the Northeast and Midwest supplied more than enough votes for electoral-college and congressional majorities, both parties had usually devoted their energies and their ticket picking to those two regions. Since 1896, the emergence of Bryan and a southern/western coalition had partially altered the Democrats' strategy, but they reverted to nominating a northeasterner in 1904 and to selecting a northeastern/midwestern pair in 1912, 1916, and 1920.

In operation, the geography of ticket picking had an even tighter focus within this regional coalition. Electorally, from the end of the Civil War to the middle of the twentieth century, New York enjoyed a dominance unmatched by any state before or since. Twenty of the twenty-one presidential elections from 1868 to 1948 featured a resident of New York on a major party ticket. Fifteen of those elections put forward a New Yorker as the presidential choice, and the number rises to sixteen if Theodore Roosevelt's second-place finish in 1912 as the Progressive Party nominee is counted as a major-party candidacy. In two of these elections, 1904 and 1944, both presidential contenders hailed from the Empire State, and all but one of the elections without a denizen of that state at the top of the ticket included one as a vice presidential choice. Given its mother lode of electoral votes, New York's enjoying a reserved seat on national party tickets is easy to understand.

Not so readily apparent is the basis for Indiana's claim. By the standard of electoral riches, Ohio should have enjoyed a semipermanent place on the other end of the seesaw. Fittingly, for presidential nominations, the Buckeye State came in a respectable second, supplying the top choice in seven of the twenty-one elections from 1868 to 1948. Three of the five elections between 1900 and 1920 featured Ohioans as presidential candidates, and in 1920 both parties' nominees came from that state. Curiously, however, an Ohioan received the vice presidential nod only once, in 1944. The best explanation for why Indiana earned the nickname "home of vice presidents" in this era seems to lie in two circumstances. First, although it was not such a big electoral prize as Ohio, Hoosierdom had been a more hotly contested two-party state in national politics before 1896 and still was at the state level in these decades. Second and probably more weighty was the circumstance that in 1904 and 1912 two well-placed men happened to come from Indiana.

Of the three vice presidents of this era after Roosevelt, the one who least deserved his comparative obscurity was his immediate successor, the first of the two Hoosiers. This was Charles W. Fairbanks. At the time of his nomination in 1904, the fifty-two-year-old Fairbanks was the senior U.S. senator from Indiana, and he cut a formidable figure in his home state, on Capitol Hill, and in the national councils of the Republican Party. He also epitomized the party's ideal type at the end of the nineteenth century.

Literally born in a log cabin, Fairbanks had worked his way through college and law school and then amassed a large fortune in railroads, which he used to finance his political career. In the 1890s, he had skillfully risen to a dominant position in the state organization. He also became a close friend and early backer of McKinley and staked out ultraorthodox stands on the core party issues of sound currency and tariff protection. In 1897, Fairbanks won his first office, his Senate seat, by virtue of Republican majorities in the Indiana legislature. Once in Washington, he immediately joined the inner circle of congressional barons who allied themselves with President McKinley to rule their party at the national level.

That position as an insider, together with his closeness to McKinley, gave Fairbanks the preferred track for the vice presidential nomination in 1904. Roosevelt's adroit use of presidential patronage, along with his tremendous popularity and the death of Mark Hanna, his only possible rival for the top spot, allowed him to bring off his own political miracle by becoming the first vice presidential successor in American history to win his party's nomination. But his miracle exacted its price. Roosevelt recognized that the second spot would have to go to someone acceptable to party leaders, most likely to a person strongly identified with McKinley and his policies. With Hanna gone, no one filled the bill better than Fairbanks. In the months since McKinley's assassination, the Indiana senator had delivered the most widely noted and best received eulogies of the fallen president. Curiously, in view of the way in which he himself had come to the White House, Roosevelt took scant interest in choosing his running mate. When he first learned of the likelihood of Fairbanks's nomination, the president was privately unenthusiastic. "But," he wrote with resignation to Nicholas Murray Butler in March 1904, "who in the name of Heaven else is there?"

Judging by his actions, Roosevelt never changed that opinion. Because the customary ban on campaigning by a sitting president still held in 1904, Fairbanks bore the brunt of speaking and public appearances for the Republican ticket. By all accounts, he acquitted himself well, but neither those performances nor anything else persuaded Roosevelt to make much use of him during his vice presidency. This failure to employ Fairbanks better may have been a missed political opportunity. Elevation to the vice presidency had not changed the Hoosier's standing among his party's congressional leaders, who grew steadily more hostile toward Roosevelt and obstructionist toward his reform initiatives after 1904. Yet, at the same time, the vice president remained on good personal terms with the president. In those circumstances, Fairbanks could have served as a bridge between the two antagonistic Republican power centers. He might even have dampened the smoldering conflict that finally erupted into a civil war within the party during the presidency of Roosevelt's successor.

At all events, Fairbanks remained an important Republican leader for the rest of his life. Some of his fellow congressional barons put his name forward as a possible successor to Roosevelt in 1908. After leaving the vice presidency, Fairbanks returned to Indiana, where he once more wielded great clout among the state's now fratricidally factionalized Republicans. The strongest testimony to his political staying power came in 1916, when his name again surfaced as a potential presidential nominee and he received his second vice presidential nomination, also to complement a New Yorker, this time Charles Evans Hughes. The 1916 campaign was Fairbanks's last hurrah; he died less than two years later. In all, he remained an able politician to the end, although he seemed a bit outdated in the polarized, reformist, publicity-driven environment that predominated after 1904.

The next of these vice presidents probably best deserved his obscurity. "Sunny Jim" Sherman brought little besides balance to his party's ticket in 1908. The balance he supplied was obviously geographical, since as a New Yorker he complemented the Ohio roots and residency of the presidential nominee, William Howard Taft. Sherman also balanced the ticket factionally and ideologically. Like Fairbanks before him, the fifty-two-year-old representative nicely fitted the mold of McKinley-style congressional Republicanism. The son of a banker and newspaper publisher in Utica, Sherman had stayed in his home region to attend college and law school, to practice law and participate in family business ventures, and to serve as mayor of Utica before being elected to Congress in 1886. From then on, he made himself a loyal, hardworking lieutenant to successive Republican Speakers of the House and to his state's party bosses. Sherman was mainly a manager and parliamentary tactician, rather than a legislator and orator, and he remained largely unknown outside his own district and beyond the walls of the Capitol.

His vice presidential nomination in 1908 virtually replicated Fairbanks's four years earlier. When Taft learned of the prospect of Sherman's joining him on the ticket, he wrote to Charles Nagel in June 1908, "I am a great deal troubled about that. My own preference would be to have a man west of the Mississippi, . . . some western senator who has shown himself conservative and at the same time represents the progressive movement." That kind of Republican was exactly what the old-guard leaders did not want. For them, it was bad enough to have Roosevelt foist his handpicked successor on the party; they were not about to accept the sort of "progressive" Taft wanted. In the event, the presidential nominee declined to involve himself in choosing his running mate, despite pleas from reform-minded westerners. He acquiesced in Sherman's selection, although he confided to William R. Nelson the next month, "I know that you were just as much disappointed as I was." During the campaign Sherman dutifully worked the hustings, even though he was suffering from a kidney ailment. At one point he became an issue himself, when a magazine charged him with irregularities in an earlier congressional campaign and with making shady investments. Sherman ignored the attacks, and they evidently did little harm.

Taft also never raised his estimate of his vice president and made little use of him. This time, however, no political opportunity went begging. During Taft's presidency, the Republican Party broke asunder between the progressive insurgents on one side and the conservative old guard on the other. Ironically, Taft and Sherman wound up on the same conservative side, linked in opposition to Roosevelt, who contested Taft's renomination in 1912 and then bolted to run as the nominee of his new Progressive Party. Sherman's chief contributions to this political donnybrook consisted of continued active membership among the congressional barons and fierce opposition to Roosevelt's efforts to reassert his influence in the New York Republican Party. Common cause did not endear Sherman to Taft, although no question seems to have been raised about his renomination. The vice president took almost no part in the 1912 contest; early in the campaign he fell ill from his long-standing kidney ailment and died just a week before the election. In the end, Sherman left the national political scene almost as obscurely as he had entered.

By the measure of merited obscurity, the last of the post-Roosevelt trio stands in the middle, between the least and most deserving, and he presents a more complicated case for judgment. Thomas Riley Marshall, the second Hoosier, was the only Democrat among these four vice presidents and the only one to be elected to more than one term. He remains slightly better remembered than his two predecessors, although the memories of him do not enhance his historical reputation. Not surprisingly,

Marshall bore some resemblances to Fairbanks, with whom he maintained a friendship across party lines. Also from a family of modest means, he had worked his way through college, read law, and practiced successfully. Unlike his compatriot, however, he did not get rich or previously play a big role in his party's affairs. He ran for office for the first time in 1908, at the age of fifty-four, when Indiana's faction-riven Democrats nominated him as a compromise gubernatorial candidate. Narrowly elected in part through the efforts of liquor interests, Marshall proved to be a surprisingly strong, progressive governor. His office and record made him Indiana's "favorite son" candidate for his party's 1912 presidential nomination and a serious prospect to be a compromise choice in the event of a convention deadlock.

Although the Democrats did come close to deadlocking in 1912, Marshall eventually had to settle for second place. His vice presidential nomination repeated not only the experiences of his two predecessors but also one element of Roosevelt's as well. Marshall, too, had a party boss who wanted to get him out of their home state's politics. At a critical moment in the horse trading for the presidential nomination, that boss, Thomas Taggart, exchanged Indiana's votes for a promise from Wilson's managers that Marshall would get the second spot. Like Roosevelt and Taft before him, Wilson initially balked at his suggested running mate. "But," he remonstrated, " . . . he is a very small caliber man." Wilson's managers did not apprise the nominee of the promise to Taggart but argued that the need to balance the ticket geographically and carry Indiana made Marshall an ideal running mate. After a few minutes, Wilson relented, saying, "All right, go ahead." In the ensuing campaign, Marshall hit the hustings energetically but attracted little attention, particularly because the titanic clash and brilliant debate between Roosevelt and Wilson overshadowed everything else.

Nor did this vice president make much of a mark in office in 1913 and afterward. During Wilson's first term, the Democrats enjoyed comfortable, ideologically coherent majorities in Congress, and others, such as Bryan, who became secretary of state, and Marshall's fellow Hoosier, Sen. John W. Kern, who was majority leader, filled any role that the vice president might have enjoyed as a liaison with Capitol Hill. Like his predecessors, Marshall endured neglect from the White House, although he did substitute in ceremonial duties that the president found uncongenial. Also as before, nothing changed this vice president's low esteem in the eyes of his chief.

Marshall became, in fact, the only vice president in these decades to face a threat of being dumped from the ticket for reelection.

Starting in October 1915, rumors circulated about his replacement. One wire service story reported the president commenting, "It would be unlucky to run the same team twice." Marshall responded, "I don't believe the President said any such thing," and the White House issued a prompt denial. The matter did not end there, however. Right down to the Democratic convention in June 1916, vice presidential boomlets kept cropping up. The most commonly mentioned names belonged to men from such ticket-balancing states as Illinois, Missouri, and Ohio. The strongest challenge came from backers of Newton D. Baker, who until recently had been the well-publicized reform mayor of Cleveland and was now a bright new face in the Wilson cabinet, occupying the increasingly critical post of secretary of war. Right before the convention, Henry Morgenthau, a New York financier and leading Democratic campaign contributor, called for replacing Marshall with Baker. The fault lay, Morgenthau explained, not in the incumbent personally but in his office, because "as vice-president, Mr. Marshall had been unable to do anything in particular to strengthen himself with the country, and that this weakness was, in a way, thrust upon him by force of circumstances inherent in his present official position."

Within this move to replace Marshall lurked not only another missed political opportunity but also a potential turning point in the history of the vice presidency. This move to replace a humdrum running mate with a popular figure who might play a larger role in the administration recalled Roosevelt's selection sixteen years before. This time, however, the main presidential confidant was trying to get the potential hero on the ticket rather than keep him off. A prime mover in the Baker boomlet was Col. Edward M. House, intimate friend to President Wilson and perennially aspiring Democratic kingmaker. Always the big thinker, House saw grand possibilities in this ticket switch. On May 24, 1916, less than one month before the convention, the colonel broached the plan directly to the president. "We talked of the Vice Presidentcy [sic]," House recorded in his diary, "and whether to sidetrack Marshall and give the nomination to Baker."

Ironically, the traditional disdain for the office was what saved Marshall's vice presidency. Wilson believed, House recorded, "that Baker was too good a man to be sacrificed. I disagreed with him. I did not think any man was too good to be considered for Vice President of the United

States. I thought if the right man took it, a man who had his confidence as Baker has, a new office could be created out of it. He might become Vice President in fact as well as in name, and be a co-worker and co-helper of the President." In view of his previous career as an academic political scientist who had closely studied American politics and government, Wilson's indifference to the vice presidency was curious. "He was interested in this argument," House further recorded, "but was unconvinced that Baker should, as he termed it, be sacrificed. He was afraid he could not educate the people in four years up to the possibilities of the office." Wilson then closed the subject with the incorrect historical observation that "no Vice President had ever succeeded a President by election." How great a potential opportunity and turning point went awry here soon became obvious in view of America's entry into World War I less than one year after this conversation and with the president's breakdown during his next term. If he had enjoyed the gift of prophecy, Woodrow Wilson might well have seized this moment in 1916.

Instead, the convention renominated Marshall by acclamation, and, thanks to Wilson's narrow win in November, he became the first vice president in nine decades elected to a second term. He served out the next four years mostly as amiably and obscurely as he had done previously. With his folksy wit, he turned many of the jokes about his office back on himself. For example, he once told a bodyguard, "Your labor is in vain. Nobody was ever crazy enough to shoot at a vice president." Such self-depreciatory cracks helped cement his contemporary reputation as a cheerful nonentity, and those, combined with his one memorable saying— "What this country needs is a really good five-cent cigar!"—cast him in historical memory as a good-humored hack. Those impressions were unfortunate because they masked a shrewd politician of unsuspected depth. Surprisingly, no one grasped this misestimate more than Colonel House, who later remarked, "Marshall was held too lightly. An unfriendly fairy godmother presented him with a keen sense of humor. Nothing is more fatal in politics. . . . [Other politicians] looked upon him as a jester."

Behind the facade of comic mediocrity lay calculated intent on Marshall's part. Indiana's rough political school had taught him the value of getting others to underestimate him. As vice president, he wrote in his memoirs, "I soon ascertained that I was of no importance to the administration beyond the duty of being loyal to it and ready, at any time, to act as a sort of pinch hitter." Unlike Fairbanks and Sherman, who had affected airs of formality, even pomposity, Marshall "chose what I thought to be the better part: To acknowledge the insignificant influence of the office; to take it in a good-natured way, to be friendly and well disposed to political friend and foe alike." Loyalty exacted some costs. On domestic issues, Marshall was less "progressive" than Wilson, Bryan, and the Democratic mainstream. On wartime issues, however, he privately deplored the suppression of free speech and hysteria against German Americans. He also vocally opposed agitation against immigrants, sneering especially at "the yellow-peril crowd." Marshall never publicly criticized his chief and loyally supported him on the League of Nations, but he did write in his memoirs about the president's and others' postwar political stances: "I have sometimes thought that great men are the bane of civilization, that they are the real cause of all the bitterness and contention which amounts to anything in the world. Pride of opinion and pride of authorship, and jealousy of the opinion and authorship of others wreck many a fair hope."

In the end, Marshall presents an interesting political case for two reasons. First, inasmuch as he freely chose his self-depreciatory role, he probably deserves his relative obscurity more than his fellow Hoosier. Fairbanks remained more of a political force during and after his vice presidency, although Marshall did get serious consideration as a compromise Democratic nominee in 1920. By 1924, he was too old and infirm for further activity, and he died the following year. But unlike Fairbanks, who was only two years older, Marshall was really ahead of his time politically. The figures whom he most closely resembled in his calculatedly unheroic approach to leadership were Wilson's presidential successors, Warren Harding and Calvin Coolidge. Like them, he had risen through his home state's bitterly factionalized, hotly contested politics by getting others to underestimate him. It is interesting to speculate that if Marshall had succeeded during Wilson's second term the presidential methods and style of the 1920s might have arrived sooner.

The second reason that Marshall presents an interesting political case is that he almost did succeed to the presidency. In October 1919, Wilson suffered a massive stroke and nearly died of ensuing complications. As it was, he did not perform his duties at all for several weeks after the stroke, barely filled the office for another three months or so, and never fully functioned as president for the remainder of his term. This episode presents the single case of prolonged, undeniable presidential "inability" in American history. Marshall's role in these events of 1919 and 1920 forms the third overshadowing fact about the vice presidency in these decades.

To many observers at the time and to most historians, Marshall appeared to play the cowardly role of abdication. He did not help his public image by refusing to make any public comment on the president's condition. "Those were not pleasant months for me," Marshall wrote in his memoirs. "I was afraid to ask about it [Wilson's health], for fear some censorious soul would accuse me of longing for his place. I never have wanted his shoes. Peace, friendship and good will have ever been more to me than place or pomp or power." Beyond those self-exculpatory sentences, Marshall's only recollections of this time consisted of chatty reminiscences about the substitute role he played in the state visits of the king and queen of Belgium and the Prince of Wales.

As with most of his vice presidency, he did himself a disservice in minimizing his involvement. A few days after Wilson's stroke, the people closest to the president, most likely his wife and his physician, decided that the vice president must be informed but only through an indirect, informal channel. A friendly journalist, J. Fred Essary of the *Baltimore Sun*, was let in on the closely guarded secret that the president had indeed suffered a stroke and might die at any moment, and he was asked to inform the vice president in strictest confidence. Essary immediately went to the Capitol, where he met with Marshall in his office. Essary recalled almost twenty years afterward that the vice president sat dumbfounded, stared down at his hands clasped on his desk, and did not say a word after he received the news. Sometime afterward, Marshall apologized to him, saying, "I did not even have the courtesy to thank you for coming over and telling me. It was the first great shock of my life."

This overture and other discussions understandably focused on the danger of Wilson's death. But the problem of prolonged incapacity also loomed before the people who either knew or guessed at the nature of the president's illness. At a cabinet meeting on October 6, 1919, Secretary of State Robert Lansing read from the "inability" clause of the Constitution and suggested that the vice president should be consulted about the possibility of replacing Wilson. Lansing's suggestion ran into a stone wall of opposition from other cabinet members, particularly such administration loyalists as Baker and Secretary of the Navy Josephus Daniels. They insisted on calling in the president's physician, Adm. Cary T. Grayson, who gave them a misleadingly reassuring diagnosis of Wilson's condition and prospects for recovery. That episode ended any moves within the cabinet to invoke the constitutional provision, although Lansing privately voiced his concerns several times before Wilson fired him in February 1920. Meanwhile, some members of Congress also raised questions about the president's condition, and on December 5, 1919, a two-person senatorial delegation met with Wilson in his White House bedroom. Officially, they were supposed to confer about Mexican affairs, but in reality they were trying to ascertain the state of his health and mental powers. Thanks to careful staging by Mrs. Wilson and Dr. Grayson, the president brought off a performance that dazzled this "smelling committee," as it was irreverently dubbed, and no further suggestions about Wilson's removal arose from Capitol Hill.

Vice President Marshall took no part in any of these moves, but he could not help knowing about some of them. At one point, four Republican senators reportedly informed him that they and their party colleagues would support him if he assumed the presidential office. Marshall brushed aside all such talk, and at one point he told his wife, "I could throw this country into civil war, but I won't." Try as he might, however, the vice president could not ignore the situation. His secretary pressed him to think about taking over if Congress passed a resolution declaring that the president was unable to continue in office. "No," Marshall shot back. "It would not be legal until the President signed it or until it has a two-thirds vote, and a two-thirds vote is impossible." The secretary persisted: What if the Supreme Court declared the president incapacitated? The court would not do that, Marshall answered, so that possibility was not worth thinking about. Finally, the vice president conceded that he would take over only if Congress passed a resolution and Mrs. Wilson and Dr. Grayson approved it in writing. But he remained adamantly opposed to taking any initiatives. "I am not going to seize the place," he asserted, "and then have Wilson—recovered—come around and say 'get off, you usurper.'"

Marshall's reasoning not only did him credit, but it also exposed the inadequacy of the constitutional provisions for dealing with presidential "inability." As he later told an Indiana political colleague, "The Constitution, under the inability clause, did not contemplate any such steps as some persons proposed in 1919. . . . Wilson was not mentally incapacitated." Those difficulties—What was the definition of "inability"? Who should decide when the president suffered from such "inability"? How could the incumbent be removed? Might the former incumbent return to office?—all stood in the way of any effort to replace Wilson in 1919 or 1920 short of his resignation or some other voluntary, temporary relinquishment of office. It is hard to fault Marshall for his hands-off attitude and discouragement of schemes to put him in the White House. The fault really lay, specifically, with Wilson for having initially allowed the selection of a potential successor who did not enjoy his respect and confidence and then for blocking his replacement with just such a running mate. More generally, the fault lay with the traditional attitudes of neglect and disdain for the vice presidency.

The events of 1919 and 1920 showed how great an opportunity the nation had missed in 1916. What might things have been like if Newton Baker or someone else who was close to Wilson and enjoyed independent standing in the public eye had been vice president? What might have happened if Colonel House's idea of a copresidency had seen the light of day during Wilson's second term? That term, after all, brought grueling, uninterrupted labors for Wilson during the year and a half that America fought in World War I in 1917 and 1918, the year of peacemaking in Paris, and the debate over the peace treaty and League of Nations at home in 1919. Conceivably, if the president had been able to share his burdens with a powerful, respected vice president, his health might not have collapsed as it did. Even if Wilson had broken down, far better arrangements would almost certainly have been made for dealing with his incapacity. The matter of the vice presidency and who held it between 1917 and 1920 stands as one of the biggest, most painful might-have-beens in American history.

More painful yet, perhaps, was that no one at the time appears to have learned much from these events. When the party conventions met in 1920, less than one year after the president's incapacity, the vice presidential selections betrayed no concern about the nominees' qualifications to fill the top office through succession or replacement. In a peculiar way, those selections in 1920 brought the process around full circle to Theodore Roosevelt's experience in 1900. A revolt by rank-and-file delegates at the Republican convention shunted aside the leaders' choice for an ideological ticket balancer in favor of a popular hero, while the Democrats picked a distant relative and in-law of Roosevelt's with the same last name. Even so, the northeastern/midwestern balance still prevailed on both parties' tickets, and none of these actions reflected much thought about the fitness of the vice presidential nominee or the seriousness of the office.

It would take another half century—replete with three more presidents' deaths in office and several other, albeit lesser, brushes with incapacity— before real changes would occur. The Twenty-fifth Amendment to the Constitution would eventually address the problems of "inability," al- though without tackling the toughest questions. More important, during the last four decades much greater concern has usually, though not always, gone into nominating able, politically potent candidates for the vice pres- idency and into making better use of their talents in office. In that way, the American political system has moved away from the shadows that once hung over its second highest office.

The Republican Ascendancy:
Calvin Coolidge, Charles Dawes,
and Charles Curtis as Vice Presidents

ROBERT H. FERRELL

In the business of choosing the vice presidents during the 1920s, choices were made as haphazardly as in the decades before and as in those to follow. The simple truth was that vice presidents were afterthoughts and received little attention either from their running mates or from party leaders. The first two vice presidents of the Republican ascendancy were chosen by the conventions when the delegates both in 1920 and in 1924 rebelled against their leaders and made up their own minds. In 1928 the leaders made a choice and then because one of them changed his mind reversed themselves, all without consulting the presidential nominee.

The wonder of this quadrennial exercise in the 1920s was that the choices for the nation's second highest political office were as good as they proved to be. Two of the choices were presidential material, a remarkable result considering the confusions that preceded them.

The fate of these three men after their nomination and election is of more than passing interest, for it seems to say that only if a vice president rises to the presidency will he or perhaps she occupy a place in history. The presidency is the great prize, for which any politician will beg, borrow, or steal. The second prize arouses no passions and makes no reputations. In the case of Calvin Coolidge, of course, fate intervened with the death of President Warren G. Harding. Charles G. Dawes deserved the presidency, but fate looked the other way on one occasion, and Dawes nudged it into inattention on the second; after leaving office he went into political exile at the American embassy in London, where he pranced around for a while, and then retired to his Chicago bank. The third of the vice presidents of the era, Charles Curtis, virtually disappeared at the end of his vice presidential term; his sole reappearance, in a form he doubtless did not ask for, was in 1936 when newspapers across the nation published his obituary.

In 1920, at the Chicago Coliseum, late in the afternoon of June 12, delegates to the Republican National Convention were tired, having listened

24

to what seemed dozens of nominating speeches for the vice presidency. All that could be heard above the din of the new "loudspeakers"—they had come in a year or two before, and were to revolutionize American politics—was the banging of folding chairs as delegates stood up and caught their trousers in the slatted seats. A lesser noise was the thud, the tramp-tramp-tramp, as they walked down the aisles to get out. More than half of the Massachusetts delegates were strolling down Michigan Avenue toward their hotels.

This was the scene when a red-faced delegate from Oregon, Judge Wallace McCamant, stood on a chair and managed to get recognition from the complaisant chairman who did not know what McCamant wanted but soon found out. The judge had a foghorn voice and even then was barely heard until he concluded with the words, "Governor Calvin Coolidge of Massachusetts." The remaining delegates raised a cheer; they were tired of being pushed around by the senatorial clique that had arranged the presidential nomination of Senator Harding and had chosen (but not yet arranged the nomination of) Sen. Irvine L. Lenroot of Wisconsin for the vice presidency. When McCamant shouted Coolidge's name, the delegates rushed it through: 674½ votes for Coolidge, 146½ for the hapless Lenroot and his supporters.

Not long afterward, in faraway Boston, at the shabby hostelry known as the Adams House, Governor Coolidge put down the receiver and turned to his wife, Grace. "Nominated for vice president!" said he.

"You don't mean it!" said she.

"Indeed I do," was the response.

"You are not going to accept it, are you?"

"I suppose I shall have to."

It had been a strange situation in which the convention's managers failed. Moreover, during the revolt Oregon did the work of Massachusetts. The delegates of Coolidge's own state sat on their hands. As a later Speaker of the House of Representatives, Joseph W. Martin of Massachusetts, present in Chicago, described the inactivity of his delegation, it was because the governor already had been nominated at the convention, put up for the presidency. Following this nomination there had been a demonstration that lasted one minute. The convention gave Gov. Frank O. Lowden of Illinois a demonstration lasting forty-six minutes, Maj. Gen. Leonard Wood received forty-two minutes, Sen. Hiram W. Johnson of California thirty-seven. After the enthusiasm for Coolidge, according to

Martin, it was decided that the governor should not be nominated for vice president. The Massachusetts leader closest to Coolidge, W. Murray Crane, passed the word, "Don't put the Governor up. He's been beaten once, and he doesn't want a second defeat." Crane must have talked to Coolidge. He was a former governor and U.S. senator and knew that the clique was ready to nominate Lenroot.

Had McCamant chosen a vice president and president of the United States? A few years later in private correspondence there was a discussion of that question, in which the then president drew a perhaps too judicious conclusion. On November 14, 1924, John L. Rand, associate justice of the Oregon Supreme Court, wrote Coolidge that when in 1920 the senior senator from Massachusetts, Henry Cabot Lodge, told the Oregon delegates in Chicago that he and Senator Johnson had released them (Lodge was to be Johnson's vice presidential running mate, and the delegates were instructed for Johnson), Rand suggested Coolidge's name. Lodge assented, for he did not think Coolidge had a chance. (Earlier he had confessed to the reporter Henry L. Stoddard, concerning Coolidge's presidential boom, "Nominate a man who lives in a two-family house? Never! Massachusetts is not for him!") Rand went back to his delegation and made the arrangement. Because another man did not want to make the nomination, McCamant made it. Had it not been for his own suggestion of Coolidge, Rand wrote, which he made because of Coolidge's action during the Boston police strike of 1919—when Coolidge telegraphed the president of the American Federation of Labor, Samuel Gompers, that "there is no right to strike against the public safety by anybody, anywhere, any time"— Coolidge would not have been nominated. The president responded a few days later that he knew this, that McCamant had not claimed too much, for after all it was McCamant who had done the deed. He added that if Oregon had not nominated him, some other delegation would have.

Coolidge's explanation essentially was that all was well that ended that way. It sufficed for a triumphant politician who had become president of the United States upon the death of a sitting president and in November 1924 had just been elected president in his own right.

After the convention in 1920 the governor received stacks of telegrams and letters, among them one from Chauncey M. Depew: "I have been present at every Republican convention beginning with 1856, and I have never seen such a personal tribute paid to any individual, by any convention, as was paid to you in the spontaneous nomination for vice president." With them was a message from President Woodrow Wilson's vice president, Thomas R. Marshall, a well-known wit: "Please accept my sincere sympathy."

In the ensuing campaign Coolidge got out of New England, something of a miracle, for he had never done so before, save on a single and distant occasion, a wedding trip to Montreal in 1905. When nominated he had never been west of the Allegheny Mountains, and had visited Washington only once. Since the time of William McKinley all the presidents, including the forthcoming president, Harding, had been men of not merely national but European acquaintance if not experience. During the campaign of 1920 the governor moved around the country somewhat, into the Midwest and upper South, giving a speech at a fair in Minneapolis, campaigning in Kentucky, Tennessee, North Carolina, Virginia, West Virginia, and Maryland. Most of the country's attention centered on the enlarged front porch in Marion, Ohio, where Harding met people and gave most of his speeches. Coolidge went to Marion to meet his running mate, albeit after the election, on one of the pilgrimages that for a short while made the little city in central Ohio famous.

For the rest of it the vice presidential nominee leaned, figuratively, on the collection of speeches that his friend, the Boston dry-goods store owner Frank W. Stearns, had arranged for Houghton Mifflin to publish in the autumn of 1919, just after the police strike. The collection was titled *Have Faith in Massachusetts,* which was the name of the speech Coolidge gave upon becoming president of the Massachusetts state senate. It was a speech full of the apothegms that would make Coolidge famous. "Expect to be called a standpatter," was one of them, "but don't be a standpatter." A favorite of the nominee was "Do the day's work," an injunction to avoid analyzing if it amounted to no more—to carry out the work and see what the scene then was. "Give administration a chance to catch up with legislation," was another remark. When Coolidge was in his first term in the state legislature, the lower house, he was a Progressive, but he rethought his position and decided that legislation had gone beyond necessity. Other advice to the state senate was that "Men do not make laws. They do but discover them." This piece of male chauvinism came from Coolidge's Amherst College professor, Charles E. Garman, the teacher whom the later president admired beyond any other he encountered. Over the years, *Have Faith in Massachusetts* sold 7,486 copies. Stearns gave away 65,465.

For the election the omens were favorable because of the discrediting of the Wilson administration, especially its leader, before the country, as a result of Wilson's continual calls to high principle, the administration's loss of the fight over the League of Nations in the Senate, and Harding's attractive alternative of normalcy. The Harding-Coolidge ticket won by a massive majority.

For Coolidge it remained to telegraph the president-elect his congratulations, make the Marion pilgrimage, and a few days before he left Northampton go around and personally bid friends good-by. Among others he shook hands with the city shoemaker, James Lucey, a longtime supporter. Lucey looked up, and there was his friend, standing in the doorway. The vice president–elect's words were, "Well, I've come to say good-by," which he did with a shake of hands and was gone, doubtless down the street to shake more hands.

One must ask whether Coolidge sensed what lay in store, that Harding who looked the picture of health was already an ill man, suffering from cardiovascular disease, with a systolic pressure of 180. Years later two physicians said they told friends that Harding would not live out his term—that he did not look at all well. An early Coolidge biography, published in 1924, asserts that the vice president heard of Harding's ill health. Only a few weeks before Harding's death a Boston friend, the biographer wrote, called on the Coolidges in their modest Washington apartment at the New Willard Hotel. "Governor," the friend said, "I've heard bad reports of Mr. Harding's condition. You'll be President before the year is up." At that moment Mrs. Coolidge was playing solitaire on the back of the piano. Addressing the friend by name, she exclaimed, "How can you say such an awful thing!" Such was the surprised response on the part of the wife of the then vice president. There is no record of what Coolidge said.

The Coolidges had taken up residence at the Willard in the suite occupied by their predecessors, Vice President and Mrs. Marshall. The Marshalls came from North Manchester, Indiana, and residents of the hotel seem to have looked upon the Coolidges as no more conspicuous.

There was a story, apparently true, that a fire alarm one evening brought all the guests to the lobby, with many of them in less than full dress. With the fire soon under control, Coolidge started upstairs, but the fire marshal halted him. "Who are you?" asked that functionary. "I'm the vice president," Coolidge replied. "All right—go ahead," said the marshal.

Coolidge walked a step or two, only to be halted a second time. "What are you vice president of?" the marshal inquired suspiciously. "I'm the vice president of the United States." "Come right down," said the marshal. "I thought you were the vice president of the hotel."

Coolidge's anonymity was symbolized in the awarding to him of a middle initial on complimentary passes issued by the National League, which designated him as Calvin G. Coolidge, and by the American League, on whose pass he appeared as Calvin C. Coolidge.

Socially he cut no figure. He and his wife did much dining out, partly because they were asked ("Gotta eat somewhere," the vice president allegedly said) and in part because Mrs. Harding was not in good health during much of her husband's administration, suffering from a kidney ailment, and the president and wife were unavailable for dinners and other social events. But Mrs. Harding did not think the Coolidges worth much, socially speaking. A story has it that when the wife of a former Missouri senator in 1922 sought to donate her Washington mansion as a house for the nation's vice president, Mrs. Harding opposed the offer. According to Nicholas Murray Butler, president of Columbia University, something of a gossip, who was visiting the White House, Mrs. Harding said, "I defeated that bill. I just couldn't have people like those Coolidges living in that beautiful house."

Politically speaking, the vice president, other than presiding over the Senate, which he did in an impartial, disinterested manner, did not make much of an impression. If Mrs. Harding had little respect for the Coolidges socially, the president possessed no higher esteem politically, although in his decent, friendly way he refused to put the case as baldly as did his wife. He gave no attention to Coolidge, although the latter sat in on cabinet meetings. He referred to him as "that little fellow" from Massachusetts. Coolidge compounded the situation by determining not to be a maker of policies. A year or two earlier he had announced his belief in political boundaries when people within Massachusetts, knowing that he had received President Wilson when the latter arrived back from Europe during the Paris Peace Conference, asked him to take a position on the League of Nations. He informed them that Massachusetts did not have a foreign policy. Coolidge's friend Stearns told the reporter Mark Sullivan that he once talked with Coolidge about Harding's policies, and Coolidge said: "My conception of my position is that I am vice-president. I am a member of the administration. So long as I am in that position it is my duty to uphold the policies and actions of the administration one hundred per cent up to the point where I cannot conscientiously agree with them. When I cannot conscientiously agree with them it is then my duty to keep silent."

The vice president was available for speeches, and, to judge from his assignments as listed in his *Autobiography,* it does not appear as if his talents were in demand. "I was honored by the President," he wrote, "by his request to make the dedicatory address at the unveiling of a bust of him in the McKinley Memorial at Niles, Ohio." The affair made so little impression on Coolidge that he forgot it was in Canton, Ohio. He remembered a single other speech, an address at the dedication of the Grant statue in Washington.

This was the experience of the nation's thirtieth president, when not yet president, only a vice president, in 1921–1923, until August 2 of the latter year when everything changed. Then the country's reporters wondered who this wispy, slight man was, what personality he possessed if indeed he had one, and in subsequent days and weeks created one for him: that of Silent Cal, so flattering, so politically useful, that its alleged possessor kept it for the rest of his presidency. All this is evident in Sullivan's diary, wherein the day Harding died in San Francisco the diarist was thinking of the president he had known, telling a scurrilous story about a Harding girlfriend in Washington, and the next day was frantically looking for a news story, any story, about Coolidge.

Charles Gates Dawes, vice president in Coolidge's second term, 1925–1929, was in many ways an able man, and deserved the presidency when on two occasions opportunity almost beckoned. On one of them there was not a thing he could do, for fate intervened and took away the opportunity. On the other, Dawes intervened himself; had he acted differently, his personal history and American political history might have gone a different way.

Possessing a remarkable family background, Dawes should have been president if only for that reason. The first Coolidge came to America in 1630, but John Calvin Coolidge was from the Ethan Frome side of the family, not the Boston side; none of the several generations of Vermont Coolidges prior to the presidential Coolidge made a name for himself. Dawes, however, was from the dominant side of his family (admittedly, the first Dawes arrived in Massachusetts in 1635). He was related to an early Massachusetts congressman who was one of the founders of Ohio, Manasseh Cutler; he kept a massive collection of Cutler papers in his baronial house in Evanston, Illinois, which upon his death went to a library. In his family background was William Dawes, who rode with Paul Revere on the midnight ride. On the midnight ride William Dawes got through; Revere was taken prisoner. Longfellow celebrated Revere because his name was easy to rhyme, that of Dawes impossible.

From the early years of his life, Charles Dawes appeared destined for the nation's highest office. Like John Hay a generation earlier, although Dawes was a worker and Hay one of the laziest persons in the entire United States, Dawes seemed to the manor born. "Charlie" was fifteen when his father was elected to a term in Congress in 1880. This meant a trip from Marietta, Ohio, to Washington early the next year, and although the experience did not seem at first prophetic, only curious, upon Charlie's arrival at night he saw from the train one of the wonders of his age, the single lightbulb placed by its inventor in the dome of the Capitol. Weeks later Charlie left Washington, again at night, and his last memory was of the lightbulb. It was a talisman of financial success. When lightbulbs were more common, Dawes invested in a natural gas plant in Wisconsin, another in Evanston, which he sold to the Chicago electric-light magnate Samuel Insull, and became a millionaire.

Graduating from Marietta College at the age of nineteen, he attended the Cincinnati Law School, where another young man, William H. Taft, marked his final examinations. Traveling out to Lincoln, Nebraska, when the town was young, he established an office in the Burr Block where he was on the fifth floor, another lawyer on the third, the latter named William J. Bryan. Dawes and Bryan belonged to a discussion group, the Round Table, and ate at Don Cameron's lunch counter, which they denominated the Square Table, where they met John J. Pershing, a second lieutenant who drilled the cadets at the local college. Pershing asked Dawes if he should quit the army and become a lawyer. "I'd stick with the army for a while," was the advice he received.

Removing to Chicago because of his gas investments, Dawes helped organize the McKinley campaign in Illinois in 1896, and because he had written a book about banking he became McKinley's comptroller of the currency. In Washington he saw much of the president, whom he considered as a father. Quitting the administration in the summer of 1901 to run for the Senate, he lost out in an intraparty machination, this at the time when senatorial candidates were chosen by party conventions. Thereafter he devoted his attention to increasing his wealth, and his bank, the Central Trust, became the third largest in the city.

In those years there was only a single, if emotionally wrenching, tragedy that afflicted Dawes's life. In 1914 his son Rufus Fearing, about to enter the senior class at Princeton, died in a boating accident in Wisconsin.

When the United States entered World War I in 1917, Dawes applied to his friend "John" for a commission and became an instant lieutenant colonel. While managing Pershing's overseas supply he became a brigadier general. After the war he was the first director of the budget under the legislation that created the Bureau of the Budget. In 1924 the Dawes Plan redefined Germany's obligation to pay reparations to the former Allies.

But the year before the Dawes Plan, fate took away an opportunity for the presidency, if one can believe a story that his vice presidential successor in 1929, Charles Curtis, told a reporter, who revealed it after Curtis's death (Curtis had asked the reporter to hold the story). According to Curtis, just before President Harding left on a personal inspection trip to Alaska he told Curtis, "Charlie, we are not worried about that little fellow in Massachusetts. Charlie Dawes is the man who is going to succeed me." Had Harding's health held until 1924 he would have replaced Coolidge with Dawes, and anytime after March 4, 1925, he could have suffered the heart attack of 1923 and Dawes would have been president. If Harding's health had held until 1928 he could have engineered Dawes's nomination for the presidency, just as Theodore Roosevelt twenty years before had engineered that of Taft.

In the summer of 1924, Dawes received his second presidential opportunity, because nomination for the vice presidency could have given him the presidency in another four years or perhaps eight.

Dawes's second opportunity began when the Republican convention in 1924 nominated Sen. William E. Borah of Idaho as the running mate for President Coolidge, only for Borah to refuse the honor. It nominated Governor Lowden on the second ballot, and the governor refused. Coolidge's manager, William M. Butler, advised the delegates to nominate Secretary of Commerce Herbert Hoover, but they rebelled as in 1920 and nominated Dawes.

What then was necessary was for Dawes to act during the next years in a statesmanlike way and prepare for his nomination for the presidency.

During the campaign and election in 1924 everything was fine. The vice presidential nominee handled campaigning with aplomb. He made the speeches that Coolidge, because of the tragic death of his younger son, Calvin Jr., in July 1924, could not make. Dawes started off with a notification ceremony outside his house in Evanston that drew 50,000 people, and followed by traveling 15,000 miles in a special train and making 108 speeches. He calculated he spoke to 350,000 people. He defied the party's campaign manager, Rep. Everett Sanders of Indiana, by going to the second-most Ku Klux Klan–dominated state in the country, Maine (the first was Indiana), where he spoke against the Klan. Coolidge was a little unsure of his enthusiasm, and wrote from the White House that talking in generalities was "the penalty we have to pay for running in pairs." In a postscript he said, "Whenever you go anywhere, take Mrs. Dawes along." Dawes took the second piece of advice and ignored the first.

In his speeches Dawes was nought but specific. "Where do you stand?" he shouted in his high-pitched voice, his Hoover collar bouncing as he shook his finger at the station crowds. He was plainly visible, just like Roosevelt a generation before: shaking jowls, prominent nose, hair parted down the middle. "Where do you stand?" he asked. "With President Coolidge on the Constitution with the flag, or on the sinking sands of Socialism?"

After election day, with which there was no more problem than in 1920, Dawes studied the rules of Senate procedure, and made his initial vice presidential error, which he was to combine with two others and lose the presidency a second time. He decided that Rule 22 of the Senate, which required closure of debate only after a two-thirds vote, should be changed to require only a majority vote. Coolidge could have told him, and would have, had the president known what Dawes was about to do, that the Senate's Republican majority was really a minority because of the farm bloc and Progressive senators, and it was no time to tempt fate in the form of losing party votes even if that meant the education of individual senators. Dawes was determined that he would not keep his newfound wisdom to himself.

What Dawes did in his speech to the Senate of March 4, 1925, when the chamber was filled with distinguished visitors, including the president and the chief justice, was to tell the Senate off. "Under the inexorable laws of human nature and human reaction," he rasped, duly pointing his finger, "this system of rules, if unchanged, cannot but lessen the effectiveness, prestige, and dignity of the United States Senate." He compounded this error when new senators were brought up to the rostrum for swearing-in, in groups of four. He endured two groups. Then he called out to the remaining twenty-four new senators and their sponsors, "Bring them all up. This is too slow. Bring them on together!"

Hiram Johnson wrote his sons that day: "I have just come down from the proceedings in the Senate, where the vice-president was inaugurated and made his speech. He gave a disgusting and unworthy exhibition. I do not speak so much of the words that he uttered, although they were in sufficiently bad taste, as the gestures and gyrations, movements and manner. These were loutish and clownish, and made every American shrink."

"I regret that such occasion was perverted into a farce," said Sen. Claude Swanson of Virginia. Sen. James A. Reed of Missouri said of the vice president of the United States: "His melody of voice, grace of gesture and majesty of presence were only excelled by his modesty." Joseph T. Robinson of Arkansas averred that Dawes "showed as little knowledge of the Senate's rules as he did good taste—not quite as little, but nearly."

Five days later, the second day when Dawes presided from the chair, March 9, 1925, the Senate took its revenge. The issue was the confirmation of Charles B. Warren of Michigan as attorney general. The session that day went into the afternoon, six more speakers were scheduled, and both the majority and the minority leaders told Dawes there would be no vote. He gave up the chair and went back to his suite in the Willard for a snooze. All the speakers but one then dropped out. Seeing what was coming, Dawes's secretary telephoned the Willard, and Dawes scrambled downstairs and through the lobby and seized a taxicab for a wild ride to Capitol Hill. At that moment the vote was forty for confirmation, forty against. The sole Democrat voting for confirmation, Lee S. Overman of North Carolina, asked for the floor. "I am convinced that this side of the house does not want this man for attorney general," he said. "I therefore change my vote." By that time Dawes was striding into the chamber. But confirmation was lost, thirty-nine for, forty-one against.

Now it was the turn of Dawes not to receive criticism but jibes for his inexperience. Coolidge never would have made such an error as to go back to the Willard as Dawes did, even though Coolidge believed in sleep. A wag placed a sign at the F Street entrance to the Willard: "Dawes Slept Here." A day or two afterward the vice president was showing a

Chicago friend around the Capitol and the two sat down in the chamber of the Supreme Court. An uninteresting case was being argued, the lawyer arguing it was a bore, one justice was nodding, another (Oliver Wendell Holmes) was pulling on his mustache to keep awake. Chief Justice Taft scribbled a message on a piece of paper and sent it to Dawes: "Come up here. This is a good place to sleep."

In celebration of Dawes's ride, Sen. George Norris read to his colleagues a parody on "Sheridan's Ride," in which he announced Dawes ten blocks away, two blocks, entering the Senate chamber, with the outcome in the last stanza: "Hurrah, hurrah for Dawes! Hurrah, hurrah for this high minded man! And when his statue is placed on high, Under the dome of the Capitol sky, The great Senatorial temple of fame, There with the glorious General's name, Be it said, in letters both bold and bright: . . . he has lost us the fight!"

During the reading of this doggerel Vice President Dawes grinned. At its conclusion he said, "The chair cannot refrain from expressing his appreciation of the delicate tribute of the Senator from Nebraska."

For several years Gridiron dinners featured the vice president's afternoon rest, and the participants in one skit brought in an alarm clock four feet high.

Dawes never secured a change of Rule 22, in favor of a majority rather than two-thirds cloture. Sen. Oscar Underwood of Alabama sponsored a resolution in 1927, but Reed of Missouri demolished it, among other arguments advancing the point that Jesus Christ was crucified by a majority. On March 4, 1929, Dawes in his last speech to the nation's highest deliberative body intoned against the two-thirds rule. "This defect of procedure is fundamental," he said. There was a pause. A ripple of applause began. "I take back nothing!" he shouted.

Meanwhile, he made another error of judgment, which together with the others ensured his vice presidential retirement instead of presidential elevation. One of the most sensitive political problems of the 1920s was "the farm problem," which received much legislative attention. What it needed was what years later President Harry S. Truman's secretary of agriculture, a longtime official of the Department of Agriculture, Charles F. Brannan, proposed, the Brannan Plan, an arrangement whereby small farmers were to receive outright payments up to a limit, and so were large farmers, but all farmers beyond the limit were unprotected, meaning that large farmers could not continue at the federal farm trough. The Brannan

Plan failed because it was too open a subsidy, not disguised as crop insurance or some measure for conservation. In the 1920s the successive proposals toward helping the farmers, which received presidential vetoes in 1927 and 1928, were known as McNary-Haugen bills. They proposed an "equalization fee" whereby farm produce unsold in the domestic market, which was protected by a tariff, would be dumped on the world market, the fee being the loss on the latter market, to be assessed farmers according to their production. Dawes championed the fee.

Dawes's advocacy of the equalization fee for farmers meant he was a McNary-Haugenite. He was only a vice president; he was not acting in the way Coolidge once had told Stearns that he himself acted during the Harding administration. An Illinois attorney, visiting at the White House, said to the president, "Mr. Dawes seems to have a good many friends among the farmers." Coolidge's glum response was, "Yes, I have noticed that the McNary-Haugen people have their headquarters in his chambers."

Fate, noticing these errors, responded, although Dawes's presidential goose was not cooked until the Republican National Convention in 1928. When Coolidge in the summer of 1927 announced his retirement after his then term, he astonished the nation, including the nation's politicians, many of whom believed the president was being only coy. It never has been certain that he was not, although when he said, "I do not choose to run," the Vermont definition of "choose" meant withdrawal. Dawes at once, immediately, should have organized his supporters, as Secretary Hoover to Coolidge's very considerable annoyance did. The Great Engineer was vulnerable, for he did not possess much personal charm; Dawes was capable of poor judgment but in many ways was attractive. Instead of organizing, Dawes for once seems to have relied on subtlety, with the anti-Hoover forces coalescing around Governor Lowden who was a McNary-Haugenite. When the Republicans assembled for their convention in Kansas City, what happened was unclear in procedure but very clear in result. Everett Sanders, whom Dawes disliked, and who had become Coolidge's secretary, appeared in Kansas City, and shortly afterward the convention turned down the resolutions committee's minority report that supported the latest McNary-Haugen bill, refusing to have anything to do with it. This annoyed Lowden, who withdrew his candidacy. He gave no warning to his supporters, who scattered and ran to the Hoover bandwagon, leaving Dawes—who could have inherited the Lowden votes—in the dust.

The general went into exile for three years, accepting an appointment from Hoover as ambassador to London. He returned to take on the chairmanship of the Reconstruction Finance Corporation, and resigned when the RFC propped up his Chicago bank. Thereafter he roamed in the political wilderness. He died in 1951, in his armchair in the library of his house, after a tiring day in which he had arranged a local welcome for another loser like himself, Gen. Douglas MacArthur.

Two holders of the nation's second highest office during the Republican ascendancy were men of marked ability, of presidential quality. The third, Hoover's vice president, Sen. Charles Curtis of Kansas, was not nearly as well known. Unlike his predecessors he did not tempt fate. He may have been incapable of it.

Curtis made the vice presidency after a long, slow rise to public notice. He rode the GOP bandwagon over the hill into the wild country of the New Deal beginning in 1933, when one four-term president had three vice presidents, each as different as could be. He entered the House of Representatives from the Topeka district in 1893, when Grover Cleveland returned for a second nonconsecutive term. He achieved the Senate fourteen years later, and except for a single defeat in 1912, by the Theodore Roosevelt Progressives, by which he lost two years of office, stayed there. A regular Republican, no devotee of the Bull Moose, he was trusted by Harding and Coolidge; unlike the Bull Moosers he never would have been seen parading around a hall in Chicago singing "Onward Christian Soldiers." A devoted family man, he watched for years over his invalid wife, who died in 1924. After her death he moved in with his half sister, who once had been his secretary but had married a government employee, Edward Everett Gann, a Democrat, who by the 1920s was a Washington lawyer.

Curtis was majority whip beginning in 1915 when he returned to the Senate. When Senator Lodge died in 1924, the Kansas senator was elected majority leader. As a senator he did not make a large reputation as a sponsor of legislation, and it might seem that the record on which he succeeded the nationally known Lodge was so slight as to be nonexistent. A Kansas historian who wrote Curtis's biographical sketch for the *Dictionary of American Biography* has related that he was preeminently a man who could get things done and who saw to it that others received the credit. Such must have been the case. This same historian made light of Curtis's reputation for being the Senate's only Native American: Curtis, he wrote, was one-sixteenth Kaw and one-sixteenth Osage, not enough Native American blood to celebrate. He was one-eighth (possibly three-eighths) French, and spoke French as a child, which no one thought to celebrate. The Native American blood attracted, and the Speaker of the House in the 1890s, Thomas B. Reed of Maine, once shouted at Curtis who was leaving a committee meeting, "Come back in here, Indian."

Like every other senator and member of the House of Representatives, Curtis wanted the nation's highest office, and in 1924 he sought the vice presidential nomination of his party, in 1928 its presidential nomination. In 1924 he lost in the confusion caused by Coolidge, who did not want to dictate to the convention but preferred Borah. In 1928 Curtis ran in opposition to Hoover. He was explicit as to Hoover's lack of qualifications, and although he did not mention him by name said that the choice, if made wrongly, would "put Republicans on the defensive from the day he is named." When the choice was made, the error not yet in evidence, Hoover's managers asked Curtis to join the ticket.

The way in which Curtis went on the Republican ticket in 1928 was as unplanned as the vice presidential nomination of Coolidge in 1920, of Dawes in 1924. The plan at Kansas City was to name former governor Channing Cox of Massachusetts, making a coast-to-coast spread, the Bay State balancing California. According to the diary of Sen. Reed Smoot of Utah, chairman of the resolutions committee at the convention, following adjournment of the convention session on June 14, the leaders held a meeting in the Muehlebach Hotel in the rooms of Secretary of the Treasury Andrew W. Mellon and virtually agreed to take Cox. That night Smoot decided against Cox, for what reason it is difficult to know. "In thinking it over after leaving the Conference," he wrote in his diary, "I concluded it was a mistake and at 8 A.M. this morning I went to the rooms of Secy Mellon and with some half dozen others including Chairman Butler the question was reconsidered and I convinced them we should nominate Sen. Chas. Curtis of Kansas."

It must have happened in this way. The presidential nominee, Hoover, was not consulted; at the end of the meeting Smoot telephoned Curtis, who accepted. In due time Hoover would announce his enthusiasm at being joined on the ticket by such an outstanding personage as Senator Curtis.

Meanwhile, the only question was who would nominate the Kansan, and Curtis refused to name anyone for the task. As Smoot wrote, "If we wanted him we would have to get someone to nominate him." Smoot related how he was leaving the crucial morning meeting with Mellon and the group when Senator Borah came in, "and I asked him if he would nominate Curtis and he said he would." The Utah senator arranged that after the convention opened with the call for nominations, Arizona would yield to Idaho. He asked Mrs. Alvin T. Hert to second the nomination of Curtis, and she said she would if Smoot wrote her speech. "I did so and handed it to her."

After the election, between the time Curtis became vice president–elect and his inauguration, there was pressure for him to give up his Senate seat, by one interpretation so the governor of Kansas could appoint a successor, by another so his colleagues could elect a better majority leader. Coolidge would not hear of a change, and asked Curtis to stay until inauguration time, for he cherished the support Curtis could give and did not want an untried replacement. The short, paunchy, bald man with the Pershing mustache did what the president asked. He was a regular Republican.

After Curtis became vice president it might have seemed as if only a single issue arose, a matter of precedence. The matter concerned his half sister, Permelia, whom he and everyone else in the capital knew as Dolly (when she was a baby she was so small her father described her as "the doll"). Upon marriage she became Dolly Gann. Her book, published in 1933, set out the "precedence war" caused by State Department bureaucrats and encouraged by President Theodore Roosevelt's daughter, Alice, who was married to the Honorable Nicholas Longworth, congressman from Cincinnati, Speaker of the House. Mrs. Longworth believed her husband was entitled to precedence at state functions and that Mrs. Gann was only the hostess of a widowed vice president.

As Mrs. Gann sorted out this problem in her book it was serious and a real problem.

> It could not go away. Avoidance of my new duties, under the circumstances, was impossible. If I had disliked them, it would have been outrageous for me to retreat; but it happened, as I have said before, that I enjoyed my social activities, and I was especially fitted for them through long experience. The criticism which might befall me for doing my duty was of no consequence, but I should have been truly distressed if, after failing in that duty, I should find myself blamed for shirking it.

The issue indeed was constitutional. "Evidently Speaker Longworth had overlooked the fact that the Vice President, elected by the people, is under the Constitution the successor of the President in case of the latter's death or disability." Mrs. Gann had known there was trouble because Representative Longworth and his wife were absenting themselves from functions. There was no argument, she said. She liked everyone in Washington, even Alice Longworth. "In any event, we paid no attention to the protest—if, indeed, one was ever formally made."

The precedence issue out of the way, following upon Curtis's insistence that his half sister required precedence over all Washington ladies save the first lady, and following Mrs. Gann's measurement of the constitutional problem, the Curtis family's social situation stabilized. That is, until what was either an increase in leisure on the part of the vice president, caused by the economic-political convulsion of the Great Depression beginning in 1929, or Mrs. Gann's desire for more social activity. The change probably was explicable because of the convulsion. During the 1920s with the tenuous Republican majority in the Senate there was much work to be done, ideally by a midwesterner like Curtis whose farm roots were unmistakable. When McNary-Haugen legislation came along, which Curtis as a regular Republican thought extreme, he voted for it. After Coolidge's vetoes, he voted to sustain the vetoes. But then, late in 1929, the stock market plunged, and a year later in the congressional elections the Democrats triumphed, a majority in both houses. Efforts at Republican unity no longer were necessary; Democratic chaos was the pattern of the day. This opened the way for more social life. As Mrs. Gann described the situation in her book, at the outset of the administration former vice president Dawes advised her not to accept more than three invitations per week, for otherwise they would drive her and her brother crazy. She took this advice. But to say "no" was difficult, and the invitations crept up on them, and "Brother" was willing, and soon they were out every night.

The vice president received advice in 1932 not to seek renomination, but to go back to Kansas, repair his fences, and seek his old Senate seat. The issue bothered him—he spent four or five weeks in Kansas studying it—and loyalty triumphed, for the regular thing was not to desert the ship. Curtis sought renomination, and did his best during the disastrous campaign that followed. Heckled during his speeches around the country, with obnoxious questions and cries of "Hurray for Roosevelt!" he lost his temper and shouted at opponents, one time calling them dirty cowards. No words availed, and he went down with the ship.

Unlike former president Hoover who fled to California, Curtis remained in Washington, taking up the practice of law. When he died in 1936, he was buried in Topeka.

Among all the vice presidents of the twentieth century, Curtis most quickly passed into oblivion. He had voted with regularity when that quality was becoming old-fashioned, when if two or three politicians were gathered together at least two were nonpartisan. He would have credited the decline of regularity to the man who in 1912 felt like a bull moose. Although James A. Garfield deserved some blame because of his assassination, which Garfield should have prevented, the principle of civil service, introduced in his memory, interfered with regularity. Another and probably the leading reason Curtis escaped history was that he was no self-advertiser. Roosevelt was an advertiser. Wilson, a college president, of course was an advertiser. Harding was a bloviator, which was a subspecies of advertiser. Coolidge was not averse to advertising; he did not demur when the national committee in 1924 engaged the self-styled public relations counsel Edward L. Bernays to bring his qualities before the American people. In an era when women had obtained the vote, Coolidge advised Dawes to take his wife along. Dawes, to be sure, needed no instruction in public relations. In that department he was a full professor. With such competition Curtis did not shine.

Charles Curtis's reputation, to use the German phrase, has been *spurlos versenkt*. He left a few papers to the state historical society in Topeka. There is a recent and able book on his connection with national Native American policy. No one wrote a biography, unless one counts the campaign effusion of 1928 by Don C. Seitz, *From Kaw Teepee to Capitol: The Life Story of Charles Curtis, Indian, Who Has Risen to High Estate.* His *Dictionary of American Biography* author, James C. Malin, a Kansan of the Kansans who would have found anything about Curtis that was worth recording, discovered only a few scattered general articles. Even doctoral students, who are on twenty-four-hour shifts looking for dissertation subjects, have chosen to ignore Vice President Curtis.

II

NEW DEAL, OLD DUTIES, 1933–1953

"Not worth a pitcher of warm piss" was how Garner categorized the vice presidency after eight years in an office he regarded as powerless compared with that of Speaker of the House, where he might have tempered the New Deal tide.

—Elliott A. Rosen

Although he was an unusually active vice president, even one with some political strength of his own, Henry A. Wallace labored in the shadow of Franklin D. Roosevelt. Like all other holders of his office, Wallace depended ultimately on another person's power: the president's.

—Richard S. Kirkendall

Truman and Barkley were regular, trustworthy men whom the big-city bosses and party regulars from the towns and countryside could understand. Both were remarkably dedicated to the party. They looked upon politics as a great game in which loyalty was the prime attribute.

—Robert H. Ferrell

"Not Worth a Pitcher of Warm Piss": John Nance Garner as Vice President

ELLIOT A. ROSEN

Some years after departing the Washington scene, John Nance Garner, having refused offers to publish his memoirs, incinerated his papers in a backyard bonfire. The incident marked the frustrating conclusion of a forty-year career in public office. Parsimonious to a fault, and a minimalist, he witnessed nothing but aggregation as government enlarged the scope of its activity, as Congress granted the presidency increased authority over the nation's social and economic agenda, and as the federal government racked up debt on a scale unheard of in peacetime. A believer in and practitioner of self-reliance, he watched with misgiving, to say the least, as Harry Hopkins built a huge relief–public works machine in an effort to cope with unemployment in the depression era. "Not worth a pitcher of warm piss" was how Garner categorized the vice presidency after eight years in an office he regarded as powerless compared with that of Speaker of the House, where he might have tempered the New Deal tide.

As much a southerner as a westerner, like many Democratic politicos of the interwar era, Garner came of age in the post-Reconstruction years, when he ascended the economic ladder by overcoming poverty and limited education through enterprise, frugality, shrewdness, and diligence. Such "self-made" men regarded centralized power of any sort as exploitative, a view reinforced in the Gilded Age when, as they saw it, railroads and finance dominated the national economy for the benefit of the Northeast, especially Wall Street, not the small-town banker-entrepreneur. While not averse to federal aid for his beleaguered constituents in the form of better transportation or rural credits or tariff policies, he deplored large-scale governmental debt that had wrecked the economy in the South in the Civil War and its aftermath.

One needs to take to the highway between San Antonio and Del Rio, even now, in south-central Texas, en route to the Rio Grande's Big Bend, to gauge the area's rugged beauty and Cactus Jack's penchant for returning home between sessions of Congress, where it was said he represented more goats and cattle than people. Diagnosis of tuberculosis took him as a young man to the market town of Uvalde, a commercial center, where he practiced law and quickly accumulated bank stock and land, in time becoming a banker-rancher and real estate developer of considerable means. He soon demonstrated political acumen as well when as a Texas legislator he carved out for himself, as chairman of a redistricting committee, a huge, safe congressional district based in Uvalde.

Garner came to the vice presidency following three decades' service in the House of Representatives, where in time he became the ranking minority member of the Ways and Means Committee, then Speaker in 1931, when the Democrats won a small majority in the lower house. An unwilling public speaker, he made a reputation as an expert in poker and matters of taxation and tariffs and as a negotiator and student of the House's legislative machinery, which he lubricated at small conferences with bourbon and branch water. His ideology was progressive in connection with the eight-hour day, the graduated income tax, rural credits, currency expansion, and federal aid for roads and waterways, which he supported. In the 1920s, he helped to lead the fight against high tariffs as well as the Mellon tax reductions on wealth. But, by and large, he was known as a compromiser, working harmoniously with Republican Speaker Nicholas Longworth and Republican presidents, relying on the "Bureau of Education," informal conferences where House and Senate members ironed out their differences while "striking a blow for liberty."

This tendency toward accommodation with Republican opponents on both ideology and detail needs to be remarked in connection with two notable incidents just preceding his vice presidency. Immediately following the 1930 congressional elections that forecast Democratic control of the House of Representatives, the party leadership—the three living presidential candidates (James Cox, John W. Davis, and Alfred E. Smith), the Democratic chairman and executive head (John J. Raskob of E. I. Du Pont de Nemours and Jouett Shouse), joined by Sen. Joseph Robinson of Arkansas and Garner (the legislative leaders)—pledged cooperation with the Hoover administration and promised not to introduce any measures unsettling to the business community. Commendable in theory, it was intended as well to head off radical, meaning experimental, approaches to the depression crisis. Elected Speaker of the House on December 7, 1931, Garner supported the Hoover economy program, which required consideration of relief–public works appropriations within the confines of a balanced budget. He would not "sink the Treasury," the Speaker pledged, by offering legislation leading to excess expenditure, and on February 16, 1932, he appointed an Economy Committee, with the young, dynamic Lewis W. Douglas of Arizona as its catalyst.

In the process, in an environment of plummeting tax revenue, House Ways and Means Chairman Charles Crisp of Georgia joined with the conservative Secretary of the Treasury Ogden L. Mills and Garner in offering a general sales tax as the solution to the twin dilemma of massive deficits and an assault on the dollar. The famous "sales tax rebellion" ensued, an alliance of progressive Democrats and Republicans led by Fiorello La Guardia of New York, sorely testing Garner's leadership. In an emotional address, which conceded the issue, Garner requested and received a vote of confidence on the question of budget balance. While he had saved his political career, there would be no sales tax and no balanced budget.

The sales tax rebellion evidenced as readily as any event in Garner's career a tendency toward equivocation in the open arena. As his colleague Robert L. Doughton of the House Ways and Means Committee suggested, "Garner has not enhanced his standing. . . . He was first for a sales tax, then indifferent; then again for it, but took no active part in it until after the sales tax was defeated . . . when . . . he makes a 'grand-stand play' by appealing on the floor of the House and delivering a speech. Those here know that it did not make or lose a vote—the battle was over."

Roosevelt's selection of the colorful legislative leader as a running mate can be attributed to several factors aside from Garner's support on the Democratic convention's decisive fourth ballot. At age sixty-four in 1932, according to his biographer, Bascom Timmons, Garner was a proved legislative leader, adequately progressive, trusted by his colleagues, scarcely the wild man painted by conservatives who fastened on William Randolph Hearst's endorsement of the Texan for the presidency. From Roosevelt's perspective, too, Cactus Jack was popular, especially with southern legislators who monopolized committee chairmanships, their support needed to enact a legislative program in process of formulation. Identified with the South and the West, he could balance the ticket. And, as presiding officer in the Senate, the poker-playing, whiskey-drinking Speaker could now take his vote-gathering talents to the upper house.

Yet how does one explain Garner's acceptance of an office he regarded as lacking authority? He was a party man, according to Timmons, determined that there would be no repetition of the disastrous 1924 Democratic

National Convention, the scene of religious and urban-rural tension that nearly wrecked the party. Then there was Roosevelt's famed talent for persuasion at the personal level. Perhaps, too, the sales tax episode revealed Garner as out of tune with his progressive colleagues, the vice presidency offering an escape route from an untenable situation.

In the course of Franklin D. Roosevelt's first term, the vice president regularly attended cabinet meetings, rendered political advice on occasion, and helped to shepherd the New Deal through the Congress. Though Cactus Jack repaired to Uvalde, as always, half the year for huntin' and fishin', the two worked in harness, their exchanges candid but polite. In 1934, James A. Farley noted: "The more I see of Vice President Garner, the more I appreciate the man. . . . He is interested in legislation that will protect the interest of the many as against the special privileges of the few. . . . He talks freely and frankly, and at meetings of the Cabinet doesn't hesitate in no uncertain terms to disagree with the President." Indeed, the old progressive was not averse to reining in the malefactors of Wall Street regarding securities legislation or the utilities magnates. When Garner allied with Republican senator Arthur Vandenberg of Michigan in support of federal deposit insurance for small bank accounts, Roosevelt opposed the idea on the ground that it would bail out unsound practices through government guarantees. Typically, with the popular measure's passage, the squire claimed credit.

Differences were muted or kept behind closed doors. Thomas Corcoran recalled for Sam Rayburn's biographers the occasion of his first meeting with the wily vice president. "Tommy the Cork" had been dispatched by "Frankie" to head off a potential confrontation. "Have you had a drink?" Garner offered. Corcoran declined, an unusual gesture. "When I'm going to have an intellectual discussion, I make it a rule," the persuasive vice president insisted, "never to talk to a man until he has had a drink if I have had one." Upon downing a tumbler of whiskey, Corcoran forgot the nature of his mission. Roosevelt next dispatched Felix Frankfurter, who returned to the White House scarcely able to stand. "He couldn't even remember what Garner said, or what he said," Corcoran told D. B. Hardeman and Donald Bacon.

Garner was, in fact, unhappy with much of the first-term legislative program, especially spending levels. He voiced misgivings concerning the National Industrial Recovery Act, wary of Washington's managerial capacity, fearful of the NIRA's cartelizing potential. He offered behind-the-scenes encouragement to Lewis W. Douglas, Roosevelt's budget director, in his struggle for an end to deficits, which was attainable only by curbing the massive relief–public works program categorized by the vice president as "useless" and destined to "bring us grief." The Wagner Act, in his view, tilted the bargaining process toward the labor unions. Recognition of the Soviet Union, he argued, offered credibility to a regime that repudiated its obligations while maintaining a Comintern at considerable expense in order to destroy "every capitalistic government everywhere."

There occurred, moreover, as the first term drew to a close, a preview of, with a critical variation, the 1938 purge attempt, as Garner and Roosevelt contested a liberal Texas representative's bid for reelection to the House. Initially elected in 1934, Maury Maverick quickly became just that: the leader of a group of congressional radicals, Progressives, and Farmer-Laborites, including Vito Marcantonio, Mon Walgren, and Tom Amlie, and Republicans Usher Burdick and William Lemke. When Eleanor Roosevelt learned from Maverick that Garner openly opposed him in the critical primary election, she telegraphed FDR: "Do you want me to send him [Maverick] some word or will you." The squire cautioned in reply, July 16, 1936: "Cannot take part in primary election but man in question is being helped."

A reversal of that position in 1938 cost dearly. But in the 1936 contest the two cagey politicos maintained their collaboration. In his only campaign address, broadcast on the radio, Garner lauded the squire: "What President Roosevelt has been doing for the past three years is really the highest type of American conservatism." Back of the statement, likely, was the traditionalists' perception that the New Deal had been fulfilled, paving the way for a business-led recovery. From this view, pursued by conservative Democrats and the financial community since 1935, the time had come to digest and consolidate gains, eliminate the uncertainties generated by legislation hostile to business and enforced by an unhampered bureaucracy, and bury costly programs such as public works and relief that unbalanced the budget and created a dependent class. Roosevelt was inclined otherwise.

Virtually coinciding with the opening of Roosevelt's second term, "striking a blow for liberty," Garner's bourbon-and-branch-water routine now took on a more literal meaning. The vice president's office became the nerve center for opposition to Roosevelt's attempt to increase presidential authority at the expense of the other two, presumably coordinate, branches of government, to punish anti–New Deal Democrats, to tilt toward organized labor and continued deficit spending required to fund relief and public works programs. In time, the third-term issue, broached by Garner as a matter of principle, hung on ideological differences, meaning the direction the Democratic Party should take.

The huge gap between Democrats and Republicans in the House and Senate following the 1936 landslide troubled Garner. The GOP, he believed, should have stayed the course with Hoover, who could not have won but would have rallied more Republicans at the ballot box than a politically inept Landon. In any event, he attributed Roosevelt's failure to consult with legislative leaders as he prepared the proposal for packing the Supreme Court to the lack of a viable opposition. Tellingly, whereas Maury Maverick introduced the bill into the House, following Roosevelt's announcement of his plans for enlarging the court on February 5, 1937, Garner, who never openly opposed the bill, vented his opinion to a group of senators by holding his nose. By mid-June, Republicans sitting cleverly on the sidelines as Democrats became divided on the issue, with the fight raging in the Senate, its presiding officer, "my ears ringing," entrained for Uvalde. An unhappy Cap'n soon pleaded for the VP's return, pledging a hardening of his attitude toward labor extremists, a balanced budget, and lauding Garner's "great help" on other issues critical to his administration. "I miss you," the suitor cooed; Garner kept on huntin' and fishin'.

The sudden death of Senate Majority Leader Joe Robinson in mid-July ended the bloodletting, for Roosevelt's plan depended on Robinson's support, and Robinson's support depended on the promise of an appointment to the enlarged court. Garner, who had joined the party's legislative powers at Little Rock, Arkansas, for the funeral, entrained with them for Washington, counting noses as usual, reporting to the president on July 20. His biographer describes the scene as vintage Garner, pithy, to the point. How was the court fight going? FDR wanted to know. Garner: "Do you want it with the bark on or the bark off, Cap'n?" FDR: "The rough way." Garner: "All right. You are beat. You haven't got the votes." Delegated the task of finding a compromise, Garner, Roosevelt later claimed, negotiated a surrender.

Hubris led to another tactical error: Roosevelt's meddling in the Senate's selection of a successor to Joe Robinson. The chief contenders for the Senate majority leadership were the independent-minded fiscal conservative Pat Harrison of Mississippi, who early on was supportive of the

New Deal, and the loyalist Alben Barkley of Kentucky, no giant. Barkley's victory, aided by administration maneuvering involving Chicago's Boss Kelly and a compliant Sen. William H. Dieterich of Illinois, heightened conservatives' suspicions of a presidency bent on intruding in the prerogatives of the legislative branch as well as on the independence of the Supreme Court. Issues were social and economic as well as constitutional in nature. Harrison had tired of New Deal spending and its anticorporate taxation policies and, like most southern Democrats, suspected the potential of a liberal court in connection with the race issue. Too, as Jim Farley recorded on the train that returned from Little Rock to Washington, the party's leadership and its Wilsonian Old Guard, prompted by Bernard Baruch, were determined to tackle the administration on the relief issue.

The late summer of 1937 witnessed the formation of a coalition of conservative southern and border-state Democrats, including as well midwesterners such as Nebraska senator Edward R. Burke and New York's Royal Copeland, Republicans following a strategy of allowing the Democrats to tear themselves to pieces. Self-styled Jeffersonians Harry F. Byrd and Carter Glass of Virginia and North Carolina senator Josiah Bailey, joined by Pat Harrison and James F. Byrnes of South Carolina, rallied against the "Dealers and Dreamers," so labeled by Joseph Lash, Frankfurter's "happy hot dogs," in Hugh Johnson's memorable identification of Corcoran, Cohen, and Landis, also against Harry Hopkins's influence. Garner, the unofficial head of the traditionalists, was particularly distressed by John L. Lewis's funding of Roosevelt's 1936 campaign, convinced that the White House Janissaries, unelected and unelectable, intended to convert the democracy to a New Deal (labor) party, purified of southern conservatives, led by Harvard intellectuals.

By early 1937, CIO-led sit-down strikes humbled the auto giant General Motors, as well as United States Steel. Garner, infuriated by what he regarded as the unlawful seizure of private property and Roosevelt's public silence on the issue, attempted to force discussion at cabinet meetings. On one occasion, Labor Secretary Frances Perkins was reduced to tears; at another the president and vice president engaged in a rare shouting match. Led by Byrnes and Vandenberg in the Senate (Byrnes feared use of the tactic in South Carolina's textile mills), the group failed to insert an anti-sit-down proviso in the Guffey Coal Act.

Equally unsettling to the vice president were Roosevelt's continued requests on behalf of Hopkins's WPA, on the grounds of creation of a permanent dependent class viewed by WPA administrators as "clients," as well as fiscal policy. With the 1937–1938 depression (Roosevelt was finally persuaded by Leon Henderson, Marriner S. Eccles, and Hopkins toward stimulation of demand through expanded federal spending), Garner and other conservatives insisted, as they had earlier, on business-confidence theory. Traditionalists were also wary of the Fair Labor Standards Act because of its provision for minimum wages–maximum hours and a powerful labor board, viewed as tilting the negotiating process toward the unions.

Growing opposition to the New Dealers by emboldened conservatives, determined to check expansion of federal overhead management and the power of the executive over independent regulatory agencies and the bureaucracy, led to a struggle over FDR's reorganization plan and the questioning of appointments, such as that of Felix Frankfurter to the Supreme Court and Michigan's Frank Murphy to attorney general (Murphy had refused, as governor of Michigan, to expel the sit-down strikers). This is not to suggest that Roosevelt lost on every major issue, or that conservatives were necessarily a unified group. But Garner, still outwardly loyal to his chief, chafed especially at the proposition, offered by Roosevelt, that the national emergency had not ended and that conservatives might well take leave of the Democratic Party. When FDR acted on this proposition in the 1938 primaries, the failed purge of "disloyal" Democrats, Garner had his fill, and the two engaged in an acrimonious debate on December 18, 1938, their last private meeting, Garner arguing for a party based on a coalition of disparate elements.

In the course of these events, Roosevelt's pledge that he would not seek a third term became increasingly suspect. According to Jim Farley, the president regarded Garner as "impossible," a "blind for those opposed to the administration." At the same time Garner told Bascom Timmons that Roosevelt would never leave office until either political defeat or his death. Yet the minuet continued, at least for public consumption. Garner refused to openly criticize the Cap'n and often rounded up the votes for administration legislation or, if opposed, remained neutral. In an article published in 1939, Ulric Bell derided the two for the harmonious front presented at the annual January Jackson Day dinner, wondering when their Gallagher and Shean routine would end. Taking his argument further, Bell claimed that Garner lacked the fortitude to openly challenge his ideological adversary, hesitation based on a lack of formal education and inability to grasp the major issues of the times. Whereas Timmons explained confinement of the vice president's opposition to the smoke-filled room in terms of a lifetime of party loyalty and playing by the rules, Bell charged: "Jack is a mole rather than an eagle. . . . He is . . . wary knowing that he is best behind guarded doors and that a scrap in broad daylight is not his style, for he is not fast enough on his feet, not profound enough in his conviction, not versed enough in intricate government problems, to stand up and slug toe to toe."

Behind closed doors Garner and Farley, avowed opponents of a third term in principle, motivated also by ambition for the brass ring, played musical chairs with the party's 1940 nomination for the presidency and vice presidency. In June 1939 a Garner-for-President movement was launched in Texas, and in December he announced his candidacy. Polls showed him as the party's front-runner—in the event FDR should refuse a third term. In the end, "the Sphinx" allowed himself to be drafted, and Cactus Jack, challenged for control of the Texas delegation by ambitious politicos such as Sam Rayburn and Lyndon Johnson, entrained for one last time to his beloved Uvalde, following the Roosevelt-Wallace inauguration in January 1941. He never "wore Washington very thick," Garner told Timmons, and he never again returned to the nation's capital, living into his early nineties, managing his property, growing pecans, huntin' and fishin'.

"Worst damn-fool mistake I ever made was letting myself be elected vice president of the United States," Garner is quoted by Alden Whitman of the *New York Times*. "Should have stuck with my old chores as Speaker of the House. I gave up the second most important job in the Government for one that didn't amount to a hill of beans." In *Franklin D. Roosevelt: His Life and Times,* Otis L. Graham Jr. reverses the equation. He is "struck by Garner's lack of gifts for the office of the presidency," his lack of vision for a reconstituted political economy, his inadequate grasp of depression causation, and his inability to communicate beyond the cloistered confines of the smoke-filled room, surrounded by convivial politicians who knew the rules of the game. From this perspective, one concludes that the international and domestic crises of the 1930s revealed both Garner's capacities for the nation's highest office and the process of selecting a vice president as flawed; from another that, despite these limitations, Cactus Jack served as a useful ideological balance wheel in the Age of Roosevelt.

In the Shadow of FDR:
Henry A. Wallace as Vice President

RICHARD S. KIRKENDALL

Although he was an unusually active vice president, even one with some political strength of his own, Henry A. Wallace labored in the shadow of Franklin D. Roosevelt. Like all other holders of his office, Wallace depended ultimately on another person's power: the president's. Roosevelt chose him for the job in 1940 and demanded that other Democrats accept him for it; Roosevelt cooperated with party leaders who wished to dump Wallace in 1944. In behaving in these contradictory ways, FDR made Wallace's vice presidency the major turning point in his political career.

Wallace did have some political strength that contributed to his selection for the vice presidency. Although he had come to Washington in 1933 as a representative of the commercial farmer, moving up from the editorship of *Wallaces' Farmer,* by the late 1930s he had become more than that by adding strong concerns for the rural poor and urban workers. These changes placed him on the New Deal's cutting edge and made him the choice of many New Dealers for the presidency, should Roosevelt decline to run for a third term. FDR did decide to run again, but Wallace's status as a New Dealer and the strength it gave him, coupled with his internationalism, made him attractive to the president in 1940, although not his first choice.

Roosevelt, however, had to give Wallace a strong hand to raise him to the vice presidency. He had foes as well as friends at the Democratic National Convention. Some distrusted Wallace, seeing him as impractical, radical, and not really a Democrat; all had choices of their own for the job, so FDR had to pressure the convention, even to threaten not to run again, to get the nomination for Wallace.

The Roosevelt-Wallace ticket won in November, but even before Wallace's vice presidency began, two events damaged it for leaders in the Roosevelt administration, including the president. During the campaign, a strange set of letters, the so-called Guru letters, came to the surface. The public did not learn of them, but Republican and Democratic leaders and some members of the press did. They concerned Wallace's close ties in the mid-thirties with Nicholas Roerich, a Russian artist and mystic. Wallace had come to know him while exploring varieties of religious experience. The letters included disparaging comments about some members of the Roosevelt administration, including FDR himself, and suggested to the president as well as others that in his religious views, the Democratic vice presidential candidate was not a typical American. Although the Democrats managed to keep the letters out of the public arena, they raised doubts in Roosevelt's mind about his running mate.

Iowa voters raised additional doubts. After supporting the Democratic ticket in 1932 and 1936, they failed to do so in 1940, even though an Iowan occupied second place. Wallace, in other words, had failed to carry his home state as he had been expected to do. His aides, much into public-opinion polling, sought to persuade the president that unhappiness with his foreign policy, not with Wallace and his farm policy, explained this election result.

In spite of the doubts that had been raised, Roosevelt gave his vice president large roles to play. Wallace did not merely preside over the Senate. He took on wartime administrative responsibilities, chiefly as chair of what became after Pearl Harbor the Board of Economic Warfare (BEW), and he spoke out frequently on the meaning of the war.

In playing his wartime roles, Wallace attempted to make American war efforts lead to more than military victory. He tried to make them serve democratic purposes as well and do so both outside and inside the United States. And his conception of democracy harmonized with and extended the intellectual position he had embraced by the late 1930s. It emphasized what he took to be the meaning of democracy for the economy. It was not enough, he now believed, as had Thomas Jefferson and others before him, for a society to have a democratic political system. In fact, a political system could not be truly democratic if it were not linked to a democratic economy.

Although Wallace relied heavily on his top lieutenant, Milo Perkins, to look after the day-to-day operations of the BEW, his ideology exerted a large influence on the agency. Established in the summer of 1941 as the Economic Defense Board, the BEW grew rapidly after December 7, 1941, in both personnel and responsibilities. At first, the assumption was that it would have only a small staff, but by 1943 it had more than four thousand people, many of them stationed outside the United States. Authorized to concern themselves with both exports and imports, they tried to guarantee that the United States and the Allies got the supplies they needed to fight the war and that the Axis nations did not.

Wallace's influence appeared most clearly in the "labor clauses" that the BEW promoted. Regarded as an essential feature of procurement contracts with foreign countries, they were designed to raise the living standards of the workers who supplied the commodities the United States purchased in Latin America and elsewhere. Board officials argued that such provisions served the interest in victory for improvements in living and working conditions and the pay made workers more efficient and countered Axis propaganda about U.S. imperialists exploiting foreign workers. The BEW, in line with Wallace's longtime and large interest in foreign trade as a key to prosperity and peace, also maintained that if their workers had more money to spend, other countries could become the large markets the United States would need after the war. Wallace was interested in those markets and in victory; he was also interested in creating conditions that could strengthen democracy's prospects, especially in Latin America. By 1943, hundreds of contracts contained labor clauses.

At the same time that Wallace oversaw the work of the BEW, he emerged as a major interpreter of the war. He gave many speeches. The most widely discussed speech, presented in May 1942 under the title "The Price of Free World Victory," challenged Henry Luce's prediction that the war would establish the "American Century" and predicted instead that it would usher in the "Century of the Common Man." Rejecting Luce's conception as imperialistic and defining his own as democratic, Wallace maintained that the common man would become a more productive and valuable member of society. Behind the speech lay Wallace's interest in promoting the modernization of agriculture, industrialization, and full employment. The labor clauses embodied the philosophy of the speech.

This speech, perhaps more than any other Wallace gave, had a large impact. It was frequently reprinted and widely distributed. It contributed to the warm welcome he received in Latin America in March and April 1943. He spoke of the "century of the common man" there, doing so in Spanish. In the United States, many liberals, including the president's wife, became more enthusiastic about him than ever before. They welcomed his ability and willingness to articulate a democratic philosophy and saw him as the person who should succeed FDR. Conservatives, on the other hand, such as Clare Booth Luce for example, recoiled in horror, insisting that the speech demonstrated that the man who might succeed Roosevelt was radical and unrealistic. In addition to their dislike of the speech itself, they grumbled about the use made of it in American propaganda campaigns and his repetition of its themes in later speeches, such as the one before the Congress of American-Soviet Friendship in November 1942.

The BEW also generated enthusiasm among liberals and opposition among conservatives. Operating under mandates from Roosevelt that were not clearly defined, the agency moved into areas previously occupied by others, including the State Department and the Reconstruction Finance Corporation (RFC), and produced conflicts that involved more than struggles for power. The issues included the pace of procurement and the ideologies that should govern U.S. relations with other nations.

Wallace, pressed by Perkins and his lieutenants, sought to gain for the BEW the power it needed to do its work, and in doing so, he clashed frequently with the secretary of state, Cordell Hull. They disagreed about each agency's responsibility for and authority over foreign trade and economic development; Wallace charged that State Department restrictions hampered the board's efforts to acquire needed supplies, and Hull and his subordinates objected to the labor clauses, portraying them as a form of imperialism. Roosevelt assured the department it was in charge of the nation's foreign relations, but this did not end the tension between the two parts of government: one old, the other new; one conservative, the other liberal. Hull also objected to Wallace's speeches on foreign policy. Far apart on the issues, the vice president and the secretary of state developed a strong dislike for one another.

The battle with the Reconstruction Finance Corporation had even greater significance for Wallace's political career. The person in charge of the RFC, Jesse Jones, was, like Hull, a southern Democrat. From Texas, Jones was a businessman as well as secretary of commerce. In this battle, much like the other, the BEW criticized the pace at which the RFC acquired essential commodities such as rubber. Wallace and his colleagues believed that Jones was banker oriented rather than production oriented. For his part, Jones objected to the labor clauses, regarding them as impractical, expensive, and radical. Low labor costs were, after all, part of what made Latin America attractive to American investors, and the BEW was working to raise the cost of labor. In his fight with the board, Jones had support from key senators, most notably Harry Byrd of Virginia. By June 1943, hostility between the vice president and the secretary of commerce had reached a high level, and they violated Roosevelt's rule against public quarrels among wartime administrators, but Wallace suffered more severely for in July the president abolished the Board of Economic Warfare, depriving the vice president of his base for the implementation of his ideas.

After the Roerich and Iowa episodes in 1940, FDR may have decided to test his vice president. He had given him opportunities but not clearly defined authority and had brushed aside his repeated pleas for clearer as well as broader definitions and stronger support. He had pushed him into an arena in which he had to contend with the heads of well-established agencies and then had punished Wallace but not Hull or Jones. It appears that by mid-1943 the president had concluded that his vice president had failed the test.

Roosevelt's treatment hurt Wallace. The vice president had known of differences between himself and his chief, especially in their willingness to speak out on certain issues, such as the southern race system, British imperialism, and the shape of the postwar world, but Wallace had believed FDR was generally satisfied with what his vice president was saying and doing. Now he felt betrayed, and rumors circulated of a split between the two men.

There was no split. Wallace began to blame the people around the president, not Roosevelt himself, and praised him publicly, urging other liberals to maintain their confidence in the president. FDR advised Wallace that circumstances forced him to do what he had done in the Jones controversy and assured him that the episode had not lessened his personal affection for his vice president.

Deprived of one role and fearful that the country was swinging sharply to the right, Wallace continued to make speeches. He spoke out frequently during the second half of 1943, often sharply critical of big business and what he called American fascism, and in doing so he challenged the movement of the political culture. He did so even though the president did not. While Roosevelt announced that "Dr. Win-the-War" had replaced "Dr. New Deal," Wallace insisted that the Democratic Party, which he continued to regard as superior to the Republican, must be the liberal party and carry forward the work of the New Deal, developing an economy of abundant production and full employment.

By 1944, Wallace had a substantial following. It included, in addition to Eleanor Roosevelt, Jim Patton, the dynamic president of the National Farmers Union; Hubert Humphrey, the rising star of Minnesota politics; southern liberals such as Sen. Claude Pepper of Florida and Gov. Ellis Arnall of Georgia; and leaders in the Congress of Industrial Organizations (the CIO, the left wing of the labor movement) and the National Association for the Advancement of Colored People (the leading representative of the rising civil rights movement). Some of these people pressured Wallace to do even more than he was willing to do on behalf of the liberal movement and his own political future. He believed the latter was in Roosevelt's hands.

Roosevelt encouraged Wallace's speech making, usually doing so behind the scenes, and early in 1944 the president, by calling for an "economic bill of rights," seemed to bring himself into harmony with Wallace, but pressures against the vice president gained strength. Two new officials of the Democratic National Committee, Bob Hannegan (the chair) and Ed Pauley (the treasurer), provided much of the leadership in a campaign against Wallace. In their efforts, they sought to conceal from the president the widespread support Wallace did have and to persuade him that Wallace would hurt the ticket. Behind their campaign lay concern about the president's health and a conviction that a person elected vice president on the Democratic ticket in 1944 would indeed succeed Roosevelt, perhaps sooner rather than later. As representatives of the big-city machine and business factions of the Democratic Party, Hannegan and Pauley feared a Wallace presidency.

Wallace's ideology contributed to their fears. With its emphasis on democracy and the rise of the common man, it threatened several groups of large importance for the Democratic Party and the Roosevelt administration. They included most southerners, business leaders, and the British. The southerners, a long-established component of the Democratic coalition, were determined to maintain the system of white supremacy, while business leaders, a group of major importance in the war effort, worried about rising labor costs. The British were the nation's closest allies in the war and proponents of an Anglo-American alliance for the postwar period. Wallace opposed such an alliance, believing it would threaten what he regarded as the key to peace: good relations between the United States and the Soviet Union. Still more, the British were as determined as the southerners to maintain what they had. For the British, it was the British Empire that Wallace's democratic ideology threatened.

In waging their campaign against Wallace, Hannegan, Pauley, and their allies got a satisfactory reception from the person that Frank Friedel labeled the "key player of the vice presidential poker game." That, of course, was Roosevelt. Perhaps he had been made receptive by the anti-Wallace efforts of members of the White House staff and cabinet, by fear of a southern revolt, and by his own worry about attacks upon Wallace as a man of the Left. All of these had emerged before Hannegan and Pauley mounted their campaign. Even earlier, the Guru letters, the loss of Iowa, and Wallace's public row with Jesse Jones had softened FDR's support for his vice president. Still further, Roosevelt did not have enough energy to wage a fight for Wallace and feared that forcing Democrats to accept him would split the party, perhaps destroying his own reelection prospects.

Whatever the most powerful forces were, they overwhelmed Roosevelt's personal affection for Wallace and the efforts on his behalf by Eleanor Roosevelt, Sidney Hillman of the CIO, and others. The president wavered when Wallace had a chance to offer evidence of his support. Drawn from the Gallup Poll and other sources, the overall assessment of Wallace as vice president indicated that Hannegan and others had not told FDR the whole truth. But in the end, while expressing a personal preference for Wallace, he declined to demand his nomination as he had in 1940 and as some people, including Eleanor Roosevelt but not Wallace, wanted now. Still further, FDR wrote in a letter, which Hannegan gave wide circulation, that he would accept Sen. Harry Truman as his running mate and then pressured him to make the race. Truman did so, and the Democrats nominated him on the second ballot.

Disappointed in the outcome, Wallace knew that Roosevelt, by the help he gave Truman, had let him down. In this mood, Wallace saw himself as a victim of one of FDR's bad habits. On December 7, 1944, the outgoing vice president complained in his diary about his chief's "brilliant improvisations":

> These . . . nearly always lead to some kind of intra-administration crisis later on because in the process of improvising the President puts the person for whom he improvises in a position to step on a great many toes. The President gives the man responsibilities without power and the man, trying to carry out his responsibilities, inevitably gets into trouble. I think the President gets a

certain amount of satisfaction out of improvising this way and then watching the results.

It seems obvious that Wallace was thinking about his own experiences with the Board of Economic Warfare and recognizing a connection between them and his failure to win renomination.

Nevertheless, Wallace accepted another opportunity—and another test —that Roosevelt offered to him. Although Wallace, without the support he needed from the president, failed at the Democratic National Convention, he demonstrated there that he had substantial political strength of his own. Convention delegates staged a huge demonstration for him and gave him nearly enough votes to put him over on the first ballot, and, although Hillman and other CIO leaders deserted him for Truman on the second ballot, other supporters, including Humphrey and the Minnesota delegation, stuck with him to the end, and many people in and out of the convention expressed deep disappointment in the outcome. He repeated the demonstration of strength in the reelection campaign. Fearful that liberals would desert the Democrats and then the Republicans would win, Wallace pushed aside his unhappiness with Roosevelt (although not with the Democratic National Committee) and worked hard for Roosevelt's reelection. In doing so, he drew large and enthusiastic crowds. Following the victory, Eleanor Roosevelt, Jim Patton, and other liberals reaffirmed their support for him and looked to him for leadership in liberal campaigns.

FDR, recognizing Wallace's strength and his loyalty, liking him as a person, and willing to test him once again, offered him his choice from among several cabinet posts. Sensitive to Hull's feelings, Roosevelt did not place secretary of state on the list. Wallace chose to become secretary of commerce, convinced that it offered power to push his ideas about trade, economic development, and full employment.

The choice meant that Wallace would face a severe test, and Roosevelt made it even more difficult than it needed to be. To take on the new position, Wallace had to displace one of his major rivals, Jesse Jones, a prospect that enhanced the attractiveness of the position for Wallace. The Texan, however, had great strength among southerners and businessmen, and Roosevelt gave Wallace's opponents a weapon when, rather than emphasize his qualifications for the job, which were substantial, he explained his decision as a reward for loyal support during the campaign. Rumors about Jones's disloyalty had persuaded FDR that his commerce secretary had contributed to the Texas revolt against the president and the New Deal. The Senate accepted Wallace but only by a narrow margin and after depriving him of powers that Jones had had and that Wallace would need. These included control of the RFC, which, as a large loan-making agency, was capable of stimulating and guiding the economy.

From our vantage point, we can see that Wallace's political career had taken a turn, but he could not see that. He had progressed rapidly upward into 1943, moving from farm editor to secretary of agriculture and then to vice president and gaining an ever wider circle of supporters as he moved, but his career began its decline in 1943. The enthusiasm of his many fans, however, before, during, and after the 1944 convention and again during the battle over his nomination as secretary of commerce, encouraged him to believe he had a bright political future. Then, immediately after FDR's death, he received additional evidence of support. Some of it came from prominent people. Eleanor Roosevelt, for one, wrote to Wallace that she wanted him to know that she felt he was "peculiarly fitted to carry on the ideals" that were close to her "husband's heart" and that she knew Henry "understood," and Hubert Humphrey wrote that he wished Wallace "were at the helm."

Three years later, Eleanor Roosevelt, Humphrey, and most other former Wallace enthusiasts would contribute to his overwhelming defeat for the presidency. That defeat would complete a line that ran back to the termination of the BEW in 1943 and included the dumping of Wallace a year later. Soon after 1948, he would retreat to his farm and once again focus his large energies and talents on agriculture.

The vice presidency was the great divide of Henry A. Wallace's political career, and Franklin D. Roosevelt, more than anyone else, made it so. The president gave his secretary of agriculture the boost he needed to move up in 1940 but declined to provide his vice president with the help required four years later to hold on to the job. Had Roosevelt supplied that assistance, Wallace—not Truman—would have become FDR's successor.

Seasoned Politicians: Harry S. Truman and Alben W. Barkley as Vice Presidents

ROBERT H. FERRELL

The two vice presidents of the middle 1940s and early 1950s were regulars of the Democratic Party and therefore fitted the pattern of vice presidents of the century's first half. Regular party members believed that the office of vice president of the United States was no place to install political innocents, for the vice president's office could lead to the presidency. Indeed, among all the vice presidents from Theodore Roosevelt in 1901 through Alben W. Barkley during President Harry S. Truman's second term, it is impossible to find anyone save a single vice president—Henry A. Wallace during Franklin D. Roosevelt's presidency—who was not a seasoned politician, a regular among party members, a man who, as Truman liked to put it, knew how to ring doorbells and poll a precinct.

The Wallace case in 1940, when the Democratic Roosevelt forced his secretary of agriculture on an unwilling party, was something to remember with a shudder. In the Chicago convention that year two southern governors were engaged in a discussion of who should become vice president, and the subject came around to Wallace. "Why," said the one, "he's my second choice." Astonished, the other governor asked who was his first choice. The answer: "Any black, yellow or white s.o.b. you can name."

Truman and Barkley were regular, trustworthy men whom the big-city bosses and party regulars from the towns and countryside could understand. Both were remarkably dedicated to the party. They looked upon politics as a great game in which loyalty was the prime attribute. This is not to say that these two vice presidents, one of whom to be sure became president, the other who admired the presidency from a distance for many years, were not men of independence. There were obvious lines beyond which neither one could be pushed. They were decent, honorable men who played the game with scruples beyond which they would not go. But the party was their life—they were party men.

Because Truman received the great prize itself—the White House—his rise beyond the vice presidency generated a dislike within some sections of the Democracy that verged on hatred. His rise to real power, not merely the dignity of the nation's second highest office, generated some of the same irritabilities that surrounded the life and actions of Truman's presidential predecessor. Whether such feelings would have followed upon Barkley's accession, had it happened, is difficult to say. They probably would have. In the public mind, however, long after the two erstwhile vice presidents had passed on, Truman was seen as the stronger personality and thereby, to his detractors, the more vulnerable personality.

Truman's background is familiar to most Americans, and needs little attention. He was two years younger than the president under whom he served from January 20 to April 12, 1945, as vice president. Born in the farm village of Lamar, 120 miles south of Kansas City, he grew up on a succession of farms and in Independence, then a country town east of Kansas City, now a suburb. He always believed that a political leader needed three experiences: knowledge of the farm, of finance, and of the U.S. military. From 1903 to 1906 (after which he went back to the farm for eleven more years, until 1917) he worked in two Kansas City banks as a teller and bookkeeper. During the years 1905–1911 he was a member of a Kansas City light artillery battery; he rejoined in 1917 and rose to the rank of captain of Battery D, 129th Field Artillery Regiment, serving in France in 1918–1919 and seeing serious action.

It was the army experience, of leading a group of 196 officers and men, that took Truman into politics, this after the ill-fated experiment with a haberdashery in Kansas City. After ten years in county government, ten more in the U.S. Senate, he found himself vice president for a few weeks and then president.

The very interesting, indeed fascinating, aspect of Truman's vice presidency is not what he did in that office, for he could do very little in the short time he occupied it, but the extraordinary way in which he came into the vice presidency at a crucial time, when President Roosevelt's health was rapidly failing and it was perfectly clear to Democratic Party insiders that whoever occupied the nation's second highest office was going to be president. Roosevelt had decided to run again in 1944 (two years earlier he had told his postmaster general, Frank C. Walker, he would run). The presidential running was necessary for the party in 1944, which faced the strongest Republican nominee in many years, Gov. Thomas E. Dewey of

New York. Roosevelt, his party's biggest vote getter, "the champ," the most attractive Democratic nominee since Andrew Jackson, would win. And he could not possibly survive a fourth term.

The party leaders wanted Vice President Wallace out of office; they determined to get him out, for he was not a regular member of the party and had never run for office until he went on the ticket with Roosevelt in 1940. At the outset, early in 1944, when the choice of a vice presidential running mate for Roosevelt was about to be made, the only question was who they could put in to replace him.

Getting Wallace out of the vice presidency was a virtual plot, necessary because of the delicacy with which the leaders had to approach the subject with Roosevelt, for if they approached it wrongly they would be saying to the president that they did not expect him to live through his forthcoming term. That they could not say, for the president did not appear to realize that his health was moving downward. He was the most powerful man in the party, who over the years had wielded an enormous influence over appointments and dismissals. He was highly intelligent, shrewd, and vain. If there was to be a kingmaker, he would be it, not the men who pulled the strings across the country. Between the leaders and FDR there was a careful bonhomie. They drank his martinis, which were mixed in the presidential office or in the blue oval room upstairs in the White House, next to the president's bedroom. They carefully told him they were the best martinis in the world. (One of the president's secretaries many years later remembered them as the worst.) The leaders waited on the president. The president liked it that way.

In passing one might remark that the leaders did not know what ailed Roosevelt, why after he returned from the Teheran Conference in December 1943 he seemed to have continual bronchitis, why he looked so fragile, even frail, why his attention often wandered. They may have suspected cancer. They knew only that he showed the unmistakable signs of failing health. They did not know that in March 1944, months before the national convention in Chicago, he was seen by Dr. Howard G. Bruenn, a cardiologist at Bethesda Naval Hospital, who found him in heart failure.

In passing one might also remark that it is possible Roosevelt knew he was dying and in the manner of a Hudson River valley patrician chose to believe the event would not occur. That is what the cardiologist's wife, pondering the event with her husband in the company of the present writer, once guessed. A single evidence, albeit a stark evidence, says that

Roosevelt knew his medical condition was cardiovascular and therefore irreparable in an era before blood pressure pills and heart pumps, and decided to ignore it. He never asked Dr. Bruenn what his blood pressure readings were, although Bruenn was taking them as many as five times a day. Bruenn said Roosevelt was the only patient he ever had who never asked. The physician was uncertain if the president knew he was a cardiologist, a faculty member in that specialty at Columbia-Presbyterian Hospital in New York City. But the night before Roosevelt died, he was talking with his secretary of the treasury, Henry Morgenthau, who had journeyed down to Warm Springs and taken dinner with the president and a few friends. Morgenthau that night wrote up the conversation for his diary. The secretary had told the president that Mrs. Morgenthau was ill in a hospital in New York with a heart condition. The president said he knew a doctor at Columbia-Presbyterian who was a cardiologist.

The party leaders did not know all this and could observe only the visible signs, and move in the most gingerly fashion possible to get Wallace out and a reliable party member in. In the spring of 1944 the party treasurer, a big, hulking oilman from California, Edwin W. Pauley, enlisted the president's appointments secretary, Maj. Gen. Edwin M. (Pa) Watson, for this purpose, and the two undertook to bring delegates to the forthcoming convention who were anti-Wallace into the president's office and exclude pro-Wallace delegates, so the president would get the message. They brought into their group the current national chairman, Robert E. Hannegan of St. Louis; two former national chairmen, Postmaster General Walker and Boss Edward J. Flynn of the Bronx; the party's secretary, George E. Allen; and the party's forthcoming host at Chicago, Mayor Edward J. Kelly.

The president by late spring 1944 had gotten the message, and the leaders could talk safely with him about how Vice President Wallace's candidacy for a second term during the president's fourth term would harm the party in a difficult race against Dewey. The problem thereupon became twofold, one part being that Roosevelt did not seem concerned about the choice of a vice presidential running mate and perhaps because of his illness did not easily put his mind to the problem. The other was that in his usual murky way of handling political matters, his desire not openly to offend anyone, he seemed willing to allow Wallace's candidacy, if personally pushed by the vice president, and simultaneously allowed his "assistant president," former senator James F. Byrnes, an exceedingly ambitious individual who easily scented the presidency, to sponsor himself as Wallace's replacement. The leaders considered Wallace, of course, impossible; they thought Byrnes too ambitious.

During a White House meeting on July 11, a bare eight days before the convention was to open, attended by all of the conspirators, Roosevelt opted for Truman, who possessed a long elective experience, including his second Senate term during which *Time* named him as the upper house's most outstanding member because of his chairmanship of a special committee to investigate the war effort that saved taxpayers billions of dollars. The Missourian also came from a border state, which made him acceptable to the Deep South but did not entrap him in the racial politics of that section. He was of a good age, sixty, and in excellent health.

The wayward president then scared everyone but himself by letting Wallace and Byrnes go to the convention, each with a presidential endorsement. Chairman Hannegan meanwhile had managed at the end of the meeting on July 11 to extract a handwritten presidential letter of endorsement for Truman.

At the convention in Chicago the president's fine hand was evident in innumerable ways, and one was the manner in which he also endorsed Justice William O. Douglas of the Supreme Court and then, even before the endorsement, made sure Douglas's candidacy would fail. In politics the president was devious to a fault. He had a liking for Douglas, who may have impressed him as the sort of man FDR would have liked to have been, had infantile paralysis not struck him down years before. The raffish justice was full of gossip and dirty stories, and Roosevelt liked to bring him to the White House dinner table. But beyond such recommendations the president was a party man, and in party matters a cold man; he could make calculations without personal feeling. Months after her father's death the president's daughter, Anna, who knew him well, far better than her mother, from whom he had been estranged for many years, explained what happened to Douglas. She explained all this, in indirect fashion, to Secretary of the Interior Harold L. Ickes, who described the matter to his diary. As Anna told it, her father despised drunken women, and once at Pa Watson's house in the president's presence Louise Hopkins had been so drunk she fell off a chair. The episode reminded Anna that she had seen Douglas out West on two or three occasions, drunk and surrounded by people of a low type. She told Ickes that in the summer of 1944 her father asked her to check into Douglas's drinking habits. Her subsequent comments to her father are not difficult to guess. In Roosevelt's endorsement of Truman to Hannegan he placed Douglas's name after that of Truman—that is, endorsed both. At the convention the endorsement of Douglas amounted to nothing, because Douglas attracted the same delegates who were holding out, until the last moment, for Wallace; a Douglas movement could not begin until Wallace withdrew, which as matters turned out (and Roosevelt probably knew they would go that way) was too late.

It was said that Chairman Hannegan ensured that his friend, the senator from his own state, became the vice presidential candidate and thereby president. It was said at the time and later that Hannegan from the outset pushed for his own man, Truman, to place in power a man who was obligated to him. In the tight senatorial primary race in Missouri in 1940, Truman squeaked through to victory because of eight thousand machine votes from St. Louis, "delivery ward" votes controlled by Hannegan. His plurality in the state was less than eight thousand votes. For years a story went the rounds that in Roosevelt's endorsement of Truman the president actually had placed the senator's name second, after Douglas, and Hannegan in asking the president's secretary to type the handwritten note juxtaposed the names. The secretary, Grace Tully, said as much in her memoirs. But she did not type the note, her assistant did, and Justice Douglas wrote an introduction to the book and may well have remembered what happened in a form that served his own version of what happened. Hannegan, like the other party leaders in 1944, was looking only for an acceptable party man, and came out for Truman when other possible candidates (Speaker of the House Sam Rayburn and the industrialist Henry J. Kaiser) eliminated themselves for varying reasons.

Of the electoral campaign that autumn of 1944, and the few weeks of Roosevelt's fourth term, it is unnecessary to relate details, except that Truman's contacts with the president were slight, as they had been over the years when he was a senator. He liked to relate that he saw Roosevelt many times during the third term when his importance in the Senate was undoubted. He said he used to slip in by the "back door," the east wing, and escape notice by newspapermen. Of this there is no proof, and at the Chicago convention Truman confessed to a reporter that he had not seen the president since March. He saw Roosevelt thereafter in mid-August. As vice president he saw the president a bare half-dozen times, only twice by himself.

During the vice presidency Truman broke two tie votes, the more important pertaining to the nomination of his erstwhile adversary Wallace as secretary of commerce. Whether his former colleagues, the senators, arranged that tie to embarrass Wallace and the president is difficult to say, but it was entirely possible. Truman had told a reporter for the *New York Times*, who quoted him in the paper's Sunday magazine, that Wallace had not known a half-dozen senators, had stayed aloof from them, had shown no interest in his constitutional duties, and that he, Truman, was going to do better. Senator Barkley in his memoirs included a sarcastic appraisal of Wallace, that when the latter had failed to do his two most important duties of presiding over the Senate and watching over administration measures, he, Barkley, had taken "Henry" aside and instructed him in his duties, that Henry had promised to do better, and reneged. The Senate could have been waiting for Henry and put the issue up to Truman, and the vice president as a loyal party man, as the senators knew he would, came through by breaking the tie.

For the rest of it Truman and his wife, Bess, socialized, attending receptions and dinners, in the manner of Vice President Calvin Coolidge's "gotta eat somewhere." Also, just as Coolidge substituted for President Warren G. Harding whose wife often was ill, Truman substituted for Roosevelt who could not get around easily for social functions and was out of the country for most of Truman's vice presidency, attending the Yalta Conference in the Crimea, with before-and-after stops at Malta and Egypt.

Vice President Truman surely was not surprised when around five o'clock in the afternoon of April 12, 1945, having a drink with Speaker Rayburn and a group of cronies in the Speaker's House hangout, the so-called Board of Education, he received word that he should come to the White House immediately, and as inconspicuously as possible. He had known that he would be president since just before the Chicago convention of the previous year, when Hannegan called to tell him the results, although not in detail, of the July 11 meeting. The only question was when. As his limousine wound its way through five o'clock traffic from the Capitol to the White House it is possible that he was thinking, as he later wrote, of the death of an Episcopal bishop, a friend of the president's, and that Roosevelt was in town for the funeral, but he must have been thinking of the office he was about to fill.

Barkley, vice president from January 20, 1949, until the same date in 1953, was a political regular like Truman, with the same spiny sense of how far he could go against his own beliefs. Like the man of Independence, he was no party hack. "I have been a loyal, regular Democrat all during my career," he wrote in his memoirs. "I believe in the principles of the Democratic party and I have fought for them as hard as I could fight." That did not prevent him from recognizing "a lot of good things" emanating from the opposition. He was his own man.

Like Truman, he rose from humble origins. He was born in a log cabin in 1877, in a little locality named Wheel, between the villages of Lowes and Fancy Farm, in Graves County, Kentucky. His given name was Willie Alben, which he changed to the better-sounding Alben William. He did not graduate from high school, but managed to enroll in a tiny Methodist institution, Marvin College, in Clinton, Kentucky, and upon graduation in 1897 sold cooking crock ware to finance himself through law school. The crockery cracked upon use, and he was reduced to going back to purchasers and paying them for their losses out of his own pocket. Eventually, he removed to Paducah where with a few shirts, fifty cents in change, and a letter of introduction to a local lawyer, he began reading law. After election to county attorney and then county judge he ran for the U.S. House of Representatives in 1912 and won, entering Congress the next year. He went to the Senate in 1927 and ten years later was elected majority leader by his Democratic colleagues, receiving election by a single vote.

It was in February 1944 that Barkley as majority leader showed his spine against President Roosevelt. At the president's request the senator sponsored an administration tax bill, and did his best with it. The nation's chief executive vetoed it, and wrote in his veto message that the bill was "not a tax bill but a tax-relief bill, providing relief not for the needy but for the greedy." Barkley thereupon created one of the most emotional scenes ever witnessed in the upper house. "That statement," he shouted, " . . . is a calculated and deliberate assault upon the legislative integrity of every member of the Congress of the United States." He announced he would resign as majority leader, and urged his fellow senators to override. Roosevelt immediately backed down, protesting that he never meant to attack the Kentucky senator's integrity or that of other members of Congress, and that he hoped the Democratic senators would reelect the majority leader immediately and unanimously—which they did.

Barkley always believed that he thereafter lost the vice presidential nomination, the nomination that Truman received, and thereby the presidency, and it is possible he was right, but it is not very likely. FDR possessed an elephantine memory, was extremely sensitive to slights, and Barkley not merely had acted against him but did so openly, and lèse-majesté could have entered into what happened at the leaders' meeting. But several of the leaders afterward related that the president did not show the slightest animus against Barkley. The people present themselves apparently passed over the Kentucky senator because of his age: Barkley in 1944 was five years older than the president, that is, sixty-seven.

Barkley's nomination as vice president during Truman's second term, interestingly enough, was handled badly by Truman, almost as badly as Roosevelt may have treated him, although the outcome was entirely different. The president had allowed his special counsel, Clark Clifford, to offer the nomination to Justice Douglas. It was a foolish thing to do, one of Truman's few political errors during his long career. Douglas was unreliable. The justice was no regular Democrat. The president soon discovered that fact, for Douglas not merely turned down the nomination, but was ungrateful enough to tell friends that he could not serve under Truman: he reportedly said he could not be a number-two man to a number-two man. By that time Barkley was believing that the vice presidency was like a biscuit passed around until it had become cold. He was pouting when Truman called him to ask, in a rather roundabout fashion, why Barkley had not told him he wanted the vice presidential nomination. At that juncture, Barkley in good party fashion said that, of course, he would take the biscuit.

Reportedly, Truman went to Barkley because the latter, who was an orator of the William Jennings Bryan school, had enlivened the party's national convention in Philadelphia. The president's appointments secretary, Matthew J. Connelly, thought the speech so attractive that Barkley was trying to take the presidential nomination. The president disagreed, saying he could trust Barkley to do the right thing, which the senator quickly did.

For the campaign the president in the traditional way of electioneering employed the train, and Barkley showed the way to the future by persuading the national committee into leasing a United Airlines DC-3, on which he flew 150,000 miles and gave 250 speeches in thirty-six states. "I wrote my speeches in the air and delivered them on the ground," he told his audiences, while the Republicans (with Dewey again their presidential nominee and Gov. Earl Warren of California his vice presidential running mate) were "always up in the air so far as their speeches were concerned."

For the president's running mate the campaign had its amusing moments. Like Truman, Barkley refused to mention Dewey by name. But on one occasion in Dover, Delaware, he told his audience he was going to shorten his speech, which was unbelievable, for he was a southern stemwinder and needed a half hour to get started. But he told them that, and explained that he did not want them to get wet, nor even to get Dewey. He had a joke for every occasion. One was about a fellow who had two sons; one went to sea and the other became vice president, and the father never heard of either again. Another was about a fellow who came into a bar to get a drink but could not remember the name of it; he told the bartender all he could say was that it was "tall, cold, and full of gin," whereupon a man leaning on the bar turned to him and snarled, "Sir, you are speaking of the woman I love."

Achieving office, Barkley received no further elevation to the presidency, as he had known would be the case, for Truman was healthy as a Missouri mule. As always, there were a few voting ties to break in the Senate. In March 1949, he ruled on a southern filibuster opposed to a civil rights bill, in favor of civil rights. He did it with humor. Before presenting his ruling he led off with an anecdote: "The Chair feels somewhat like the man who was being ridden out of town on a rail. Someone asked him how he liked it. He said if it weren't for the honor of the thing, he would just as soon walk."

In October 1949, he broke a tie in favor of a farm bill allowing 90 percent parity for corn, cotton, peanuts, rice, and wheat. In June 1952, he broke another that saved the Wage Stabilization Board, an arbitrating and mediating panel.

Besides breaking ties, little else of importance happened. The vice president constitutionally possessed duties that resounded in their recitation but were less than they seemed. He could appoint five cadets each year to West Point and five to Annapolis, appoint a few Senate committees, sign congressional resolutions, and represent the government on the Smithsonian Institution's board of regents. President Truman invited him to cabinet meetings, which he attended, and showed no hesitation in offering his opinions. He attended meetings of the National Security Council, although Truman refused to allow him to chair them in the president's absence, passing that responsibility to the secretary of state.

Barkley flourished in other ways, brightening other corners, some of his own choice, others by happenstance. His ten-year-old grandson announced to "gramps" that "Mr. Vice President" was too much of a mouthful and it would be better to take the initials "VP" and place two *e*s between them. Barkley told a press conference, the word got out, and he became the Veep. In 1949 he met a St. Louis widow thirty years his junior, Jane Rucker Hadley. The Veep was a widower, and because of his experience with the DC-3 in the campaign resorted to the airplane for a courtship between the nation's capital and Ms. Hadley's home city. To the enchantment of his fellow citizens he married the young widow.

And then there was always the amusing behavior. Tall and courtly, as befitted a man of his years and high office, paunchy as befitted a devotee of quart-sized portions of coffee ice cream and pound-sized snacks of chocolate almonds, the vice president performed his social duties with éclat. Many of them included visits to festivals across the length and breadth of the Union where he crowned cherry queens and apple queens. Part of the crowning consisted of a kiss from the vice president, with reporters and press cameramen egging him on, especially if he chose to place a mark of affection only on the queen's forehead or cheek instead of, properly, her mouth. As he described this occupation in his memoirs, he soon "manfully faced up to his duties." On one occasion, he averred, he met in his office Ms. Marie McDonald, "known in the cinema world, for reasons not too difficult to discern, as 'The Body.' " The photographers implored him to kiss Ms. McDonald, but he withstood the demands, perhaps because they would have been improper under the great chandelier of Theodore Roosevelt's White House and amid the other antiquities of his august Capitol office. A day or so later, he wrote, the beautiful lady came down with the measles.

But it was in his offhand remarks, which he delivered on innumerable occasions, that he endeared himself to his countrymen, in the way that Vice President Marshall once whispered to a Senate official during a debate the remark about the five-cent cigar. President Truman, solicitous for the Office of the Vice President, decided that the Veep needed his own flag and seal, and set the heraldic branch of the U.S. Army to work designing these important gewgaws. In due course a two-star general arrived at the vice presidential office to present the new adornments. The general explained at length the characteristics of the flag, and in the midst of his discourse advised Barkley, "I do not know whether the eagle on this flag is a male eagle or a female eagle." At that point the vice president closed the proceedings by asking, "What difference would that make except to another eagle?"

Then there were the funny remarks in the speeches, as when he inserted an alleged letter to the well-known female newspaper columnist Ms. Dorothy Dix, who offered advice to the lovelorn. A young man, the orator announced, wrote as follows: "Dear Miss Dix: I am in love with a beautiful girl of fine character and want to marry her. But there is one thing in my background I am ashamed of. She knows about my sister who is a prostitute, my brother who is in the penitentiary and my uncle who is in an insane asylum. But she doesn't know I have two cousins who are Republicans. Shall I tell her?"

In such ways the vice president of the United States during the second Truman term filled out his time: he did what he needed to do, enjoyed the role, and added enough humor that his time in office would be remembered long after he passed on.

Barkley suffered one major political disappointment in his life, and its very mention displayed what often happened to front-ranking political leaders who did everything anyone could have asked of them, and whose qualities were such that they deserved the nation's first political office, but, alas, only obtained the second. In Barkley's case the desire for the presidency was present to the end of his life, however he papered it over with understanding that fate had not given him the great prize. By 1944 it should have been clear to him that his age made him a marginal candidate for the presidency, whatever the effect of his defiance of the president. It never was clear to him. After the congressional elections in 1950, during which he served as a major party orator, he learned that he suffered from a "tired heart." His eyesight was failing—he was going blind. But knowledge that he not merely was old but was wearing out did not dim his ambition. On March 1, 1951, when he was presiding over the Senate, President Truman came into the chamber and presented him a gavel made from wood used in rebuilding the White House in 1817, after the British troops had burned the building. The wood had been removed in 1949 when the building was gutted, only the walls left standing, for a complete renovation. In response Barkley pointed out that years ago some of his teachers had predicted he would be president of the United States. It was a revealing remark. "I have disappointed those teachers," he said. "I have not made the White House; I have not been able to enter it in the capacity in which they predicted I would. So it is very gracious and thoughtful of you to bring a part of the White House to me."

Another and equally pathetic illustration of his disappointment occurred the next year, 1952. During the Jefferson-Jackson Day banquet in Washington, a great affair, the high point, almost, of the occasion occurred when the president arose, followed by the vice president, and from opposite ends of the Washington National Guard Armory the two men walked toward each other. As they met and shook hands the applause turned into a deafening roar. At that moment Truman told Barkley quietly what he was going to say later that evening, that is, announce his own withdrawal from the forthcoming presidential race. Barkley then got into action and tried for the nomination. In his memoirs he devoted two chapters to the effort, for he was serious. At last, during the Chicago convention, after he arrived in the city and walked nine blocks to the hall to prove his vigor, representatives of American labor withdrew their support of his candidacy, cruelly saying he was too old. He received a forty-five-minute ovation when he announced his withdrawal.

After the vice presidency the old fire horse waited out a year and then took a worthy if inept Kentucky Republican's Senate seat, that of John Sherman Cooper. Two years later, April 30, 1956, he made an address before the student body at Washington and Lee University. He spoke of his new and lowly position in the Senate, in a back row, for he had lost seniority: " . . . and now I am back again as a junior Senator," he shouted. "And I am willing to be a junior. I'm glad to sit in the back row, for I would rather be a servant in the house of the Lord than sit in the seats of the mighty." He perhaps was speaking of the vice presidency. He probably was referring to the presidency. A roar of applause greeted the remark. He stepped back and bowed his head to the audience. Suddenly he fell over backward, dead of a heart attack.

III

THE SPRINGBOARD, 1953–1963

It is sometimes asked whether the American vice presidency is a "making" or a "maiming" experience. For Richard Nixon it was, quite simply, both. If there were limits of advocacy and activism beyond which his relationship with Eisenhower did not permit him to go, it is nevertheless true that Nixon made the most of the opportunities that came his way. As a result, he enjoyed vastly more latitude as the administration's chief foreign representative, domestic campaigner, and liaison to Capitol Hill than any of his predecessors.

—RICHARD NORTON SMITH

Johnson's service as vice president frustrated and pained him. But his presence in the office had schooled him in the workings of the executive branch and had helped prepare him for the heavy burden of responsibility he assumed with John Kennedy's tragic death in November 1963.

—ROBERT DALLEK

"You Can Be President Someday": Richard M. Nixon as Vice President

RICHARD NORTON SMITH

On the evening of May 8, 1952, California senator Richard Nixon had a job interview. He did not know it at the time, but that is what his appearance before the New York State Republican Party's annual fund-raising dinner amounted to. The program, like virtually everything associated with the state party, was subject to the approval of Thomas E. Dewey, who, in the words of one irreverent associate, had a habit of getting reelected governor every time he ran for president. Dewey the kingmaker had already settled on Gen. Dwight Eisenhower as his candidate for 1952; now he was in the market for a dauphin.

As a former prosecutor, Dewey was predisposed to Nixon as the man who had nailed Alger Hiss. Beyond this, he sensed that the senator's youthful conservatism and western background might perfectly complement the establishment connections and military glamour of Eisenhower, the political virgin. Nixon aided his cause with a forceful speech, delivered without notes, in which he asserted the need for any GOP ticket to attract millions of Democratic and independent voters. When he concluded, the dapper governor stamped out a cigarette and gave his guest some advice. "Make me a promise," Dewey told Nixon. "Don't get fat, don't lose your zeal, and you can be president someday."

Dewey's prophecy bore first fruit two months later, at the GOP convention in Chicago. In the convention's aftermath, reporters seeking a story camped outside the Nixons' home in northwest Washington. Among them was Jacqueline Bouvier, then "the Inquiring Photographer" for the old *Washington Times Herald*. As it happened, the future first lady got no more than a brief street-corner interview with the Nixons' four-year-old daughter, Julie, who, when asked if she played with Democrats, responded, "What's a Democrat?"

Nixon's running mate knew what a Democrat was, but otherwise his political insights were decidedly limited. Indeed, one close Eisenhower associate once observed to me that the problem with Ike—whom he greatly admired—was that as soon as he learned how to spell *precinct* he thought he knew everything worth knowing about politics. The problem was not one of naïveté: no one rises to the rank of a five-star general of the army without the ability to manipulate men and events. But Ike was no party politician; to the contrary, he liked to imagine himself a man above party. It was this broad unifying appeal that made him an irresistible candidate and, for his vice president, saddled with the heavy lifting of partisan politics, a difficult, often mercurial, superior.

The time-honored notion of a balanced ticket rests upon the even hoarier belief that opposites attract. Yet it is just as likely that opposites will remain opposites, and for good reason. Certainly, the Eisenhower-Nixon marriage had its rocky moments. Following their pairing in Chicago, Ike the outdoorsman invited his understudy for a postconvention fishing trip to Colorado, where he instructed Nixon in the fine art of trout casting. On his first three attempts Nixon hooked a tree limb. The fourth time he caught Eisenhower's shirt. So much for balance.

That fall the Democrats conducted their own fishing expedition when press reports of a so-called secret fund contributed by wealthy supporters in California briefly jeopardized Nixon's place on the ticket. Once more taking Tom Dewey's advice, Nixon seized the initiative by going on national television. By the time he finished delivering what has been both immortalized and trivialized as "the Checkers speech," the self-made grocer's son from Yorba Linda had created an indelible self-portrait and an enduring bond with the flag-waving, country-loving strivers whom FDR had called "the forgotten man" and whom Nixon himself would later enshrine as the Silent Majority.

Thanks to his half-hour address, Nixon was assured of a vast national constituency before ever taking the oath of office as vice president. Off-setting this, it must be added, was a countervailing army of detractors for whom the very mention of Checkers was a desecration on the memory of FDR's sainted (and politically useful) Scottie dog, Fala.

Of course, a vice president must ultimately rely on, and answer to, a constituency of one. Eisenhower the warlord, accustomed to making life-and-death decisions on his sole authority, could hardly fail to note that by taking his case directly to the viewing audience, Nixon had, in effect, taken the decision regarding his own future on the ticket out of the general's hands. Inevitably, the affair bred in Eisenhower and key members of his White House circle, led by the imperious chief of staff, Sherman Adams, a certain ambivalence toward Nixon that would subtly color the next eight years.

Rarely has this country witnessed so dramatic a change as took place on January 20, 1953. After twenty years in the political wilderness, a divided Republican Party was returned to power. While most observers understandably dwelt on the contrast between the outgoing and incoming presidents, an even greater gulf separated seventy-four-year-old Alben Barkley from Richard Nixon, who had turned forty just a week before inauguration day. Truman once complained that it took Barkley five minutes to sign his name. His "veep's" tub-thumping oratory, liberally flavored with branch water and "My Old Kentucky Home," seemed even then more appropriate to the age of William Jennings Bryan than *I Love Lucy*.

Not surprisingly, Truman's vice president had played little role in the administration's foreign policy initiatives. For Nixon, by contrast, foreign affairs had been a subject of consuming interest ever since his first election to the House in 1946. He was not the first vice president to travel overseas at the behest of his chief; Franklin Roosevelt had dispatched Henry Wallace to China in May 1944, although it was widely viewed as FDR's way of sidetracking a controversial vice president during the critical weeks leading up to the convention that would decide Wallace's political fate.

Richard Nixon was no Henry Wallace. At Eisenhower's urging Nixon became the first truly global vice president, visiting fifty-eight nations and carrying out a number of sensitive diplomatic assignments. In the autumn of 1953, for example, he embarked on an Asian odyssey that was both a learning experience and a foreshadowing of policies Nixon would pursue in his own presidency. He impressed Malcolm McDonald, Great Britain's representative in Singapore, with his open-minded attitude toward the Communist Chinese, whose future entry into the United Nations Nixon refused to rule out.

Nixon paid calls upon Japan's emperor and an Indian mystic. In French Indochina, the American vice president sampled monkey stew in Vietnamese military camps and Boeuf bourguignon in a French officer's mess. He came away deeply pessimistic about French colonial rule, and convinced that the nationalism espoused by Ho Chi Minh held far greater appeal than the Old World condescension exhibited by France's military and political leaders. In South Korea, Nixon pressed the country's seventy-eight-year-old president, Syngman Ree, for a firm commitment not to attack the Communist North. It took two meetings and several difficult hours, but Nixon finally obtained the assurances sought by Eisenhower as a precondition of continued American assistance.

Seventy days after setting out, the vice president and his party returned to Washington. At the end of a two-hour presentation before the National Security Council (NSC), Nixon received a standing ovation from the president and others in the room. A few days later he took to the airwaves to share his Asian observations and demonstrate yet again his mastery of the communications medium that was already coming to dominate American public life.

Nixon's foreign travels increased his personal stature even as they raised the vice presidency to new heights. But it remained a Janus-faced office, one whose occupant could all too easily become a victim of his own success. With increased visibility came demands to match, especially in an administration dominated by nonpolitical businessmen and led by a president who fancied himself above the partisan fray. To Nixon fell the unenviable task of bearding Wisconsin's Joseph McCarthy in his senatorial lair, while simultaneously defending the White House and congressional Republicans against Democratic charges of anti-Communist witch-hunting. For his pains the vice president earned McCarthy's contempt, Adlai Stevenson's sarcasm, and some unusually warm praise from Ike. McCarthy's censure in December 1954 prompted Eisenhower to exclaim, "McCarthyism is now McCarthywasm." Ike's famous "hidden hand" may have pushed McCarthy off the cliff, but it was his vice president who bore the scars of battle and who suffered guilt by association.

Nixon was still walking the McCarthy tightrope when Ike handed him another treacherous assignment, this time as the administration's point man in the 1954 off-year elections. Unable to dent Eisenhower's overwhelming popularity, Stevenson went after his embattled vice president, accusing him of practicing "McCarthyism in a white collar." Nixon returned the criticism with interest, singling out for abuse Americans for Democratic Action—the ACLU of its day. So rough was the fall campaign that in its last week, stung by editorial censure and the eye-gouging attacks of cartoonists such as the *Washington Post*'s Herblock, Nixon impulsively decided to quit politics. He quickly changed his mind after GOP losses were held to a minimum and his own vigorous campaigning was given much of the credit for the party's unexpectedly strong showing.

In retrospect Stevenson and his allies were doing Nixon a favor. In casting him as a Republican hatchet man, the vice president's critics all but guaranteed Nixon to be the Republican hero. Party allegiances meant a lot more in the 1950s than they do today, and party loyalists were just that: intensely loyal to the hard-hitting vice president whose denunciations of Korea, communism, corruption, and controls contrasted favorably in their eyes with Ike's disengagement. Twenty years later Spiro Agnew would take a page out of the Nixon playbook. By making himself the darling of grassroots Republican activists, Agnew made it impossible for then President Nixon to dump him in 1972. In both cases the undesirable had become the indispensable, one difference being that Nixon, a far more substantive figure, did not have to rely upon speechwriters to supply him with his verbal indignation. He could not if he had wanted to; as late as 1960 the vice presidential budget did not allow for the hiring of a full-time speechwriter.

In a sense it did not matter. Thanks to television, the jet plane, and political opportunities unique to the good, gray Eisenhower White House, Nixon was in a position to command attention as few vice presidents before or since. Yet for all his activism he could not escape the paradox of the modern vice presidency: the proximity to power resting upon a relationship that is both a vice president's greatest strength and his greatest frustration. A vice president is judged on his loyalty, and loyalty can sometimes get in the way of leadership.

It must also be said, however, that probably no vice president has made more out of adversity than the author of *Six Crises*. In September 1955, Eisenhower suffered a heart attack while visiting his in-laws in Denver. Before the news was made public, White House Press Secretary Jim Hagerty informed Nixon, who responded by summoning his old friend Bill Rogers, then acting attorney general in the Eisenhower cabinet. Neither man had any idea what, if any, legal position the vice president occupied under such circumstances. An embarrassed Rogers began looking for a copy of the Constitution. Unable to find one in his son's schoolbooks, he picked up the phone to call his office at the Justice Department.

"For God's sake, don't do that," Nixon told him. "If it ever gets out that the vice president and the attorney general don't know what the Constitution says, we'd look like a couple of complete idiots."

As the nation held its breath over the first serious presidential illness of the nuclear age, Eisenhower's concept of a governing team was put to the test as never before. By all measurements Nixon passed the test with flying colors. Moderating rather than presiding over meetings of the cabinet and the NSC, Nixon was careful to downplay talk of any power struggle. He refused to criticize Chief of Staff Sherman Adams, whose attempt to fill the White House vacuum made Al Haig's famous "I'm in charge" statement at the time of Ronald Reagan's shooting look positively self-effacing. In the words of historian Stephen Ambrose, Nixon "was a model of propriety" at a time when a single misstep might have proved fatal to his political future.

Given this solid performance, one is moved to ask what can possibly account for the awkward and embarrassing Alphonse and Gaston act played out by Eisenhower and Nixon in the months leading up to the 1956 GOP convention. At one point, the president went so far as to offer Nixon a cabinet job during the second term, ostensibly to bolster his administrative credentials, a proposal that can only be called surreal. Privately, Ike expressed disappointment over his teammate's failure to "mature" in office. Republican National Committee Chairman Len Hall did not help matters when, pressed by reporters as to what would happen if Ike did not run that year, he replied, "We will jump off that bridge when we come to it."

In the end the Republican voters of New Hampshire came to the vice president's rescue, as more than twenty-three thousand took the trouble to write in Nixon's name in their state's primary. This spontaneous gesture all but ended the "Dump Nixon" movement. Nixon's resentment lingered on, however. When he came to write *Six Crises* in 1961, Nixon described Eisenhower as "far more complex and devious" than most people realized. A generation later, with Ike in his grave and Nixon himself a former president seeking to influence the judgment of history, he was rather more candid in appraising Eisenhower's occasionally ruthless treatment of subordinates. In his postpresidential memoirs Nixon cited the example of Eisenhower's World War II chief of staff, Gen. Walter Bedell Smith, a Washington neighbor with whom the vice president sometimes met at the end of the day to discuss current issues over cocktails. One night, weakened by the flu, General Smith let a couple of drinks go to his head. Expressing sympathy for the way Nixon handled press attacks aimed his way by journalists who were too timid to go after Eisenhower personally, Smith recalled similar treatment accorded him during the war. "I was only Ike's prat boy," a tearful Smith confessed. "Ike always had to have a prat boy, someone who'd do the dirty work for him. . . . Ike always has to be the nice guy. That's the way it is in the White House, and the way it will always be in any kind of organization that Ike runs."

One need not wade far into the treacherous waters of psychohistory to consider personal factors that may have undercut the Eisenhower-Nixon relationship. The vice president was a much younger man, one whose career clearly was before him. Eisenhower's Jekyll and Hyde attitude toward the political wars made him all the more dependent on his vice president—a partisan of shrewd instincts and sharp elbows. This was an exact reversal of the role Ike was accustomed to playing. Is it an exaggeration to suggest that Ike's frustration over his own advancing age and deteriorating health combined with his sometimes fanciful notions of what was possible in the two-party system of his day to vent themselves on his dutiful vice president? Nixon's outward loyalty could not disguise his emerging status as Eisenhower's likeliest successor. And no one likes to be reminded of their mortality—even their political mortality.

There is another factor worth considering. Ike's failure to institutionalize what he liked to call "modern Republicanism" coincided with Nixon's soaring popularity among party conservatives. Yet, as the 1960 election would demonstrate, Nixon was a very modern Republican indeed; if anything, Eisenhower may have underestimated their common achievement in dispelling much of the GOP's negative image among an electorate still used to being governed in the long shadow of Franklin Roosevelt.

That the vice presidency under Nixon was a very different office from the constitutional fifth wheel he had inherited from Alben Barkley is apparent from the wild scrimmage that took place on the floor of the 1956 Democratic National Convention once Adlai Stevenson invited delegates to choose a running mate for him. That national figures of the caliber of Jack Kennedy and Estes Kefauver should battle each other for second place on what few observers expected to be a winning ticket was no small tribute to the newfound prestige enjoyed by the vice presidency. Moreover, for all his frustrations, Nixon was the first vice president since Theodore Roosevelt to be seen as a presumptive presidential candidate. Since then, every American vice president has been automatically admitted to that select circle.

Eisenhower contributed to the process following his stroke in November 1957. Mindful of Woodrow Wilson's tragically diminished presidency, Ike drafted a four-page letter providing for the transfer of executive authority to his vice president, a document so skillfully drawn that it prompted Attorney General Rogers to remark that Eisenhower would have made an outstanding lawyer. At its heart, Eisenhower's solution to the constitutional vacuum was to provide for joint consultation between himself and Nixon concerning the president's ability to fulfill his responsibilities.

Should Eisenhower be incapable of participating in such discussions, then Nixon, on his own, and following "such consultation as seems to him appropriate under the circumstances," would serve as acting president until the president could resume the full exercise of power. Eisenhower's letter had limited standing under the law. Yet it represents a historical milestone, for it anticipated the Twenty-fifth Amendment to the Constitution, which, as Nixon biographer Jonathan Aitken has pointed out, actually places less confidence in a vice president than Ike did in his, since it entrusts the final decision on a president's capacity to discharge his duties to the vice president and a majority of cabinet officers or others as determined by Congress.

Nixon's stature grew markedly during his second term, ironically aided by confrontations with anti-American demonstrators in Caracas during his 1958 South American tour and still more by the famous "kitchen debate" in which he was pitted against Soviet Premier Nikita Khrushchev in the spring of 1959. The theatrical showdown in Moscow produced a surge in Nixon's poll numbers, all the more welcome as the debate came in the wake of the disastrous off-year elections of 1958 and on the eve of the 1960 presidential race.

At times that year Nixon's vice presidency seemed less a springboard than a trapdoor. Defending the Eisenhower stewardship while presenting himself as an agent of change was akin to squaring the circle. He was, in effect, forced to argue that voters had never had it so good, when he—and they—thought it might be better. While JFK prosecuted a nonexistent missile gap, Eisenhower's vice president fought with one hand tied behind his back, denouncing the idea of a Cuban invasion lest the administration's plans for just such a military action be compromised. In selecting Henry Cabot Lodge to be his running mate, Nixon followed Ike's wishes. But Lodge turned out to be a political bumbler who cost the Republican ticket more votes than he gained.

In a final crowning irony, Eisenhower was kept off the campaign trail at a time when his presence might have closed the gap between Nixon and John Kennedy, this after Mamie Eisenhower persuaded Nixon that her husband's health might not withstand the rigors of the closing stretch. Having risen to the occasion in two earlier bouts of presidential illness,

Nixon now was to be denied the benefits of Ike's undiminished popularity as he surged toward a photo finish with JFK.

In the wake of his narrow loss, Nixon became the first vice president since John C. Breckenridge in 1860 to announce an opponent's electoral-college victory. He prepared to leave Washington. After fourteen years in public life his family's net worth was forty-eight thousand dollars. His Secret Service protection evaporated at high noon on inauguration day. Nixon's car and driver would vanish, like Cinderella's carriage, at midnight. That evening, as jubilant Democrats in limousines and flowing gowns celebrated their return to power, the former vice president went to the Capitol. A surprised guard let him in. His footsteps echoing on the bare stone floor, Nixon made his way to a balcony overlooking Washington's Mall and the marble monuments of earlier American leaders. "As I turned to go inside," he wrote later, "I suddenly stopped short, struck by the thought that this was not the end—that someday I would be back here."

It is sometimes asked whether the American vice presidency is a "making" or a "maiming" experience. For Richard Nixon it was, quite simply, both. If there were limits of advocacy and activism beyond which his relationship with Eisenhower did not permit him to go, it is nevertheless true that Nixon made the most of the opportunities that came his way. As a result, he enjoyed vastly more latitude as the administration's chief foreign representative, domestic campaigner, and liaison to Capitol Hill than any of his predecessors. As he gazed out over the west front of the Capitol on the frosty night of January 20, 1961, Nixon might well have reflected that as much as he had changed during the last eight years, it was nothing compared with how much he had changed the nation's second highest office.

Frustration and Pain:
Lyndon B. Johnson as Vice President

ROBERT DALLEK

Lyndon Johnson was a reluctant vice president. He had hoped and planned for the presidency, but fate or the limitations of his time, place, and personality had cast him in the second spot. And he despised it. From his earliest days in the Texas hill country, he had aspired to be the best, to outdo friend and foe. He needed to win higher standing, hold greater power, earn more money than anyone else. Some inner sense of want drove him to seek status, control, and wealth. Throughout his life he demonstrated a compensatory grandiosity that spawned legends. In one of them, German Chancellor Ludwig Erhard asked Johnson whether he had been born in a log cabin. "No, no," LBJ answered. "You're confusing me with Abe Lincoln. I was born in a manger."

For Johnson, gaining the presidency meant fulfilling fantasies about becoming a great man who gave all Americans a richer life. Shaped by the poverty he saw and experienced growing up in rural Texas and inspired by FDR, the greatest liberal reformer in the nation's history, Johnson had indeed produced "good works." His commitment to New Deal, and Fair Deal, programs, the liberal nationalism of the 1930s and 1940s, helped transform America, particularly his native South and West. Aid to education; dam building providing flood control; conservation; cheap rural electrification; public works modernizing the nation's infrastructure; low-cost public housing to shelter millions of the country's least affluent citizens; expanded Social Security benefits; an increased minimum wage and farm subsidies serving the elderly, unskilled workers, and farmers; federal protection for black civil rights; and the creation of the National Aeronautics and Space Administration (NASA): all had benefited from Johnson's public service.

After thirty years of accomplishment, however, LBJ found himself in a dead-end job. Or so the 172-year history of the vice presidency suggested. There were no notable achievements by a vice president to give him comfort, and no vice president had succeeded to the presidency by election since Martin Van Buren in 1836. Johnson was mindful of Woodrow Wilson's observation: "The chief embarrassment in discussing his [the vice president's] office is that in explaining how little there is to be said about it, one has evidently said all there is to say."

John Kennedy added to Johnson's sense of being eclipsed and useless. Harvard educated, handsome, charming, urbane, a northeastern aristocrat with all the advantages, JFK appeared to be everything LBJ was not. As painful to Johnson was that Kennedy's claim on the presidency seemed unmerited alongside his own. "It was the goddamnedest thing," Johnson later told Doris Kearns. "Here was a whippersnapper. . . . He never said a word of importance in the Senate and he never did a thing. But somehow . . . he managed to create the image of himself as a shining intellectual, a youthful leader who would change the face of the country." Behind Kennedy's back, Johnson called him "sonny boy," a "lightweight" who needed "a little gray in his hair." When forty-three-year-old Kennedy, the youngest man ever elected to the presidency, declared in his inaugural speech that "the torch has been passed to a new generation of Americans," Johnson saw the reference as applying not only to Eisenhower, at age seventy, the oldest man then to have served in the White House, but also to himself. To be sure, Johnson had established a record as an exceptional Senate leader and had made a significant contribution to JFK's victory in November 1960, helping him carry Texas and six other southern states. But whatever his political savvy as a legislator and a campaigner, he was now an outsider, a marginal figure in a Kennedy White House keeping its distance from familiar faces and programs as it sought to conquer "the New Frontier."

Johnson had no intention of remaining a fringe player in the Kennedy administration. From the moment he had decided to accept the vice presidential nomination in the summer of 1960 he had sought to increase the importance of the office. Presiding over the Senate and casting rare tie-breaking votes—a vice president's only constitutional duty—was not Lyndon's idea of how to achieve four more years as vice president and a record to run on for the presidency. A promise from Kennedy to House Speaker Sam Rayburn that he would give Lyndon "important domestic duties and send him on trips abroad" was music to Johnson's ears. During the 1960 campaign one of Johnson's aides told him that the Founding Fathers "intended the vice president to be the number two man in the government" and that a larger executive role for the vice president should complement a significant part for him in rallying Congress behind the president's program. Johnson wanted the memo published in a national magazine.

Johnson's plan to make himself a powerful vice president ran into insurmountable obstacles. On January 3, seventeen days before taking office, he tried to assure himself an unprecedented congressional role. At a Democratic Senate caucus, Mike Mansfield of Montana, Johnson's hand-picked successor as majority leader, asked the sixty-three Democratic senators to let Johnson preside over future caucuses. The proposal angered several senators, who saw this as a power grab and a challenge to the traditional separation of congressional and executive authority. Liberal senator Albert Gore Sr. of Tennessee spearheaded the opposition: "This caucus is not open to former senators," he declared. Although a vote of forty-six to seventeen gave Johnson a large majority, it left no doubt in his mind that most senators opposed the plan. "You could feel the heavy animosity in the room, even from many who voted for Lyndon," Gore asserted. The reaction of his Senate colleagues humiliated and enraged Johnson. "I now know the difference between a caucus and a cactus," he told someone who leaked his remark to reporters. "In a cactus all the pricks are on the outside."

Johnson suffered another humiliating defeat within days after becoming vice president. In his eagerness to establish an important role for himself, Johnson proposed that Kennedy sign an executive order giving the vice president "general supervision" over a number of government agencies, including NASA, and directing cabinet heads and department chiefs to give Johnson copies of all major documents sent to the president. Knowing a power grab when he saw one, Kennedy simply ignored the memo. But White House aides, determined to put Johnson in his place at the start of the new administration, leaked the incident to the press and compared Lyndon to William Seward, Lincoln's secretary of state, who had made a similar unsuccessful proposal.

Yet, in turning aside Lyndon's reach for power, Kennedy did not want to alienate him and destroy his usefulness to the administration. Indeed, Kennedy was sensitive to Lyndon's plight: the powerful majority leader of 1955–1960, whom the younger, less experienced JFK had to court for favors, was now the supplicant asking for a share of power. Kennedy had no intention of letting Lyndon become a dominant figure or more than a well-controlled functionary in the administration. But neither did he wish to provoke him into becoming a covert opponent, as John Nance Garner, FDR's first vice president, had been. "I can't afford to have my vice president, who knows every reporter in Washington, going around saying we're all screwed up, so we're going to keep him happy," JFK told White House aide Kenneth O'Donnell. Having won the presidency by a paper-thin margin over Nixon and needing southern Democratic support to pass significant legislation and win reelection to a second term, JFK saw LBJ as a useful political ally.

Kennedy tried to assuage Johnson's huge ego with the trappings of power. He raised no objection to letting Lyndon hold on to his majority leader's office, a seven-room suite across from the Senate floor, known as the Taj Mahal or the Emperor's Room. Decorated in royal green and gold with crystal chandeliers and plush furniture, the office featured a lighted full-length portrait of Johnson leaning against a bookcase and two overhead lamps projecting "an impressive nimbus of golden light" as Lyndon sat at his desk. In addition, although Kennedy rejected a request from Johnson for an office next to the president's, he assigned him a six-room suite on the second floor of the Executive Office Building (EOB) next to the White House. Since many, including Presidents Truman and Eisenhower, believed that the vice president was a member of the legislative rather than the executive branch, Johnson's presence in the EOB had significant constitutional implications. Kennedy also invited Lyndon to attend cabinet meetings, weekly sessions with House and Senate leaders, prepress conference briefings, and National Security Council meetings, as required by law.

Kennedy insisted that his staff treat Johnson with the same respect they would have wanted him shown if the positions were reversed. "You are dealing with a very insecure, sensitive man with a huge ego," JFK told O'Donnell. "I want you literally to kiss his fanny from one end of Washington to the other."

New York Times columnist Arthur Krock remembered Kennedy "often" expressing concern about Lyndon, saying, " 'I've got to keep him happy somehow.' " To appease Johnson, who would often descend on him with personal complaints, Kennedy worked out a routine with O'Donnell. JFK would first hear Lyndon out and then call in O'Donnell for a tongue-lashing about Johnson's problem. Johnson would then "go away somewhat happier." He had been treated "better than any other vice president in history and knew it," Johnson later told Secretary of State Dean Rusk.

Johnson's satisfaction was hardly Kennedy's first priority. His problems with the Soviet Union, Cuba, Southeast Asia, the domestic economy, black pressure for equal rights, and the political survival of his administration left him little room to fret over a discontented vice president. Yet he had genuine regard for Johnson as a "political operator" and even liked his "roguish qualities." More important, he viewed him as someone who, despite the limitations of the vice presidency, could contribute to the national well-being in foreign and domestic affairs and, by so doing, make Kennedy a more effective president.

JFK gave some careful thought to Johnson's role in the administration. He did not want him managing its legislative program and creating the impression that the president was following the lead of his vice president, a more experienced legislator. Kennedy was happy to have Johnson gather intelligence on what senators and representatives were thinking, but he had no intention of allowing him to become the point man or administration leader on major bills. Besides, he understood that Johnson no longer had the means he used as majority leader to drive bills through the Senate. Instead, he wanted Johnson to head the new Committee on Equal Employment Opportunity (CEEO), chair the National Aeronautics and Space Council, and represent the United States on trips to foreign countries.

Kennedy knew that civil rights was going to be a major issue during the next four years. The campaign in the fifties by Martin Luther King and the Southern Christian Leadership Conference against racial segregation made civil rights a compelling question for JFK's administration. He doubted, however, that a cautious Congress dominated by southern Democrats would be favorably disposed to a bill assuring black Americans both the right to vote and access to public facilities across the South. Consequently, he planned to rely on executive action as an immediate device for advancing black equality. Specifically, JFK wanted the CEEO to combat discriminatory hiring practices in the federal government and by private businesses with federal contracts. Lyndon was to be one of the principal figures implementing this strategy. As a southern moderate, who had led a major civil rights law through the Congress in 1957 and believed the national well-being required equal treatment for blacks, Johnson could be invaluable in advancing a rational response to a highly charged issue and preventing southern alienation from the administration.

At the same time, Kennedy wanted Johnson, the legislative father of NASA, to have a significant part in shaping space policy. Again, he would not let Lyndon eclipse him on an issue given high public visibility by Soviet space launches, but he was eager to use Johnson's expertise on a matter of vital national concern. Moreover, in giving Johnson some prominence as an architect of America's space program, Kennedy was making him a political lightning rod. Should an effort to catch and pass the Soviets in space technology fail or suffer a well-publicized defeat, Lyndon would be out front taking some, if not much, of the heat. As for trips abroad, they were ceremonial givens of the vice president's office, but Kennedy also saw them as an outlet for Johnson's restless energy.

None of what Kennedy asked him to do made Johnson happy. He resented the president's unwillingness to rely on his legislative expertise, telling people that his knowledge and contacts on the Hill were not being used. He had little enthusiasm for foreign travels that would be more symbolic than substantive. Although he saw some political benefits coming to him from chairing the CEEO and the Space Council, he also saw liabilities that could work against his having another vice presidential term or ever getting to the presidency. As important, he viewed both jobs as relegating him to a distinctly secondary role in the administration, which, of course, they did.

Initially, one of the hardest assignments for Johnson to accept was that of goodwill ambassador. In the nearly three years he served as vice president, he spent almost two and one-half months making eleven trips to thirty-three foreign lands. Most of it consisted of showing the flag. But Kennedy saw it as a good way to fill Johnson's time and improve his disposition. Kennedy told Florida senator George Smathers, "I cannot stand Johnson's damn long face. He just comes in, sits at the Cabinet meetings with his face all screwed up, never says anything. He looks so sad." Smathers suggested that the president send Johnson "on an around-the-world trip . . . so that he can get all of the fanfare and all of the attention and all of the smoke-blowing will be directed at him, build up his ego again, let him have a great time." Kennedy thought it "a damn good idea," and in the spring of 1961 he sent Johnson to Africa and Asia.

Johnson was reluctant to spend his time on what he saw as mostly frivolous business. But his craving for center stage, which he could have while traveling abroad but not at home, quickly made him an enthusiast of foreign trips. Indeed, they became a kind of theater in which he could act out his zany, irreverent, demanding, impetuous characteristics that amused and pleased some and offended and amazed others. They also gave him an opportunity to bring a message of hope to needy people in distant lands. In Africa and Asia his trips partly became a crusade for the New Deal reforms that had transformed America. Eager to combat Communist appeals to poor developing nations, Johnson pointed to economic change in his native South as a model for Third World advance.

A four-day trip to Senegal in April 1961 was part comic opera and part serious diplomatic mission. Kennedy's decision to send Lyndon there largely rested on a desire to compete with Communist efforts to woo emerging nations. For Johnson, it immediately became a chance to play the great man offering enlightened guidance to an impoverished people. He insisted that a seven-foot bed to accommodate his six-foot, three-and-one-half-inch frame, a special showerhead that emitted a needlepoint spray, cases of Cutty Sark, and boxes of ballpoint pens and cigarette lighters with his initials inscribed on them travel with him to Dakar.

There, he ignored the diplomatic niceties urged upon him by the U.S. embassy. One morning at four-thirty he and Lady Bird traveled to a fishing village, where the American ambassador refused to leave his limousine. "It was too smelly a town for him," a Johnson traveling companion recalled. The ambassador counseled Johnson against any contact with the people, whom he described as dirty and diseased. But the vice president strolled among the villagers handing out pens and lighters, shaking hands with everyone, including a few fingerless lepers, and advising the bewildered natives that they could be like Texans, who had increased their annual income tenfold in forty years. When he returned to the United States, Johnson told black civil rights leader Roy Wilkins that Senegalese mothers, into whose eyes he had looked, were just like Texas mothers; all of them wanted the best for their children. The trip was a microcosm of Johnson's career: a grandiose, temperamental man doing outlandish things simultaneously to get attention and to improve the lot of the poor.

Johnson's behavior abroad makes it easy to poke fun at him as a comic figure or some sort of fabulous Texas character, a man with a monumental ego whose priority was more the selling of Lyndon Johnson than the advancement of any foreign policy goal. There is, of course, a certain truth to this. Johnson was a larger-than-life character with self-serving impulses that entered into everything he did. Yet he was also someone who never lost sight of bold public designs. Johnson's trips were a kind of New Deal crusade. They were an attempt to get out and meet the people and sell them on the virtues of American democracy and free enterprise. However parochial it may have been, Johnson, like Woodrow Wilson and other evangels of democracy, was a crusader for the American dream, an exponent of the idea that inside of every impoverished African and Asian there was an American waiting to emerge.

In April 1961, after a Soviet cosmonaut became the first man to orbit the earth and the failure at the Bay of Pigs had embarrassed the United States, JFK asked Lyndon to make "an overall survey of where we stand in space. Do we have a chance of beating the Soviets by putting a laboratory in space, or by a trip around the moon, or by a rocket to land on the moon, or by a rocket to go to the moon and back with a man?" Johnson replied that the Soviets were ahead "in world prestige attained through technological accomplishments in space." And other nations, identifying space gains as reflections of world leadership, were being drawn to the Soviets. A strong effort was needed at once to catch and surpass the Russians if the United States was to win "control over . . . men's minds through space accomplishments." Johnson recommended "manned exploration of the moon" as "an achievement with great propaganda value." "The real 'competition' in outer space," he said, was between the communist and free-enterprise social systems. The control of outer space was going to "determine which system of society and government [would] dominate the future." When people complained about the cost of space exploration, Johnson replied: "Now, would you rather have us be a second-rate nation or should we spend a little money?"

Kennedy needed no prodding from Johnson to make the case for some dramatic space venture. At the end of May 1961, JFK asked the country to commit itself to the goal of landing a man on the moon and returning him safely to earth before the decade was out.

Yet, Kennedy worried that a highly publicized American space effort that ended in failure would further damage the nation's prestige and inflict a political wound that could jeopardize his hold on the presidency. Alan Shepard's successful suborbital flight in May 1961 had encouraged Kennedy's hopes that America might catch and pass the Soviets, but he remained concerned about future mishaps. In June when Shepard drove with the president, LBJ, and Newton Minow (head of the Federal Communications Commission) to speak before the National Convention of Broadcasters, Kennedy poked Johnson and said: "You know, Lyndon, nobody knows that the vice president is the chairman of the Space Council. But if that flight had been a flop, I guarantee you that everybody would have known that you were the chairman." Everyone laughed, except Lyndon, who looked glum and angry, especially after Minow chimed in: "Mr. President, if the flight would have been a flop, the vice president would have been the next astronaut."

The possibility that he would be a sacrificial political lamb for a faulty space effort did not dampen Johnson's enthusiasm for a manned mission to the moon. In 1963, when criticism from academics, journalists, and political conservatives began to be heard against "the moon-doggle," Johnson told Kennedy: "The space program is expensive, but it can be justified as a solid investment which will give ample returns in security, prestige, knowledge, and material benefits."

Johnson's greatest challenge as vice president was chairing the CEEO. The goal of helping black Americans win equal access to jobs appealed to his sense of fairness and compassion for a disadvantaged minority, concerns dating from early in his political career. To be sure, his congressional voting record on civil rights before 1957 in no way distinguished him from southern segregationists. But his inner convictions were different: for the South to come into the mainstream of the country's economic and political life, he believed that it would have to abandon the system of segregation that consigned blacks to second-class citizenship and separated the South from the rest of the nation.

The chairmanship at the CEEO had the added advantage of disarming northern liberal hostility, which Johnson saw as a potential obstacle to a presidential bid in 1968. Yet, at the same time, Johnson feared that chairing the CEEO might trap him into antagonizing northern liberals, who would complain he did too little, and southern conservatives, who would attack him for doing too much. Reluctant to put himself between the clashing forces on the most visible domestic problem of 1960–1961, Johnson did not want to take the job, telling Kennedy: "I don't have any budget, and I don't have any power, I don't have anything." But Kennedy would not let Johnson off the hook, saying, "You've got to do it because Nixon had it before, even though he didn't do anything; you're from the south, and if you don't take it, you'll be deemed to have evaded your responsibility."

Although he saw political liabilities resulting from almost anything he did at the CEEO, Johnson was determined to get something done. This was partly a matter of personal temperament and ego; the assignment was a fresh challenge, a test of Lyndon Johnson, a questioning of his capacities as a leader and a politician. As with every job he ever confronted, it triggered his competitive urges, driving him to do his best, disarm critics, and win praise for a gold-medal performance.

At the same time, he believed that racial discrimination had no legitimate place in American life. When Harris Wofford, an early supporter of JFK and a leading civil rights advocate in Kennedy's White House, tried to persuade Roy Wilkins of the National Association for the Advancement of Colored People (NAACP) to back Kennedy in 1960, Wilkins said that "of all the men in American political life, I would trust to do the most about civil rights, . . . it would be Lyndon Johnson." "And," Wofford added, "I think Roy was not too far wrong on that. Civil rights really was something that, by this time, was burning pretty strongly in Johnson."

Kennedy and Johnson believed that the CEEO could make a difference in giving blacks a fairer chance at more and better jobs. A federal workforce of more than 2 million and government contracts paying the salaries of another 15.5 million Americans gave the government considerable leverage to advance the interests of black wage earners. JFK asked Johnson to draft an executive order that would set the CEEO in motion. Relying on his old friend Abe Fortas, a prominent Washington attorney, Johnson pushed to have "this Executive Order go as far as an Executive Order could go." When Kennedy pressed Johnson through White House aide Richard Goodwin to get the order out, Lyndon replied: "We are trying . . . to make [the committee] more workable and more effective, . . . we don't think it has produced much results in eight years." In particular, Johnson insisted that all contractors doing business with the government sign statements denying discriminatory practices and that the committee be free to cancel contracts with businesses violating their commitments.

At the same time, though, Johnson was the soul of caution. Discrimination against blacks was wrong: it violated the spirit and letter of American ideals; it limited the country's economic output and injured its prestige abroad. But it was part of the southern landscape, and moving too vigorously to break old habits would produce social divisions and political losses that neither Kennedy nor Johnson was prepared to accept, at least not in 1961–1962.

Johnson was also reluctant to compel southern accommodation to his committee's equal employment demands. "This is not a persecuting committee or prosecuting committee," he announced in March 1961. "In most cases, we believe and hope the situation can be straightened out through persuasion and . . . appeals to good will." Johnson had an excessive faith in volunteerism. In a meeting with forty-eight of the nation's largest defense contractors in May, he described the urgency of the situation. Discrimination was a reality of American life, and sympathy for its victims was an inadequate response. "They need jobs—and it is not enough to tell them that if they are patient their children or their grandchildren will have justice. We must act now." His committee had considerable power to force nondiscrimination, Johnson pointed out. "But I do not think this problem will be solved by threatening people or bullying them. . . . We are going to operate on the rule of good faith." Lyndon's inclination to rely on the goodwill of defense contractors in the South had less to do with their demonstrated readiness to respond than his reluctance to force an issue that could hurt him and the administration.

Nevertheless, in 1962–1963, Johnson used the CEEO to expand black job opportunities in the government and the private sector. Federal jobs held by blacks increased 17 percent in fiscal year 1962 and another 22 percent in fiscal year 1963. In addition, Johnson's committee directed private contractors to correct nearly seventeen hundred complaints lodged against them by black employees, doubling the rate at which the CEEO had required "corrective actions" in one year. Yet these CEEO gains barely made a dent in black unemployment or satisfied the demand for comprehensive civil rights legislation that would challenge the whole Jim Crow system of segregation across the South.

By the fall of 1963, Lyndon was largely a forgotten man in the country. An article in the *Texas Observer*—"What Is an LBJ?"—reported that comedians and newspapers were having a field day with Johnson's obscurity. When the popular CBS television show *Candid Camera* asked a random sample of Americans, "Who is Lyndon Johnson?" the on-camera replies demonstrated LBJ's public invisibility. "No, I don't know him," one man said. "I'm from New Jersey." Another replied: "There's a lot of Johnsons around here. Does he live on a farm?" Three ladies said they did not know who he was, though one thought "he [had] something to do with the President," and another answered: "He's not president. Am I getting close?" A man working in a warehouse said he did not know him and suggested that they look him up in the telephone book.

As the reality of Johnson's eclipse registered on him, he became sullen and depressed. When his former Senate aide Harry McPherson went swimming with him one afternoon at his home, McPherson thought he "looked absolutely gross. His belly was enormous and his face looked bad, flushed, maybe he had been drinking a good deal. . . . His life was not causing him to come together physically, morally, intellectually, any way. On the contrary, . . . it must have been a tremendous frustration." When Elizabeth Wickenden told Abe Fortas, both old Johnson friends, that Wilbur Cohen, a prominent New Dealer, thought Lyndon would succeed JFK in the White House, Fortas said: "Oh, get on the phone. Call him up right away and tell him because he's so depressed." Daniel Patrick Moynihan remembered looking into Vice President Johnson's eyes and thinking, "This is a bull castrated very late in life." Johnson himself made no bones about the vice presidency. He later described the office as "filled with trips around the world, chauffeurs, men saluting, people clapping, chairmanships of councils, but in the end, it is nothing. I detested every minute of it."

Yet he never gave public expression to his disgruntlement. As he had told JFK almost a year after their inauguration, "Where you lead, I will follow." And he did. Although he disagreed with Kennedy on a number of issues that arose during his presidency, Lyndon had swallowed his objections. He would not let on to reporters that there was ever the least difference between him and the White House nor would he speak in other than "measured phrases" about the president in private. During cabinet and National Security Council meetings he invariably backed Kennedy's policies. He cleared all major speeches at home and abroad with the White House. When journalist William S. White, his old friend, visited him at his office, Johnson suggested that they see less of each other as a way to avoid suspicions that any critical White column originated with him. "Johnson showed great self-discipline and strength" during his vice presidency, Dean Rusk said. "I think it was a major effort of self-control to fit into that role—with all that volcanic force that was part of his very being."

But Johnson was containing that "volcanic force" in hopes of using it another day. His self-discipline partly stemmed from the conviction that a vice president owed his president full loyalty. It was an unspoken contract Johnson had accepted when he signed on as Kennedy's second in command. But beyond that there was the hope that after eight years of unstinting service he would have Kennedy's backing for his own presidential term. Johnson understood that any number of things could sidetrack his ambition, including a shift in political circumstances that would lead Kennedy to drop him from the ticket or JFK's defeat in 1964. Both these possibilities nagged at him, but he had tried to forestall them and advance his prospects for 1968 by being as disciplined and devoted a member of the Kennedy administration as he could.

Johnson's service as vice president frustrated and pained him. But his presence in the office had schooled him in the workings of the executive branch and had helped prepare him for the heavy burden of responsibility he assumed with John Kennedy's tragic death in November 1963.

IV

TRAGEDY AND CRISIS, 1965–1973

In many respects, the vice presidency of Hubert Humphrey was among the most tragic episodes in the history of our most anomalous office. Humphrey entered office a popular and dynamic political leader whose skills were widely admired. His term began flush with hints of historic new responsibilities. Within months, he was portrayed as an insignificant figure, often ignored or ridiculed. During a confinement of four years he was repeatedly subjected to petty humiliations, surprising in their occurrence and unprecedented in their range.

—JOEL K. GOLDSTEIN

Agnew had found his niche as a political-campaign assault weapon. But when he was required to employ some humility and quietly assume the role of second in command, he was miserable. His attempts to plunge into policy waters that were clearly over his head only further alienated him from a White House staff and a president who already viewed him as a boor.

—JOHN ROBERT GREENE

More Agony than Ecstasy:
Hubert H. Humphrey as Vice President

In many respects, the vice presidency of Hubert Humphrey was among the most tragic episodes in the history of our most anomalous office. Humphrey entered office a popular and dynamic political leader whose skills were widely admired. His term began flush with hints of historic new responsibilities. Within months, he was portrayed as an insignificant figure, often ignored or ridiculed. During a confinement of four years he was repeatedly subjected to petty humiliations, surprising in their occurrence and unprecedented in their range.

Humphrey himself later wrote that as vice president "he had been trapped, vulnerable and alone," a complaint unduly mild in its indictment of his subjugation. Author Jules Witcover was surely right in his book *Crapshoot: Rolling the Dice on the Vice Presidency* when he pronounced Humphrey's vice presidency "more agony than ecstasy." Although this portrayal accurately depicts Humphrey's experience, it should not obscure the very real contributions that Humphrey's tenure made to the development of the vice presidency as a political institution, for Humphrey became vice president at a time when the office was in the midst of a transformation from an insignificant office to a station of some import. Notwithstanding the disparity between promise and reality, Humphrey's tenure contributed importantly to the development of the vice presidency as a significant political institution.

Speculation regarding Lyndon Johnson's running mate began within days of his succession to the presidency. John Kennedy's assassination and Johnson's prior health problems focused attention to an unusual degree on the possibility of presidential vacancy. One of the persistent myths of American politics is that nobody runs for vice president. In fact, most recent vice presidential nominees have campaigned for the office, albeit not in the same public way politicians seek other positions. Humphrey was no exception. He conducted a curious campaign orchestrated to influence an electorate of one: President Johnson.

From the outset, Humphrey was clearly among the handful of most eligible candidates. He met with advisers early in 1964 to determine a strategy to secure the vice presidency. Associates contacted friends across the nation to enlist support. Politicians were urged to exploit visits to the Oval Office to lobby Johnson on Humphrey's behalf. Ultimately, forty senators endorsed Humphrey as did leaders in more than half of the states.

Johnson himself encouraged Humphrey's activities, both by word and by deed. Yet the president was not willing to commit to Humphrey until the last possible moment. He considered naming Secretary of Defense Robert McNamara, a risky choice since McNamara had never held elective office and his credentials as a Democrat were suspect. Johnson floated trial balloons for improbable candidates such as Sen. Mike Mansfield, Mayor Robert Wagner, and Gov. Pat Brown. Yet, Johnson's main purpose was to remove Atty. Gen. Robert F. Kennedy from consideration. He feared that Kennedy, who was interested in the second spot, would try to force his way onto the ticket. Finally, in late July, Johnson summoned Kennedy to the White House to tell him he would not be selected. To avoid the appearance that Kennedy alone had been eliminated, Johnson announced on July 30, 1964, that he had "reached the conclusion that it would be inadvisable for me to recommend to the convention any member of the Cabinet or any of those who meet regularly with the Cabinet," a subterfuge that fooled no one. Even as polls demonstrated his popularity, particularly when matched against his Republican rival, Sen. Barry M. Goldwater, Johnson continued to suggest that he needed a Catholic running mate, one of several factors that led him to consider Humphrey's junior colleague from Minnesota, Eugene McCarthy.

Although the choice of Humphrey seemed clearly warranted to most, the lone decision maker kept his counsel, his cards close to the vest. The toll on Humphrey was considerable. Two weeks before the convention, recalled Eric Goldman in his account *The Tragedy of Lyndon Johnson*, Humphrey was "a man who was being drained." Even when McCarthy finally withdrew his name from consideration at the convention, having concluded that the choice of Humphrey was inevitable, Johnson arranged for Connecticut senator Thomas Dodd to accompany Humphrey to the White House on August 26, 1964, to continue the charade.

Johnson had parlayed the uncertainty over his choice of a running mate into a world-class drama. It was, after all, the main suspense at the

Democratic convention. Although Humphrey had received some inkling that he would be the choice during the convention, he had no commitment from Johnson until his meeting at the White House on August 26. Johnson had thoroughly investigated his options, including Humphrey, through their mutual friend, Washington attorney James Rowe; Rowe, no doubt at Johnson's behest, had arranged for Humphrey to assure the president before the convention that, if chosen, he would be loyal. After Johnson emphasized to Humphrey at their August 26 meeting the need for the vice president to share any policy disagreements only with the president, Humphrey again pledged loyalty.

Johnson had declared, during a televised interview on March 15, that the only criterion for a vice president should be "is this the best equipped and best trained and best fitted man to serve as President should he be called upon to do so?" The selection of Humphrey seemed to meet that test. He came to office with broad support within the Democratic Party, a record of legislative accomplishment, and the admiration of politicians in both parties, the media, and the intellectual community. As Johnson told the Democratic convention on August 26, his choice of Humphrey was "not just merely the way to balance the ticket. This is simply the best man in America for this job."

Humphrey's role was not, of course, critical in securing the Democrats' landslide victory in 1964; virtually any reputable Democrat would have coasted to victory in the second spot on that ticket given Johnson's popularity and public concerns regarding Goldwater and his philosophy. But Humphrey's positive performance, if anything, enhanced his public reputation.

There was much reason to expect the Humphrey vice presidency to be successful. His friendly relationship with Johnson extended more than a decade. They had long worked well together in a relationship that in some respects mirrored that of president and vice president—Johnson as the leader, Humphrey as the subordinate—in the Senate Democratic leadership (where they had promoted each other's ambitions) and during the fourteen months while Johnson completed Kennedy's term. During that time Johnson relied on Humphrey to spearhead efforts on behalf of his legislative program, particularly the civil rights bill of 1964.

Moreover, circumstances appeared opportune for an active, contributing vice presidency. Humphrey came to the office a legislator widely admired for his intelligence, creativity, energy, and skill, traits that would seem likely to enhance an active administration. He was revered by important components of the Democratic coalition who traditionally had been suspicious of Johnson: liberals, labor, blacks, Jews; presumably these relationships could lend strength to Johnson's administration. Johnson, having served almost three years as vice president, was well aware of both the frustrations and the possibilities of the office, knowledge that theoretically would have enabled him to spare Humphrey the tribulations many of his predecessors had experienced.

Further, the vice presidency itself enjoyed an enhanced stature that seemed likely to translate into more opportunities for its new incumbent. Humphrey's immediate predecessors, Johnson and Richard M. Nixon, had been more visible and active than most prior vice presidents, thereby creating increased expectations for the office. The Kennedy assassination and smooth and effective transition had focused new attention on the problem of presidential succession and increased interest in making sure that the vice president was informed and ready to succeed.

Indeed, proposals to amend the Constitution to provide better for presidential succession and disability were pending in Congress. The leading proposals were all premised on the notion that the vice presidency had achieved new significance, that it had become an indispensable part of the executive branch.

Finally, Johnson publicly and repeatedly proclaimed his intention to involve the vice president in important fashion. He told a press conference on July 30 that "the Vice President ought to be a very intimate, close part of the Chief Executive's responsibilities, and work with him in discharging them." He promised to expand the vice president's duties. Humphrey, he told the Democratic convention on August 26, would "help make the Vice Presidency an important instrument of the executive branch." He would "help connect Congress to the White House" and "help carry America around the world." Johnson felt "strengthened knowing that he is at my side at all times in the great work of your country and your Government."

Johnson told a press conference on November 28 that he planned to consult with Humphrey on the budget, to involve him in formulating the legislative program, to rely on Humphrey's "counsel and leadership" to combat discrimination, and to engage him in special assignments. Johnson assured the press that day: "I have an extremely high regard for his capacity and he has a rich background. I want to call upon him every place I think he can make a contribution."

Johnson had sketched an image of a robust vice presidency, an office of far greater substance than ever before. The plan envisioned a close working relationship between Johnson and Humphrey. Ultimately, it depended on Johnson's willingness to involve Humphrey, for the vice presidency brought no ongoing responsibilities of significance. The workload of any vice president depends heavily on presidential assignments. Yet, Johnson never translated the portrait of the office into reality. On the contrary, Johnson began to exclude and humiliate Humphrey from the early days of the administration.

On the surface, there were some indications that Humphrey would be truly involved. In the early months of 1965, Johnson proliferated Humphrey's assignments. Johnson named Humphrey to chair the National Advisory Council of the Peace Corps on January 26, the space council, the President's Council on Equal Opportunity on February 5, the Cabinet Committee on Employment on April 26, and the Task Force on Youth Opportunity on May 22. In the heady climate of the early Great Society, when optimism ran high regarding America's ability to solve problems of prejudice and poverty, these assignments seemed to place Humphrey in positions where he could help the administration achieve some of its lofty goals in significant areas.

Yet other more ominous signals foreshadowed the troubled times ahead for the Humphrey vice presidency. Three days into the new administration, Johnson was hospitalized with chest pains. His prior history—he had a serious coronary in 1955—heightened concern over this new episode. In view of the increased interest in issues relating to presidential succession and disability, one might have expected that Johnson would take steps to ensure that Humphrey could act in his stead if need be. Indeed, only a few days later Johnson was to urge Congress to propose a constitutional amendment to better handle presidential disabilities. But the vision Johnson demonstrated regarding the problem of presidential disability in the abstract did not extend to his own health situation. Instead, Johnson denied Humphrey any information regarding his medical condition and insisted that Humphrey fulfill his prior commitments—a parade in St. Paul and opening an antipoverty program on an Indian reservation in Tucson, Arizona—to minimize concern for Johnson's condition.

When Winston Churchill died a few days later, Johnson created a controversy of sorts when he did not designate Humphrey to lead the

American delegation to the funeral. Political satirist Art Buchwald suggested that Humphrey was not sent because he was incapable of looking sad, an account that amused but did not edify. Some thought Johnson was not anxious to allow Humphrey the media attention that the role would bring; perhaps he feared his health was precarious and did not wish the vice president out of the country at the time. Johnson claimed on February 4 that he "had no particular reason for not asking" Humphrey to go; he had not realized "so vividly that it was the duty and the function of the Vice President to be present at all official funerals." Of course, no one suggested that Humphrey needed to attend *all* official funerals, but his exclusion from Churchill's seemed a slight, and Humphrey later concluded in his autobiography, *The Education of a Public Man,* that whatever Johnson's motives, "it would have been better for me had Johnson sent me."

But the most disturbing development for Humphrey's vice presidency during its first few weeks related to Vietnam. The issue that would ultimately undermine Johnson's presidency damaged Humphrey's vice presidency. On February 6, 1965, a Vietcong assault on the U.S. compound at Pleiku killed nine Americans and wounded more than one hundred. Most of Johnson's principal advisers on Vietnam favored retaliatory bombings in North Vietnam. In a meeting on February 10, 1965, Humphrey, along with Undersecretary of State George Ball, argued against air strikes while Soviet Premier Aleksei Kosygin was in Hanoi. Humphrey also forcefully opposed reliance on bombings to induce North Vietnam to negotiate and counseled against a massive infusion of American ground forces in South Vietnam.

Five days later, Humphrey prepared a twelve-point memorandum for Johnson arguing against escalation of the war. In the document, which he reproduced in *The Education of a Public Man,* Humphrey, after renewing his August vows of fidelity, expounded on the "politics of Vietnam." He warned that just three months after the election, Johnson was perceived as adopting the very Goldwater policies the Democrats had denounced. He argued that a military solution was inconsistent with the Democrats' historic approach and risked fracturing the party. Escalation of the effort in Vietnam would jeopardize other international policies in which the administration had a "heavy investment." He worried that the administration risked "creating the impression that we are the prisoner of events in Vietnam," which "blurs [our] leadership role and has spillover effects across the board" by eroding "confidence and credibility in our policies." He doubted that the public would support the war effort, in part because the government of South Vietnam seemed unworthy and the struggle appeared to be a civil war. Humphrey urged that 1965 presented the time of minimum risk to disengage. A negotiated settlement would enhance Johnson's stature and produce "enormous" domestic political dividends.

Of course, it is impossible with certainty to predict what would have transpired had Johnson accepted Humphrey's counsel. However, it is difficult to believe that the history of America or of the Johnson presidency would not have been improved. Interestingly, aside from some vague allusions to "spillover effects across the board," the memorandum failed to state explicitly that the war jeopardized the ambitious domestic programs of the Great Society. In any event, Humphrey's memorandum was prescient in analyzing the obstacles to success and in anticipating the political costs of the Vietnam War.

Yet, Humphrey's arguments, at the meeting and in the memorandum, created another casualty; they caused Johnson to ostracize him from administration councils on the war. Johnson may have viewed Humphrey's advocacy as disloyalty or as a violation of his instruction that Humphrey should not disagree with him in the presence of others. In any event, Johnson was "so annoyed at [Humphrey's] cautionary words that [he] was thereafter excluded from our meetings for many months," Ball recalled in his memoirs. The vice president was, of course, by statute a member of the National Security Council. Johnson called fewer meetings of that body, relying instead on informal conferences to plan war strategy to which Humphrey was not invited. Johnson even reprimanded Humphrey for communicating his views to him in writing, no doubt fearful of leaks and suspicious that Humphrey was preserving the historical record.

The exclusion of Humphrey from inner councils on Vietnam had multiple effects. It denied him access to important information and the opportunity to influence government policy. Moreover, the exile no doubt damaged Humphrey's reputation in Washington. Administration officials take their cues from the president. The prestige and influence of those he values rise; the standing of those he keeps at bay suffers. Word of Humphrey's demise spread. By July 1965, satirist Tom Lehrer was singing "Whatever became of Hubert?" America was feasting on news of Humphrey's fall from grace, and it was laughing. The visible signs that Humphrey was "out" no doubt undermined his influence with others.

Although Ball and Humphrey frequently discussed Vietnam, Ball avoided making common cause with Humphrey in opposing the war; he recognized that Humphrey's endorsement would not help persuade the president.

Although excluded from participating on the most significant foreign problem, Humphrey remained active on domestic policy. Humphrey was engaged advancing Johnson's legislative agenda; Johnson had anointed him as "my man on the Hill" at a meeting with legislative leaders. Johnson's recent landslide election, large Democratic majorities in Congress, and the tenor of the times combined to make early 1965 a propitious time to advance the ambitious Great Society domestic agenda. Humphrey was busily engaged as a legislative liaison and public proponent of these programs. Author Albert Eisele, who later served as press secretary to Vice President Walter F. Mondale, observed in his book, *Almost to the Presidency*, that Humphrey "helped push dozens of major laws through the first session of the Democratic-controlled Eighty-ninth Congress, including programs which had long been his personal goals."

Johnson had given Humphrey a range of domestic portfolios. Although some involved relatively trivial matters—promoting domestic travel, for instance—others had real substance. Johnson's appointment of Humphrey to chair the President's Council on Equal Opportunity on February 5, 1965, seemed most promising. Johnson wrote Humphrey on that day that the council would provide "a most effective means of insuring cooperation, coordination and harmonious working relationships" among those in the federal government dealing with civil rights; the president was "pleased" that Humphrey was "personally undertaking the coordination" of the programs that would benefit from Humphrey's "special qualifications."

The chairmanship of the President's Council on Equal Opportunity, an entity designed to address discrimination in government contracts, placed Humphrey, in the words of Joseph Califano, "at the center of the administration's civil rights action," a critical part of the agenda of the Great Society. By late summer, Humphrey had organized a series of meetings with cabinet members and heads of government agencies and had issued directives to them to address discrimination in a range of institutions.

During the same period, Humphrey's activity as chair of a presidential task force on youth opportunity won him credit for producing more than 880,000 new work and training opportunities for young Americans between sixteen and twenty-one years old. At a session in the cabinet room on August 21, 1965, Johnson, after accepting Humphrey's report, lavished praise on Humphrey:

> I thought, as you were speaking, I guess if we had a man-of-the-year poll . . . that the Vice President would be voted the one person in the Government that is everybody's best friend. If the Secretary of State, Defense, or Labor or any of them had a peculiar and particular and delicate situation on their hands, I imagine they would want to talk to him—and they usually do—to get not only sympathy and understanding, but to get some energy and some effort and some constructive leadership. I know that is true of the Cabinet. It is particularly true with me. In a very wide range of fields and complex subjects, I find the Vice President specializes in practically all of them.

News of Humphrey's popularity no doubt surprised administration watchers. Humphrey must have been particularly shocked, albeit pleasantly so, to learn of the demand for his participation, talents, and "constructive leadership." Yet, Johnson allowed him little time to savor his status as "everybody's best friend" before again ushering him toward the exit signs. Johnson had become impatient with the pace of administration efforts on civil rights and questioned whether Humphrey was forceful enough to accomplish the mission. He decided to reorganize the government's efforts, transferring authority from Humphrey. Having received a plan from aides, Johnson proceeded to advise Humphrey, in the presence of others, that he was being stripped of his responsibilities.

Johnson had carefully choreographed the scene, the atmosphere, and the presentation to allow Humphrey no option but to acquiesce to the inevitable. Califano, who was present and who has provided an account of these events in his memoirs, *The Triumph and Tragedy of Lyndon Johnson*, recalls that the ever loyal Humphrey again assured Johnson of his support. Johnson then decided that, in view of Humphrey's expressed support for the plan, Humphrey should be presented as its architect.

At Johnson's direction, by the next morning Califano prepared and presented to Humphrey for signature a vice presidential memorandum to Johnson recommending the changes. "Humphrey's" memorandum, which was made public on September 25, 1965, suggested that "whenever possible operating functions should be performed by department and agencies with clearly defined responsibilities, as distinguished from interagency committees or other interagency arrangements," a principle that, though plausible, threatened many of the duties Humphrey had been assigned. Since Humphrey was "convinced" that the functions of the committee he had chaired "can be even more effectively administered if transferred to existing agencies," Humphrey recommended abolishing his committee. After Humphrey dutifully signed the document, Johnson decided that in view of Humphrey's enthusiasm for the change (as reflected by the memorandum that Johnson's staff had drafted for Humphrey), Humphrey should announce the reorganization at a White House press conference.

The events of the first year underscored the dependence of a modern vice president on the chief executive. Since neither Constitution nor statute assigned the vice president meaningful ongoing duties, Humphrey, like other contemporary vice presidents, relied on the president for assignments to make his political life meaningful. After only eight months on the job, Humphrey had been dealt out of decision making on Vietnam, the most significant international issue of the time, and deprived of his portfolio on civil rights, the signal domestic issue. As Humphrey learned, "He who giveth can taketh away and often does."

Humphrey's humiliation was not defined solely by exclusion from major substantive issues. Johnson concocted other ways to embarrass the vice president. When Humphrey entertained friends and supporters one night on one of the presidential yachts, he had the misfortune to pass a boat carrying Johnson. Johnson instructed his captain to call the yacht bearing Humphrey to find out who was using it. Thereafter, whenever Humphrey wanted to use one of the presidential planes or boats he needed to send a written request for the equipment to a top White House aide who would forward the request to Johnson. Approval was not automatic.

To be sure, Humphrey was not totally free of fault. At times during the first year and later, he made policy statements that went beyond administration programs or was the source (or was believed to have been the source) of leaked information. But such offenses were probably inadvertent and surely did not merit the punishment applied.

Humphrey's year in political Siberia ended in late December 1965 when Johnson sent him to four Asian nations (the Philippines, Formosa, South Korea, and Japan) to explain America's role in Vietnam. The following month Johnson designated him to lead the American delegation to the funeral of India's prime minister, Lal Bahadur Shastri. The trip demonstrated that Humphrey could look sad at funerals; more important, it provided Humphrey with the opportunity for several talks with the new Soviet premier, Aleksei N. Kosygin. Although the wide-ranging talks failed to produce any movement toward a negotiated settlement in Vietnam, they constituted the first high-level meetings between the United States and the new Soviet leadership that had been installed in October 1964. For Humphrey, the trip provided the benefits that foreign travel gives vice presidents: information, new contacts, and, perhaps most important, favorable exposure. Cynics dismissed the missions as attempts to restore Humphrey's popular approval; Goldwater termed them "Operation Help Hubert," which he described to *Time* as "the most valiant rescue effort since the evacuation of Dunkirk."

Humphrey did not have to wait long after his return from New Delhi for his next significant assignment. Johnson, after returning from meetings in Honolulu with the leaders of South Vietnam, dispatched Humphrey to Saigon and other Asian and Pacific nations. Ironically, the trip occurred almost a year to the date of the fateful meeting following the assault on Pleiku at which Humphrey's performance contributed to his ostracism. The ostensible purpose of the mission was to explain to allies in the region the results of the Honolulu conference and to allow Humphrey and his colleagues opportunity to review developments in Vietnam.

Yet, Johnson had a broader agenda in sending Humphrey to Vietnam. Liberals and other important constituencies in the Democratic Party were becoming more vocal in their questioning of America's involvement in Vietnam. Johnson hoped to parry their criticisms by thrusting Humphrey to the forefront of the administration's defense of its policy.

The conditions under which the trip occurred were miserable: Humphrey and his staff had less than twenty-four hours' notice to embark on a two-week, forty-three-thousand-mile journey to nine countries. There was little time to arrange passports and shots, or to pack; adequate briefing was impossible. Johnson sent with Humphrey not only ranking diplomats but also Jack Valenti, one of Johnson's most faithful White House aides, to report daily on Humphrey's performance. Valenti's participation signaled that even abroad the White House was intent on maintaining tight reins on Humphrey.

Moreover, the trip carried obvious political risk for Humphrey. He lacked the authority to decide American policy on Vietnam; indeed, he could not even influence the administration's deliberations since he was not invited to those discussions and had been told not to write Johnson memos on the subject. Yet he was now being positioned to spend his credibility with his long-standing allies by championing a policy they detested and he had questioned.

Humphrey had no real option but to accept this mission impossible. His first year in office had no doubt reminded him of the perils of his position. His standing with the electorate had plummeted; a national poll at the end of 1965 revealed that 58 percent did not want him to be president. He had become totally dependent on Johnson for his political survival, and Johnson clearly had the will and skill to exploit Humphrey's subordination.

Johnson wasted little time before he put Humphrey on center stage in efforts to build domestic support for the administration's policies. Johnson embraced Humphrey upon his return in a welcoming ceremony on the south lawn of the White House on February 23, 1966, and pronounced Humphrey's "mission of peace" a success. Humphrey announced that he was "encouraged because the tide of battle in Vietnam has turned in our favor," reported that the Asian and Pacific Rim countries wanted their own " 'Great Society,' " and proclaimed his "deep sense of confidence in our cause, and in its ultimate triumph." With fanfare, Johnson arranged for Humphrey to conduct separate briefings the following day for the bipartisan leadership of Congress and for two hundred members of congressional committees dealing with foreign affairs and defense.

Humphrey had been relegated to the sidelines since February 1965 when he dared to raise questions in administration councils or in a private memorandum to Johnson. Now he was back on the active roster, and prominently so. Indeed, during speeches and press conferences during the winter and spring, Johnson invoked Humphrey's findings as support for his actions in Vietnam.

Following the trip, Humphrey became, in the words of *Time*, "the Administration's most articulate and indefatigable exponent of U.S. Asian policy." Humphrey defended Johnson's policies in speeches around the country. The trip and new salesman role certainly raised Humphrey's standing within the administration. But his influence remained limited; he was a cheerleader, not a playmaker. As Tom Wicker of the *New York Times* perceptively observed on February 27, 1966, "the Johnson Administration seems less interested in learning from [Humphrey's] experience than in using the Vice President's new expertise and customary enthusiasm to justify its established policy."

Although Johnson began to invite Humphrey to the small luncheons where foreign policy decisions were made, his inclusion now had limited impact. Johnson's policy was set, for the time being at least; moreover, Humphrey's views had apparently changed. Influenced perhaps by the views of Asian leaders or by his desire to win Johnson's favor, Humphrey had become a convert to the administration's policies. He continued to champion those policies well into 1968.

Humphrey's role as salesman for the war cost him, especially among liberals, his traditional constituency. "I think he has lost all his persuasiveness among people who think," said Sen. Wayne Morse in February 1966. "I never expected my Vice-president to make this plea for war that he is making." *New York Post* columnist James Wechsler compared Humphrey's "righteous rhetoric" to Richard M. Nixon, an association Humphrey and his allies would have found repugnant.

Yet it would be inaccurate to regard this middle period of Humphrey's term, 1966 and 1967, as simply a dark chapter for Humphrey. He made other well-publicized trips: to the Dominican Republic to attend the inauguration of President Juan Balaguer, to Europe (where he met with the leaders of England, France, West Germany, Italy, and other allied nations), and to Africa. These journeys provided Humphrey with visibility and some opportunity to contribute substantively. For instance, Humphrey returned from his trip to Europe to receive a south-lawn welcome from the president, cabinet, and congressional leaders with full military honors. Johnson spoke of the "importance" of Humphrey's mission in fostering better relations with Europe.

Humphrey made a second voyage to Asia, including Vietnam, in autumn 1967. During that visit, Humphrey warned its leaders of growing American impatience. In his autobiography, Humphrey relates that his old misgivings returned following this trip and caused him to warn Johnson about the lack of support for the Thieu-Ky government and to suggest curtailing bombing missions and reducing America's combat presence.

Humphrey remained active on domestic issues. At a cabinet meeting on April 19, 1967, Johnson designated Humphrey as his chief legislative liaison, charged with the responsibility of shepherding Great Society measures through Congress. Johnson also made Humphrey his point person for dealing with the nation's mayors and governors regarding intergovernmental relations. Humphrey remained active monitoring race relations; during the summer of 1967 he worked closely with big-city mayors and officials of the federal government to devise programs to improve the lot of urban youth.

Humphrey's ability to influence administration policy varied according to his unpredictable relationship with Johnson. Reporter Douglas Kiker related in the January 1967 issue of *Atlantic Monthly* that Johnson decreed that Humphrey not be advised of the contents of the State of the Union address until after the administration briefed the White House press corps on its contents. "Thus it was that the relationship between Johnson and Humphrey in mid-January was such that every newspaper reporter in Washington knew the contents of the State of the Union message before the Vice President of the United States did," wrote Kiker. Alexander Haig, in his memoirs, *Caveat*, recalled attending a meeting at which Johnson allotted Humphrey five minutes to make a presentation to congressional leaders and members of the National Security Council. Johnson conspicuously monitored his watch as Humphrey spoke. And as Humphrey exceeded his limit, Johnson, according to Haig, physically pushed Humphrey from the room.

On other occasions, Johnson would summon Humphrey for lengthy conversation, for breakfast, drinks, or dinner, repeatedly. Or Johnson would extol Humphrey publicly as he did at a press conference on March 9, 1967, when he said, "I have never known a public servant that I worked better with or for whom I had more admiration, or who I thought was more entitled to the public trust than the Vice President."

Humphrey's final year as vice president exposed the strengths and weaknesses of the office as a springboard to the presidency. Humphrey must have felt real frustration as the year began. Colleagues in the administration such as George Ball and Larry F. O'Brien have confirmed in their autobiographies that Humphrey was unhappy with the president's conduct of the war in Vietnam. Domestically, Johnson continued to shower Humphrey with chairmanships of relatively trivial task forces. In March 1968 alone, Humphrey was appointed chair of the President's Council on Physical Fitness and Sports, the National Council on Indian Opportunity, and the Council of Recreation and Natural Beauty. These assignments hardly suggested that Humphrey was at the cutting edge.

Humphrey's prospects changed on March 31, 1968. After Johnson announced that he would not run for reelection, Humphrey soon emerged as the administration candidate. Although two formidable candidates were in the race—Sen. Robert F. Kennedy and Sen. Eugene McCarthy—and the war was unpopular, particularly in the Democratic Party, Humphrey stood atop delegate counts even before Kennedy was assassinated in June 1968. Since Humphrey was essentially precluded from entering primaries in view of his late entry into the race, his support came from states where local party leaders controlled the state delegation. Humphrey's delegate strength traced in large part to the favor he had won with party luminaries for partisan work done as vice president and from Johnson loyalists whose endorsement he inherited.

Yet, once again, being vice president was a mixed blessing. Johnson wanted to distance his administration from partisan politics; moreover, no doubt it was difficult for him to watch his aides following the leadership of his longtime subordinate. Accordingly, he ordered personnel not to participate in any campaigns, a policy that precluded some officials from supporting Humphrey's campaign for the nomination. Quite clearly, no such policy would have inhibited partisan activity had Johnson, not Humphrey, been the likely beneficiary.

Most significant, Humphrey's position as vice president compromised his ability to distance himself from the administration's policies on Vietnam. Many Humphrey allies suggested that the vice president opposed Johnson's policies on Vietnam and encouraged Humphrey to say so publicly. For months Humphrey refused, governed no doubt by the constraints of his office and his commitment to be loyal. He told one White House aide that he was "heartbroken" about efforts to cause a split between Johnson and him and "that he would rather lose the election than to let anything appear he is double-crossing or repudiating the President he has been proud to serve."

Humphrey's presidential prospects depended on his ability to separate himself from Johnson's policies on Vietnam and to establish an independent identity. But Johnson did everything he could to discourage these steps. Humphrey resisted the suggestions by some that he resign as vice president to liberate himself from the political baggage the job entailed. At the Democratic convention, Humphrey and his associates worked out a Vietnam plank that won approval from key doves and was accepted by Johnson's top foreign policy advisers, including Secretary of State Dean

Rusk. But Johnson deemed the provision unpalatable; rather than risk an open battle with the president at the convention, Humphrey retreated.

Humphrey chose as his running mate Sen. Edmund S. Muskie. He had previously tried unsuccessfully to convince Sen. Edward M. Kennedy and New York's Republican governor, Nelson A. Rockefeller, to run with him. Muskie was, of course, a well-regarded senator and a centrist within the party. Coming as he did from Maine, a state with only four electoral votes, Muskie did not seem ostensibly to bring as much political strength to the ticket as would New Jersey's governor, Richard Hughes, or Oklahoma senator Fred Harris, for instance. Humphrey claimed he chose Muskie because he "saw a man of ability and of character . . . and I liked the man, so I felt here's a man I can trust." Once Humphrey concluded that he could not convince Kennedy or Rockefeller, it seems plausible to conclude that Humphrey did, in fact, weigh competence and compatibility heavily in deciding on Muskie.

Johnson did little publicly to help Humphrey. Even after Humphrey was the nominee Johnson seemed somewhat ambivalent. He signed a farm bill that Humphrey deemed important to his campaign in the Midwest, but only after suggesting he might veto it. He often briefed Humphrey about developments in the peace talks simultaneously with his rivals, Nixon and Gov. George Wallace, not even giving him advance information. To be sure, Johnson did campaign for Humphrey toward the close of the campaign, but, as Johnson aide Harry McPherson has written in *A Political Education*, "the extensive help which the Administration might have given Humphrey during the campaign was missing. The machinery of government was not transformed, during the 1968 campaign, from neutral-bureaucratic to partisan-political."

Distancing himself from the administration's policies on Vietnam was not easy or without risk. If Humphrey separated himself from Johnson's policies, he exposed himself to the charge of being hypocritical and disloyal and of undermining Johnson's negotiating hand. Moreover, Humphrey's comments might prompt a public rebuke from Johnson. When Humphrey suggested in early September 1968 that some American troops might come home later that year or in 1969, Johnson said the following day that the timing of the troop withdrawal was something no man could predict. "The Vice-President ran for the office of President in full consciousness that the President was going to react one way or another to everything he had to say," wrote Sen. Edmund S. Muskie in *Journeys*.

Humphrey trailed Nixon badly in the late summer and early autumn. His dismal standing traced to the baggage he carried: public disillusionment with Johnson's policies in Vietnam, the bitter aftertaste created by confrontations between police and demonstrators at the Democratic convention, the perception of Humphrey as a political eunuch. Humphrey finally staked out some separate territory with his Salt Lake City speech on September 30, 1968, in which he said that as president he would stop bombing North Vietnam to attempt to stimulate peace talks. The difference with the administration position was subtle, but Humphrey's statement and the spin put on it finally put some distance between him and Johnson's policies and allowed him to reemerge from the dark shadows obscuring his identity. (In an act replete with poetic justice, Humphrey deferred advising Johnson of the key passages of his speech until it had been taped for television and released to the press.) Humphrey gained in the polls following the speech.

Humphrey's confidence in Muskie also proved well placed. Muskie acquitted himself well in his first national campaign, particularly when compared with his opposite number, Gov. Spiro T. Agnew of Maryland. Indeed, the Democrats attempted to exploit their advantage in the vice presidential choice in media advertisements.

Although Humphrey gained ground during the closing weeks of the campaign, he narrowly lost the election. He no doubt suffered dearly from his association with the administration, a burden Johnson did nothing to ease.

In his final State of the Union address on January 14, 1969, Johnson remarked that "I have been assisted by my friend every step of the way, Vice President Hubert Humphrey." In fact, Johnson had not allowed Humphrey to so help him. He had periodically excluded and embarrassed Humphrey, demeaning the vice presidency and its incumbent and frustrating Humphrey's ambition to contribute at the level he had hoped.

What can we learn from Humphrey's vice presidency? Certainly, Humphrey's experience represents our most powerful reminder of how dependent a vice president is on the chief executive for the work that makes his job rewarding. Formal grants from Congress, such as membership on the National Security Council, may mean little, Humphrey found, if the president wishes to exclude the vice president; he can simply transfer important discussions to another venue to which the vice president is not invited. And in normal times when the vice president's influence with the chief declines in a conspicuous manner, so, too, is his standing with others likely to suffer, thrusting the vice president into a spiraling free fall that only the president can arrest.

Although more recent developments dating from the Rockefeller or Mondale years—the White House office, the regular weekly meeting with the president, and the access to presidential papers and time—have created some conventions that have helped subsequent vice presidents, Richard Neustadt is surely right in reminding us that, based on Humphrey's experience, the president, through his management of the vice president's time and schedule, can isolate the second person. Of course, others may not be quite as pliant (and not so loyal) as was Humphrey, especially if their president is not so manipulative as was Johnson. Moreover, the more recent increase in presidential primaries leaves the president somewhat more dependent on his running mate than in Humphrey's day. The president may need his running mate to carry the torch for renomination, and the proliferation of primaries even raises the possibility that some vice president could someday challenge the chief. Still, Professor Neustadt's insight represents an appropriate and ominous warning to those, including future vice presidents, who might conclude that vice presidential power has been institutionalized or that future vice presidents will be totally immune from the agony Humphrey endured.

Given that the relationship between the president and the vice president is so critical to determining vice presidential success, the Humphrey experience suggests that predicting the chemistry between two human beings in that awkward alignment is hardly a science. Ultimately, the many reasons to expect Humphrey to thrive as vice president—his long friendship with Johnson and experience in a like hierarchy, the enhanced expectations of his office, and the immense talents and relationships he brought to an active administration—were insufficient to overcome the complications Johnson's personality imposed.

Finally, Humphrey's problems running for president are instructive. An incumbent vice president must negotiate between the desire to establish an independent identity and the likely need to avoid offending the chief executive by criticizing his policies. Future vice presidents may hope they encounter circumstances less difficult and presidents more forgiving than did Humphrey.

Humphrey endured pain and disappointment of tragic proportions as vice president; that experience provides lessons for the future. Ironically,

Humphrey's tenure represented, in another sense, a period in which the vice presidency as an institution made substantial gains. When Humphrey became vice president on January 20, 1965, the office was in the relatively early stages of a transformation from a legislative office of relative insignificance into a contributing part of the executive branch. Although the rise of the vice presidency, as historian Irving Williams put it, traced to the beginning of the twentieth century, the more significant evolution began following World War II, around midcentury. Now more than three decades after Humphrey took the vice presidential oath, the office has evolved to a position of significance, even greater in many ways than the position Humphrey hoped he was getting. Developments related to Humphrey's term contributed to that growth.

First, in regard to procedures for vice presidential selection, Johnson provided an important model in several respects. Presidential candidates since 1940 had enjoyed the right to designate their own running mate; but the extent to which Johnson as president controlled the decision was virtually without precedent (except perhaps the choice of Henry Wallace in 1940). Moreover, Johnson's decision followed a prolonged consideration of the various candidates, their strengths and weaknesses. Blessed with the luxury of time to make the choice, he engaged in a careful consideration. Finally, the selection of Humphrey made plausible Johnson's claim that he chose the person best equipped to succeed to the presidency, a standard that along with compatibility surely should inform all such decisions.

Second, the selection of someone of such high caliber as Hubert Humphrey contributed to the development of the institution. Not all vice presidents, before or since, have measured up to the high standard of excellence he brought to public life. Johnson's choice of Humphrey helped set a standard of quality for others to follow. The fact that some subsequent vice presidential candidates suffered by comparison does not diminish the importance of historical examples as a way of shaping public expectations.

Third, Humphrey's service intensified the association of the vice presidency with the executive branch. Although Nixon and Johnson had increasingly abandoned their constitutional role as presiding officer of the Senate to work with the administration, Humphrey's activities more clearly placed the vice presidency near the White House. The fact that Johnson hand-picked Humphrey emphasized the link between president and vice president. The assortment of presidential assignments Johnson gave Humphrey—commission chair, foreign envoy, legislative liaison, administration spokesman, and party surrogate—identified the vice president with the executive branch.

Fourth, Humphrey was among the first truly visible vice presidents. His foreign travel and role as salesman for the Great Society and the Vietnam War made him far more conspicuous than virtually all of his predecessors and helped establish expectations for his successors.

Fifth, Humphrey's experience emphasized the power of the vice presidency as a political springboard. As a senator in 1960 he had been unable to mount an effective presidential campaign; as vice president eight years later he essentially breezed to the nomination. Of course, other factors helped account for the change in Humphrey's fortunes, but his incumbency lent resources and advantages that were probably critical. In doing so, he became the second sitting vice president of the postwar period to win his party's nomination. Clearly, Humphrey's incumbency also complicated and damaged his race for the presidency. Still, his experience helped establish the vice presidency as the best route to a presidential nomination.

The lessons of Humphrey's tenure have helped other vice presidents structure their own service in more successful fashion. Humphrey shared insights from his vice presidency with Gerald R. Ford and Walter F. Mondale. Based in part on Humphrey's experience, Mondale avoided commission chairmanships and other responsibilities that would intrude on the turf of executive-branch agencies. Such duties were time-consuming and often placed the vice president in the middle of interagency disputes that he lacked authority to resolve. Similarly, Mondale learned from Humphrey's experience that proliferation of trivial task-force assignments demeaned the vice presidency and its occupant.

Finally, during Humphrey's term the vice presidency achieved an enhanced constitutional status. The Twenty-fifth Amendment to the Constitution, which addressed problems of presidential succession and disability, was proposed by Congress in 1965 and ratified by the states by 1967. It rested on the premise that the vice presidency had become an indispensable part of the executive branch, that the vice presidency offered the best solution to problems of presidential succession and disability, and that the vice president should be a person of stature and great ability and a close working colleague of the president.

That vision behind the Twenty-fifth Amendment very much reflected the view that President Johnson and the amendment's congressional sponsors articulated of the vice presidency in 1964 and 1965 when decision makers in the nation's capital were grappling with the problem of how to improve laws relating to presidential succession and disability. That conception of the office represents the ideal against which the Humphrey vice presidency is assessed. When measured against that standard, the Humphrey vice presidency assumes its tragic dimensions. This is not because it was a failure or because its occupant did nothing, for Humphrey was active in constructive ways, nor even because Humphrey's term revealed obstacles in making real the vision. The tragedy of the Humphrey vice presidency was that one who had so much to contribute at so critical a time in America's history was not able to do so fully in that office. Recent vice presidents have benefited from the lessons of that experience; we can hope that a better understanding of that experience will contribute to the further development of the vice presidency.

"I'll Continue to Speak Out":
Spiro T. Agnew as Vice President

JOHN ROBERT GREENE

On August 8, 1968, at about one o'clock in the afternoon, Richard M. Nixon went down to the ballroom of his Miami Beach hotel to speak with the press for the first time since winning the Republican Party's nomination for the presidency. The room was buzzing with anticipation, as everyone expected that Nixon would use the occasion to announce the name of his running mate.

Smart money was riding either on one of Nixon's two defeated rivals for the nomination—New York governor Nelson Rockefeller and California governor Ronald Reagan—or on longtime Nixon confidant Robert Finch. However, when Nixon announced his choice, the press could not contain their astonishment. As Nixon walked out of the room without taking any questions, several reporters cried out, "Spiro *who?*"

Even Nixon, whose aides had met with Spiro T. Agnew several times that spring to dangle the second spot to the Maryland governor, misunderstood the tiger he had just grabbed by the tail. The night after his acceptance speech, Nixon evaluated Agnew for speechwriter William Safire: "He can't make a speech worth a damn, but he won't fall apart."

The son of a Greek immigrant, Spiro Theodore Agnew attended Johns Hopkins University and Baltimore Law School before his education was interrupted by World War II. Upon his return, he received his law degree from Baltimore in 1947 and began a career in politics. However, Maryland was solidly Democratic, and it took Agnew ten years to get his first break: in 1957, he was appointed to the Baltimore County Zoning Board of Appeals. Five years later, in a surprising upset, he was elected Baltimore County executive. Almost immediately, Agnew began to sound out Maryland Republican leaders about a run for governor in 1966. He was not given much of a chance. But he was one of only a few Republican officeholders in the state, and as a result he had no opposition. Thanks to the rabid segregationist stand of his Democratic opponent, and the correspondingly solid support of the Baltimore black community, Agnew stunned his party by winning the statehouse.

Governor Agnew moved quickly to repay his debt to the black community. He put forth a progressive fair-housing act and appointed many blacks to statewide positions. However, his gratitude did not keep him from condemning Baltimore's black community for the riots in the city that followed the April 1968 assassination of Martin Luther King. Agnew called around one hundred of the city's black leaders to his Annapolis office and, rather than offering them sympathy and help, berated them and laid the blame for the riots squarely at their door. Agnew called them "caterwauling, riot-inciting, burn-America-down type of leaders," and saw to it that his harangue was leaked to reporters in detail.

Rather than being castigated for his remarks, polls showed that public opinion in the state was clearly on Agnew's side. Quick to sense a winning issue within his constituency, Agnew became one of the leading race baiters in American politics. For example, he observed in a press backgrounder that strict gun control would not end killing in the streets of America because African tribes "shoot little darts through a blow gun very accurately," and, to Agnew, black Americans had inherited both this precision and this technique.

Agnew's rhetoric appealed to Pat Buchanan, who was then working as a speechwriter for Richard Nixon's campaign to win the 1968 presidential nomination. Buchanan reported Agnew's tirade to his boss, who was intrigued not only by Agnew's growing standing with conservatives but also by the fact that the governor had only recently abandoned his first choice for the presidency, fellow governor Nelson Rockefeller.

Nixon arranged for a dinner between himself and Agnew. The two men were joined by Nixon law partner John Mitchell, who was then serving as Nixon's campaign manager. During the course of the dinner, Nixon asked Agnew if he would place his name in nomination before the convention. Agnew agreed, and, although a deal was not yet offered, both Nixon and Mitchell came away from the dinner convinced that the governor would make a good running mate.

It is arguable that Nixon chose Agnew in 1968 for the same reasons that Nixon had been chosen for the same position in 1952 by Dwight Eisenhower. Never having the same appeal to the conservative wing of his party that his chief opponent, Robert Taft, had enjoyed, Eisenhower chose Nixon as his running mate precisely because his conservative credentials

were so strong. In 1968, Agnew had already begun to appeal to the most recent incarnation of this same constituency: those Goldwater conservatives
who had never fully trusted Nixon. Nixon hoped that Agnew's continued
harsh rhetoric would bring these conservatives—many of whom had
begun to voice their support for Alabama governor George Wallace—
home to the Republican Party in time for the election.

In addition, Agnew's bombast would serve another equally important
purpose. With Vietnam hovering as an issue that threatened to destroy any
candidate who mishandled it, Nixon wanted to deflect as much attention
from himself as possible. Thus, as he had done for Eisenhower in 1952
with much success, Nixon assigned Agnew the task of assaulting the
opposition. He was to launch a rhetorical first strike, while Nixon stayed
above the fray and pleaded for the nation to bury its divisiveness.

Agnew, then, inherited from Nixon what Garry Wills would later label
as his style of "denigrative politics." It was a shrewd move. Agnew
enjoyed traveling the low road, and he was particularly good at it. He
brought back memories of Nixon's "Alger—I mean Adlai" speech by
accusing Democratic candidate Hubert Humphrey of being "squishy-soft
on communism." Humphrey tried to fight back, telling the New York
Liberal Party to "think as I say it—President Agnew and President [Curtis]
LeMay" (George Wallace's running mate). After the expected catcalls,
Humphrey excoriated both Nixon and Wallace for "play[ing] with our
country's destiny like that."

But Agnew did not melt under the pressure. He lashed out at criticism
that he was not campaigning in enough inner cities by snapping that
"when you've seen one slum, you've seen them all," and suggested that
all looters should be "shot down by the police." In retaliation, blacks left
a sheet and a bullwhip on the fence of the governor's mansion. Agnew's
attacks seemed to know no limits: he publicly called Maryland reporter
Eugene Oishi a "fat jap," then later apologized, claiming that they were
old friends.

Nixon, however, was far from worried. Indeed, he was thrilled that
Agnew's press contingent had doubled before October, thus deflecting
attention from Nixon's own campaign. As Humphrey threatened to close
the gap in the final weeks, thanks largely to Lyndon Johnson's well-timed
bombing halt in Vietnam, Agnew continued to draw media attention
away from the serious issues of the campaign. More important, in an
election that was so close (Nixon won with just 43.4 percent of the popular

vote), postelection polls made it clear that, as Nixon had predicted, many conservatives voted for the Republican ticket *because* of the man whom they had begun to call "Spiro our Hero."

Agnew had found his niche as a political-campaign assault weapon. But when he was required to employ some humility and quietly assume the role of second in command, he was miserable. His attempts to plunge into policy waters that were clearly over his head only further alienated him from a White House staff and a president who already viewed him as a boor.

As the first man since Calvin Coolidge to step directly to the vice presidency from a statehouse, it was logical that Agnew be put in charge of relations with other state executives. The Office of Intergovernmental Relations was thus created as part of the Office of the Vice President in 1969. However, Agnew was far from diplomatic in his dealings with his former colleagues. Rockefeller, for example, simply refused to talk with him, sending his messages to Nixon through National Security Adviser Henry Kissinger.

Yet, Agnew pushed on. As chair of the Space Advisory Committee, his persistent support of a manned mission to Mars infuriated aides who tried to warn the vice president that Nixon would never approve so costly a mission. His dogged opposition to Daniel Patrick Moynihan's welfare-reform proposals unnerved Nixon, even though the president eventually abandoned the reform.

When Agnew advocated the immediate bombing of the Vietcong sanctuaries in Cambodia and Laos during a 1970 meeting of the National Security Council, his belief mirrored Nixon's own. However, Agnew was so vocal with his support that Nixon, feeling that he had been overshadowed by an adviser, refused to invite Agnew to the meeting of the inner circle during which Nixon announced his decision to proceed in Cambodia. The CIA even reported that while on an African trip, Agnew had told leaders that he opposed Nixon's overtures to the People's Republic of China.

Thanks to his refusal to be politic, Agnew was simply cut out of the policy loop before his term of office was two years old. Nixon ordered that he be told nothing of substance and that his speeches and statements be cleared with the White House in advance. Suffering in political exile, Agnew could not even retreat into the relative obscurity of his constitutional role as president of the Senate. He had poisoned that well during his first month in office, when he left the president's chair during a session and strolled onto the Senate floor with the intention of lobbying members to vote the administration line on a surtax bill. This was an egregious breach of senatorial etiquette, and Len Jordan of Idaho stopped the vice president on the floor and chewed him out. The next day, Jordan continued his complaint about Agnew during the weekly leadership meeting. Thus, the Jordan Rule was born: all present agreed that whenever the vice president lobbied for an administration bill, the member would vote the opposite way, no matter what his personal or political beliefs.

By 1970, Nixon had quipped to Kissinger, "only facetiously" as the national security adviser remembered, that the possibility of Agnew's acceding to the presidency was Nixon's best protection against assassination. On a more serious note, Nixon began to openly speculate with aides about getting rid of Agnew by naming him to the Supreme Court. Then he could use the Twenty-fifth Amendment to name Secretary of the Treasury John Connally, Nixon's choice as his heir apparent, vice president.

Unneeded in Washington, Agnew hit the road. Using speeches largely crafted by Buchanan, Agnew lashed out at liberals and liberalism everywhere. The result was political invective the likes of which had not been heard from a Washington pulpit since Joe McCarthy. Agnew's first target was what he perceived to be a growing permissiveness on the part of middle-class America toward their children. At the University of Utah in May 1969, he railed against the appearance of college students (quipping, "I didn't raise my son to be a daughter"). The next month at Ohio State, Agnew charged that any society that feared its young was "effete." His followers loved this word, so Agnew used it again and again, as he did later that fall in New Orleans, when he attacked the "effete corps of impudent snobs" who were teaching in the colleges and universities and poisoning the minds of the nation's young. These liberal intellectuals were soon labeled with one of the most famous of the Agnew-isms, when he began to call them "Radiclibs."

But Agnew's most famous assault came in November 1969 when he took on the nation's broadcast media. In a speech at the Midwest Republican Conference held in Des Moines, he savaged a media "whose minds were made up in advance" on Nixon's Vietnam policies. Agnew charged the networks with a conspiracy to slant the news through "a handful of commentators who admit their own set of biases," and encouraged like-minded people to call in and voice their support of his attack. They did: all three networks were flooded with phone calls and telegrams. Agnew's crusade against intellectualism had struck a chord in middle America, and he had become a celebrity in the process. By the end of 1969, Agnew placed third on a list of most admired Americans, finishing behind Nixon and the Reverend Billy Graham.

Yet, Agnew's opponents were just as vocal. The media slashed back with editorials and commentary that generally mirrored the one found in the *Hartford Courant,* which sputtered, "Spiro Agnew has become this nation's great divider . . . [he] appeals to everything low and bitter and mean in the American character." Agnew defended his Doberman-pinscher tactics by arguing that "somebody has to speak out on these subjects. I spoke out, and I'll continue to speak out. . . . I feel like I'm involved in a crusade, almost."

Despite this lofty proclamation, several Republican congressional candidates publicly stated that they did not want Agnew campaigning for them in the off-year elections that fall. But Nixon wanted Agnew on the campaign trail. Using Agnew as the administration's chief campaign surrogate would allow Nixon to stay in Washington and avoid the political fallout. It would also allow the administration to strike out at Republicans who had criticized the administration's policy on Vietnam without getting the president involved.

Thus, in the fall of 1970, with Buchanan at his side, the vice president plunged himself back into the electoral fray. As had been the case in 1968, Agnew was both crude and effective. His attacks on antiwar Republican senator Charles Goodell of New York were so stinging—in a reference to the first person who had undergone a sex-change operation, Agnew called Goodell the "Christine Jorgensen of the Republican party"—that they brought private complaints from Minority Leader Gerald R. Ford. In spite of Ford's objections, it was clear that Agnew was fronting for a White House purge of antiwar liberals of both parties. Goodell lost his race, as did several other candidates who had refused to support the administration on the war, and the White House was ecstatic. So was Agnew, who, hearing on television that Goodell had lost, yelled, "We *got* that son of a bitch!"

Agnew had a new lease on life. He soon scored his first—and only—policy success as vice president, as his National Council on Indian Opportunity officially proposed the establishment of the Indian Revenue Sharing Program in October 1971. Agnew's plan was supported by the Department of the Interior and eventually adopted by the president. There would be no serious "Dump Spiro" movement in 1972. Quite the contrary: Nixon was quick to announce, during a January 2, 1972, televised interview with CBS's Dan Rather, that Agnew would stay on the ticket that fall.

The Committee to Re-elect the President had the same role in mind for Agnew that he had played four years earlier, and once again he played it to perfection. Agnew mauled Democratic presidential candidate George McGovern, calling him "one of the greatest frauds ever to be considered as a presidential candidate by a major American party." He also followed Democratic vice presidential contender Sargent Shriver from city to city, answering the speeches of the former director of the Peace Corps with speeches that specialized in claiming that Shriver's position on the ticket was a result of his being an in-law of liberal senator Edward M. Kennedy. Despite the zeal with which Agnew attacked his foes, his invective was less necessary in 1972 than it had been in 1968, as the Nixon-Agnew ticket won with 60.7 percent of the popular vote.

Immediately after the 1972 victory, the press crowned Agnew as the front-runner in the 1976 race. Agnew clearly wanted it, telling a reporter, "I wouldn't put up with this job for another four years if I weren't interested in seeking the top one." However, Nixon did not join in the speculation. Constitutionally disqualified from seeking a third term, Nixon no longer needed Agnew to rally the conservatives on the campaign trail. Agnew was stripped of the Office of Intergovernmental Relations, and Nixon told domestic policy adviser John Ehrlichman to "give him the Bicentennial to look after." Any access Agnew had to the president virtually disappeared. Nixon never considered for a moment supporting an "Agnew for President" bid in 1976. His first choice, as it had been since 1970, was John Connally. Had Watergate not interfered, Nixon was ready to announce his support for Connally before the end of 1975.

But it never came to that. In Baltimore, U.S. Atty. George Beall had found evidence that real estate developers in and around Baltimore County had been paying kickback money to Agnew since 1962. The payments began as a quid pro quo for lucrative building contracts. But one developer fell behind in his payments, and at least two installments were delivered to Agnew *after* he became vice president. Throughout the spring of 1973, Agnew had heard rumors of Beall's investigation, but the Watergate revelations had spurred the press to new heights of investigative reporting, and Agnew dared not interfere, lest an enterprising reporter pick up the scent.

Nixon, however, was one of the first to know. On April 14, 1973, during a meeting with Ehrlichman and Chief of Staff H. R. Haldeman, Nixon was given the details of the investigation. He was also told that the Agnew scandal would eventually touch John Mitchell, as one of the couriers for Agnew's money had also been passing money to Mitchell. This news descended on a White House that had long been bunkering itself against Watergate, and Nixon made it clear that there would be no attempt to cover up Agnew's transgressions.

Left without White House spin support, it was only a matter of time before the press picked up the story. On August 6, 1973, an editor of the *Wall Street Journal* called Agnew to tell him that the paper was running a story that reported there was an investigation under way. That same day, Atty. Gen. Elliot Richardson, who had been kept apprised of the investigation by Beall, met with Nixon and told him that the case against Agnew was airtight.

Nixon met with Agnew the next day. The vice president emerged to report that the president supported him in his fight against charges that Agnew labeled "dammed lies." But Nixon's support never consisted of anything more than benign neglect. Implicated House aides, including Haldeman and Ehrlichman, had been allowed to resign, as Nixon was faced with investigations by both the Congress and a Justice Department special prosecutor, both of whom wanted to hear recordings from the Oval Office taping system.

As Nixon fought the battle of the tapes, which had every indication, even as early as the summer of 1973, of being a fight that would find its way to the Supreme Court, he clearly wanted to rid himself of Agnew as soon as was politically possible. Before the end of August, he sent Alexander Haig, Haldeman's replacement as chief of staff, to ask the vice president to resign. In September, Asst. Atty. Gen. Henry Petersen examined the evidence and said that Agnew had no chance. Haig and White House Counsel J. Fred Buzhardt told Agnew this, and the plea bargaining began.

But when the *Washington Post* reported this development on September 22, a seething Agnew tried one more offensive. Ordering that the plea bargaining come to a halt, he demanded to be afforded the formal impeachment process before the House of Representatives. This terrified the administration: once the impeachment process had been dusted off and tested, Agnew's case might well serve as a model for Nixon's own. Fortunately for Nixon, Speaker of the House Carl Albert refused to intervene.

Agnew then tried one last gambit. Arguing that the Constitution prevented a sitting vice president from being indicted for a crime, his lawyers filed a suit against the Justice Department, enjoining them not to turn over any further evidence to the grand jury. Once again, however, Agnew lost. On October 4, the court ruled that while a president was protected from indictment, a vice president was not.

Agnew had no further legal avenues open to him, and his attempt to garner public opinion had failed miserably. The country was Watergate-weary; both the president and the people wanted Agnew gone, and the vice president finally accepted the inevitable. On October 10, Agnew appeared in a federal courtroom in Baltimore to plead nolo contendere to a charge of income tax evasion. He received a ten-thousand-dollar fine and a three-year jail sentence that was suspended immediately. Later that afternoon, Agnew delivered his resignation to Secretary of State Kissinger. On October 12, Nixon announced that he would nominate Gerald Ford to replace Agnew under the terms of the Twenty-fifth Amendment.

Five days after his resignation, on October 15, Agnew delivered a farewell address to the nation. It was vintage Agnew, as he continued to claim his innocence and blame the media for his problems. In the national sigh of relief that followed the Ford nomination, Agnew's protests fell largely on deaf ears. In the more than two decades after he left the vice presidency—a period that saw Agnew retreat into a retirement that did not include an attempt to return either to public office or to the public arena—he continued to maintain his guiltlessness. In his memoirs, *Go Quietly . . . or Else,* which were published in 1980, Agnew widened his indictment to include Atty. Gen. Richardson and Nixon himself.

In May 1995, the Republican-dominated Congress accorded Agnew an honor, which, to that point, he had been the only vice president not to receive. His bust was included with the other vice presidents just outside Statuary Hall on the Senate side of the U.S. Capitol. Ironically, the ceremony received a great deal of media attention.

Agnew's sudden death in September 1996 brought to an end one of the saddest chapters in vice presidential history. Like the man himself in recent years, the funeral was private, for friends and family only. As if to fulfill the title of his memoirs, Agnew went quietly.

V

RECOVERY AND REFLECTION,
1973–1981

"You know how I feel about being Vice President," he said, "but I believe I must accept."
I agreed and said so. And Rockefeller said, "Well, I will do this for President Ford, and
through him, for the country." So he accepted out of patriotism; he served in frustration;
and he left in greater frustration.

—James Cannon

Mondale played a key role in the evolution of the Office of the Vice President. Together,
he and President Carter rewrote the rules that have become the standard for all future
officeholders. Yet, Mondale's experience also highlights that changing the institutional
responsibilities does not alter the political calculus that continues to define and limit the
vice president's role.

—Steven M. Gillon

Gerald R. Ford and Nelson A. Rockefeller:
A Vice Presidential Memoir

JAMES CANNON

I have had the honor of knowing and working for the only two men who have become vice president of the United States under the provisions of the Twenty-fifth Amendment to the Constitution. In simpler terms, Gerald R. Ford and Nelson A. Rockefeller were appointed—not elected—to the office. And it is this extraordinary brush with history that has led me to write this personal reflection on their tenures in that office.

I have written at length about the Ford vice presidency in my 1994 book, *Time and Chance: Gerald R. Ford's Appointment with History*, and so I will be brief about the tense nine months from December 6, 1973, to August 9, 1974.

Gerald Ford was not Richard Nixon's first choice to fill the vacancy created by the resignation of Spiro Agnew. It was well known in the inner circles of the Nixon administration that the president wanted to appoint former Texas governor and Nixon Treasury Secretary John Connally as vice president. But the realities of politics—in the form of the congressional leadership—made it clear that a Connally nomination would not pass muster.

After both the Democratic and the Republican leaders of the House and Senate told Nixon that Connally could not be confirmed, Nixon—we now know—did consider Ronald Reagan and Nelson Rockefeller, along with Ford. But Nixon thought that choosing either Reagan or Rockefeller would split the party. More important, House Speaker Carl Albert and Senate Majority Leader Mike Mansfield told Nixon that Ford was the one person who could be quickly confirmed. The Democratic leaders of Congress chose Ford, and confirmed Ford, believing that Nixon would not finish his second term.

Initially, Ford enjoyed the job. He was free from the grind of a legislative calendar dictated by the Democratic leadership. As vice president, Ford found himself with unlimited opportunity to do what he liked best:

examine and study the mammoth and creaking engine of the federal government and look for ways to improve it.

Yet the vice presidency was not easy for Ford. He wanted to be free to express his own opinions on Watergate and other national issues, but he did not want to appear disloyal to Nixon. "So it was a very narrow path," Ford told me much later, "and not a very pleasant one." Ford's problems were compounded by a White House staff that wanted to coopt him. They wanted Ford to be a mouthpiece for the president and nothing more.

By mid-January, after giving a speech in which he said public things he did not believe, Ford realized that he was being used. "My credibility will erode overnight," Ford told his friend and assistant Bob Hartmann. "Get whatever help you need, but from now on you're in charge of speeches."

When he accepted the vice presidency, Ford was sure that Watergate was nothing but politics, as Nixon had assured him. But within six or eight weeks, Ford's belief in Nixon's innocence turned to wonder, and then from wonder to doubt, from doubt to fear, and finally—to use Ford's word—to "denial" that his old friend Dick Nixon might somehow have been involved in Watergate after all. But Ford said nothing, not even to his wife, Betty, who was his closest political adviser.

But in his own way Ford took action. His sense of public duty, and memories of his days as an Eagle Scout, told him to be prepared. He met weekly with Secretary of State Henry Kissinger or National Security Council Deputy Adviser Brent Scowcroft to be briefed on world developments and crises. He spent hours with Dixie Lee Ray of the Atomic Energy Commission, Arthur Burns of the Federal Reserve, every member of Nixon's cabinet, and staffers from the Office of Management and Budget. Ford also opened the door to his magnificent office in the Old Executive Office Building to diplomats who needed to cable home their appraisals of the man who might become president.

All through the spring and early summer of 1973, Vice President Ford walked his narrow path, trying to show, simultaneously, his support of President Nixon and his independence from him. "It was the most difficult period of my political life," Ford said later. He traveled constantly, for two reasons—one, to avoid getting caught up in Nixon's legal and political problems, and two, to show the country who he was—just in case something did happen to Nixon.

In July 1973, after the Supreme Court handed down the unanimous decision that Nixon would have to give up the White House tapes, Vice President Ford concluded that Nixon could no longer govern. But Ford said nothing, and he did nothing to prepare to take over the presidency. He had known Richard Nixon for twenty-five years, and he knew that the slightest sign that the vice president or any of his staff was plotting would provoke Nixon to fight on.

Not since the Civil War had there been a comparable constitutional crisis. President Nixon had defied Congress, defied a federal court, and considering defying the Supreme Court until, fortunately, Al Haig talked him out of it.

Even after the White House tapes revealed that Nixon had obstructed justice by telling his chief of staff, Bob Haldeman, to direct the CIA to stop the FBI investigation of Watergate, Ford waited. He would do nothing until he heard from Nixon himself that he would resign. When Ford was sworn in as president, "the long national nightmare" ended, as he said at his inaugural.

Nelson Rockefeller was vice president of the United States from December 19, 1974, to January 20, 1977—a total of two years and thirty-three days. For most of his political life, Rockefeller disdained and dismissed the vice presidency. He used to say that he had personally known every vice president since Henry Wallace, and they were all unhappy in the job.

Twice, by his account, Rockefeller turned down the opportunity to be vice president: first in 1960, when he said that Nixon offered him the vice presidency, and again in 1968, when he said that Hubert Humphrey had sent an emissary to inquire as to whether he would consider being the vice president on the Democratic ticket. Rockefeller turned down the two offers, he said, because, in his words: "I never wanted to be Vice President of *anything.*"

There was the one time when Rockefeller thought the vice presidency worth having: when he—and several of us on his political staff—first learned, very early in 1973, that Vice President Agnew might be forced out of office on charges of bribery. We calculated that this would be the best and possibly the quickest route that Rockefeller might ever find into the White House. Watergate might force Nixon out of office. And even if it did not, three years as VP would give Rockefeller his best platform for winning the Republican nomination in 1976.

In fact, by the early summer of 1973, Rockefeller was preparing to campaign to be nominated under the Twenty-fifth Amendment. But Henry Kissinger stopped that campaign before it got started. Rockefeller told me that Kissinger told him that yes, Agnew was going to have to resign, but that Nixon had already decided to nominate John Connally for vice president, and so Rockefeller would only embarrass himself if he tried to organize a political campaign.

So why did Rockefeller take the job when Gerald Ford asked him to be vice president in August 1974? The answer is complex, involving the singular events of Watergate, the cover-up of Watergate, and the constitutional crisis that forced the resignation of Richard Nixon and made Ford the president. The answer is also simple: Rockefeller felt he had no choice.

Ford, a new president assuming office in a time of political turmoil, the first president never to be elected to office, needed Rockefeller's help. Ford sensed that his new presidency required that he nominate the most qualified Republican in terms of domestic governing experience and international experience. Against the advice of staff who feared that Rockefeller would overshadow the new president, Ford chose Rockefeller.

I was at my farm in upstate New York when Rockefeller, on a rare vacation in Maine, telephoned to say that Ford had offered him the vice presidency. "You know how I feel about being Vice President," he said, "but I believe I must accept." I agreed and said so. And Rockefeller said, "Well, I will do this for President Ford, and through him, for the country." So he accepted out of patriotism; he served in frustration; and he left in greater frustration.

A week after Ford took the oath of office, he turned to Nelson Rockefeller as the best man to assist him in restoring stability to the federal government and confidence to the country. Rockefeller asked for a day to consider it, and then accepted. It was not the presidency, and offered little hope of it. Ford, when he first telephoned Rockefeller, had informed him that he—and not Nelson—would run in 1976. Ford needed his help, had asked for his help, so Rockefeller said yes, out of a sense of duty.

Certainly, Nelson Rockefeller was well qualified by experience to be vice president; but by personality, he was unsuited for the office. It was against his life experience to defer. It was simply not in him to play second fiddle—not to anyone.

His problems began with his confirmation. Ford, the first person to be confirmed under the Twenty-fifth Amendment, went through a rigorous examination by the Senate and the House, but he won the endorsement of the Senate and the House by a landslide, in part because some congressional Democrats wanted to speed up the confirmation of Ford so they could get on with impeaching Nixon.

Not so with Rockefeller. Curiosity about one of the richest men in America, combined with a legitimate look at possible conflicts of interest, prompted congressional investigators to probe deeply into the financial holdings of Rockefeller and his family.

At one point, the House Judiciary Committee demanded that he and all members of his family—more than fifty persons—disclose every share of stock, every asset they held. Rockefeller refused. He said he would withdraw his name first.

The Rockefeller family has a strong sense of privacy. Nelson was willing to disclose every financial interest he had, but he did not think it fair to his family that all be required to make such a disclosure. A compromise was reached: he disclosed his assets in detail, the family in the aggregate. Finally, after four months of accusations by liberal Democrats and conservative Republicans, Rockefeller was confirmed by the Senate and the House, and sworn in on the floor of the Senate.

A couple of days later, on a rainy Saturday before Christmas, President Ford told Rockefeller he wanted him to be involved in all national-security discussions and decisions, and he wanted him to take responsibility for domestic policy.

There were other assignments, political appearances, foreign travel, chairmanship of a commission on privacy, and, a few days later, the responsibility to head a major commission to investigate the CIA—a commission that incidentally included Gov. Ronald Reagan.

Rockefeller accepted his responsibilities, and—as was his nature—he set out to make the most of them. He assumed he would be in charge of domestic affairs in the same way National Security Director Henry Kissinger was the chief operating officer of foreign policy. And, since Rockefeller had been assigned domestic policy, he assumed that he would choose the president's director of the Domestic Council, and proposed that I be appointed to the job.

The new White House chief of staff, Donald Rumsfeld, opposed my appointment. He had his own man for the job. After a contest that was brief but divisive, Rockefeller won, and I was appointed by the president. Rockefeller then made me a great gift: he let me have his former budget director in New York, and a brilliant young lawyer, plus one of the best policy analysts he had in Albany. And he told me the first priority was to bring in the best staff in the White House—"even better than Henry's," he said.

At that point, I know that Rockefeller and I did not know exactly what the Domestic Council did, and I am reasonably sure that President Ford did not know how his staff—too much of it holdovers from Nixon— functioned. But Rumsfeld knew. Very quickly, I discovered that I was the editor of a lot of documents with an audience of one: the president.

Under Nixon, and now under Ford, the Domestic Council staff—some twenty-five bright, young MBAs, lawyers, intellectuals, and former advance men, plus an equal number of researchers and assistants—managed the flow of domestic information to the president, relayed his decisions to cabinet members and agency heads, and tried to make sure the president's orders were carried out.

We were a fire department, responsible for putting out fires that had already started and trying to prevent fires that seemed about to break out. If someone had a brilliant idea, we were the ones who had to find its natural enemies, get their views down succinctly and accurately, summarize the arguments for and against this brilliant idea, and get a report to the president—fast.

I got a taste of this early. President Ford had asked his new vice president to give him a recommendation on whether there should be a science adviser to the president. With his usual verve and enthusiasm, Rockefeller convened Edward Teller and similarly high IQs and delivered his recommendation. Ford handed it to Rumsfeld, and Rumsfeld handed it to me. "Staff this out," he said. Suddenly, I was having to review the work of my good friend and former boss.

As the new boy, I could ask President Ford what he wanted in my review, and his answer is revealing about him. "Well," he said, "I would like to know what each of the science advisers to former Presidents *think* they accomplished, and I would like some outside expert to tell me what each one actually accomplished." That was easy.

What was not easy was going over to the vice president's office to tell him I had been asked to review his recommendations. He listened, his eyes narrowing to angry slits, and said, "Why did the President ask me to make a recommendation to him, and then ask his staff to review it?"

Rockefeller and I tried to work together for President Ford on the Domestic Council. He wanted to initiate domestic policies, and we made some progress. Dick Parsons, our counsel for the Domestic Council, initiated the first ever serious, government-wide examination of the drug problem. In 1975 we saw what was coming, but we were unable to persuade Congress to address the problem.

Rockefeller proposed a $100 million extended plan to solve the energy crisis, and Ford accepted it after a lot of internal argument. But a handful of White House staffers berated the plan to the press, and we never got anywhere with it.

We proposed that the United States, which then had a near monopoly on the production of fuel for nuclear power plants, create a public-private partnership that would make the United States the energy equivalent of Middle East oil, with built-in safeguards against conversion to weapons. But Sen. John Glenn and Sen. Charles Percy shot it down, saying in effect, if the United States does not produce nuclear fuel, maybe no other country will. So we left it up to such countries as France and the USSR to produce and sell nuclear fuel.

We brought forth other good proposals, but Rockefeller soon realized that Ford had not actually granted him authority over domestic policy. In fact, no president can give up control over domestic policy any more than he can give up control over foreign policy. Ford had his own strong views about domestic policy: he was a fiscal conservative. For twenty-five years he had voted against federal social programs and federal spending. He came into office determined to shrink the government, not expand it. Indeed, in the first months of 1975, Ford had decided—at a Sunday meeting to which neither Rockefeller nor I was invited—that he would oppose any new federal programs.

Rockefeller was an expansionist, a doer, an innovator. His interest was in solving public problems. That took money. But President Ford was determined to cut the cost of the federal government. The two men had contradictory objectives. Moreover, as vice president, Rockefeller simply did not know how to conduct himself. He had been a king—not a courtier. On those few occasions when he tried flattery, he simply sounded obsequious. Maneuvering in court for power and access was not his way.

On a personal basis, he had excellent relations with the president. Ford told him his door was always open to him; he could come in anytime.

And this vice president often did. At least once a week they met one-on-one for lunch. Rockefeller would go in with a long agenda of ideas and suggestions. He did not hesitate to differ with the president in those private meetings. Ford would listen. Sometimes he took Rockefeller's advice; more often he told him why he could not.

They worked together best on foreign policy. Rockefeller was there with President Ford when the United States pulled the last Americans off the embassy rooftop in Saigon, at the time of Mayagüez, and during every other international crisis.

Rockefeller also took on all the political chores handed to him, but he did not make enough friends among the conservatives who were taking over the Republican Party. Perhaps by then Rockefeller was politically doomed.

President Ford waited too long to start his campaign for election. In May 1975 I took it upon myself to tell the president in a private meeting that he should start organizing his campaign. His response was pure Ford: "Well, I believe that if I do a good job as President, the party will nominate me and the country will elect me. That's the way I've always run my campaigns."

That summer, after President Ford did begin his campaign, the conservatives in the Republican Party began to demand that he dump Rockefeller from the ticket. At first Ford refused, but in time the challenge by Governor Reagan and other conservatives changed Ford's mind.

On the morning I got the urgent call that Rockefeller was about to sign a letter taking himself off the ticket, I raced over to the EOB and tried to dissuade him. He gave me a cold and angry look and said, "I was asked to." It was a bitter and final political blow to this proud man. He had not asked to be vice president. He accepted out of a sense of duty. He did not like the job. And now he was being politically humiliated. Ford later said, "It was the biggest political mistake I ever made." And on another occasion Ford said: "It was one of the few cowardly things I ever did in my life."

As it turned out, dumping Rockefeller did not help Ford right away. Reagan was a formidable challenger. After Reagan won North Carolina and Texas, Vice President Rockefeller delivered the New York delegation to Ford, and helped bring in other moderate Republican delegates from Pennsylvania and other states. It was a memorable act of political loyalty on Rockefeller's part, quite in character.

From that point on, Ford led in delegates all the way to the Republican convention. When Ford won the nomination, Rockefeller was a strong supporter of Bob Dole for vice president. During the 1976 campaign, Rockefeller tried to convince Ford that the country would be better off if he committed to some federal projects to help his election. But Ford would not spend federal money to get himself elected. He had never done that in his congressional races; he would not do it to keep himself in the White House.

In that campaign there was to be one more humiliation for Rockefeller. Ford's campaign advisers concentrated on the West and wrote off New York State. How could Rockefeller explain that to the New York Republicans who had supported Ford's nomination?

Ford lost to Jimmy Carter, narrowly; and we will never know whether Ford might have been elected had he kept Rockefeller on the ticket. In that event, of course, Ford might have lost the nomination to Reagan that year.

As governor of New York, Nelson Rockefeller was ebullient, confident, progressive, and dedicated to the kind of public service that improves the lives of all citizens. When he completed his two years as vice president, Rockefeller had lost much of his verve, spirit, and enthusiasm.

After he went home to New York, to Happy and his boys, I used to go up to the fifty-sixth floor of the RCA Building in Rockefeller Center and see the governor occasionally. On the wall beside his desk was an impressive Rouault, with a brass plate that read, "The Old King." The old king in the painting still wore his crown, but his face was scarred and weathered, his eyes seemed filled with bitter memories.

I used to wonder if my old friend was aware of how much that painting seemed to reflect his age and spirit. I never knew.

A New Framework:
Walter Mondale as Vice President

STEVEN M. GILLON

In June 1976, shortly after winning the Ohio primary that guaranteed his nomination on the first ballot, former Georgia governor Jimmy Carter began his search for a running mate. The lessons of the past weighed on Carter's mind. In 1972, George McGovern was forced to drop his first vice presidential pick, Missouri senator Thomas Eagleton, after the press discovered that Eagleton had been treated for depression. To avoid repeating that mistake, Carter planned a long, thoughtful process of interviewing candidates personally and carefully examining their backgrounds.

During the primaries Carter had turned his outsider status and his lack of experience in Washington into a campaign asset, but he was shrewd enough as a politician to know that he needed a party insider as a running mate. Within a few weeks Carter had narrowed the list to a handful of senators and invited them to his home in Plains, Georgia, for serious discussions. After an initial round of interviews, the Democratic nominee narrowed the list to two contenders: Sen. Edmund Muskie of Maine and Sen. Walter F. Mondale of Minnesota.

In July, as Democrats gathered in New York for their convention, Carter had still not made up his mind. On Thursday morning, July 15, Carter announced his choice. "I've asked to serve as my running mate Senator Walter Mondale of Minnesota," Carter told a packed hall. Mondale, he said, had a "great feeling of understanding and compassion for people who need government help," had earned the "trust of a wide range of Democrats," and possessed a "clear concept of what the vice presidency should be."

Like other vice presidential choices, Mondale offered ideological and geographical balance to the ticket. A prominent midwestern liberal and a protégé of Hubert Humphrey, Mondale had established close ties with the established Democratic Party during his eleven years in the Senate. His support was strongest in precisely those areas where Carter's was weakest: among liberals, Jews, organized labor, and Democratic Party activists who had opposed Carter's nomination and remained deeply skeptical about his candidacy. The support of these traditional Democratic groups was essential for the Democrats to carry the big industrial states of the Northeast and Midwest.

Mondale, understanding his role, spent most of the fall campaigning in Illinois, New Jersey, Ohio, Pennsylvania, New York, and Wisconsin, which held the largest number of blue-collar, ethnic, and urban voters. He also scored a symbolic victory in a debate with his Republican opponent, Sen. Robert Dole—the first televised debate of vice presidential candidates. Despite numerous blunders that plagued the campaign, the Carter-Mondale ticket squeaked out a narrow victory in November.

Mondale assumed the vice presidency at a critical point in the history of the office. The position's vague duties and the mediocre talent it had attracted had always made it the object of public ridicule. The resignation of Spiro Agnew and the brief Ford-Rockefeller interlude intensified the criticism of the office. "There is no escape," observed the historian Arthur Schlesinger, "from the conclusion that the vice presidency is not only a meaningless but a hopeless office."

Much of the problem stemmed from the vice president's ill-defined responsibilities. As Schlesinger commented sardonically, "The Vice President has only one serious thing to do: that is, to wait around for the president to die." Schlesinger was not far from the mark. The vice president's sole constitutional duty, other than to succeed the president, was to preside over the Senate. The vice president was not even a full member of the executive branch. The vice president could not propose legislation or sign it into law, veto bills, appoint executive officials or take over any of the significant duties of the president. Not until Kennedy became president was a vice president even given space in the Executive Office Building.

This history weighed on Mondale's mind when, in December 1976, he met with the president-elect, Jimmy Carter, at Blair House to discuss their plans for the vice presidency. Mondale presented him with a detailed memorandum outlining the role he wanted to play in the new administration. Careful research, along with conversations with Hubert Humphrey and with Nelson Rockefeller, convinced Mondale that the vice president's role had been "characterized by ambiguity, disappointment and even antagonism." Realizing that "my personal and political success is totally tied to yours," Mondale informed Carter that he hoped to break the cycle of frustration that had characterized the office.

Mondale contended that the vice president's primary role should be as general adviser to the president. Too often, he argued, presidents had failed because they had ignored independent voices. As the only other member of the administration with broad responsibility unrestricted by loyalty to a department or agency, the vice president was in the position to provide such independent analysis. In order to fulfill this function as general adviser, the vice president needed access to the same information as the president, especially the daily briefings from the CIA and other intelligence agencies; a close relationship with other members of the executive branch; participation in meetings of key groups; an experienced staff member on both the National Security Council and the Domestic Policy Council; and finally, close and frequent access to the president.

Carter, who felt that fear of political competition had prevented previous presidents from taking full advantage of the vice presidency, had no such concerns about Mondale and no hesitation about permitting him to play an active role in his administration. He agreed that Mondale should receive the same intelligence reports as the president and attend cabinet meetings, National Security Council briefings, and Economic Policy Group discussions. Carter offered a standing invitation for Mondale to attend all of the president's political meetings. They also agreed to schedule a regular Monday lunch where they could discuss in private important business. "What was unique about their relationship was that it was across the board," recalled Domestic Policy Adviser Stuart Eizenstat. "Carter saw Mondale as his most senior advisor. No one else had that breadth of relationship with the president."

As evidence of his faith in Mondale and his desire to make the vice presidency an important institution, Carter signed an executive order making Mondale second in the chain of command for the control of nuclear weapons. Since 1958, when Congress passed the National Security Reorganization Act, the secretary of state had served as the deputy commander in chief. During the next four years the constant presence of a military aide carrying the "Black Bag"—the locked briefcase that contained the codes needed to unleash the nation's nuclear arsenal—served as a sobering reminder of that responsibility.

After agreeing to their groundbreaking institutional relationship, they turned to the more mundane questions of where Mondale's office would be located and how to organize their respective staffs. Mondale wanted to be "in the loop" with an office in the west wing of the White House rather than in the Executive Office Building where most vice presidents had spent their time. "The White House operates not by structure but by osmosis," recalled a Mondale adviser. "Most of the business is done by floating in and out of each other's offices, bumping into people in the hall, dealing in the White House restaurant. If you are out of the loop, it is very hard to be part of the process." Mondale did not select the office that was traditionally held by the chief of staff because he did not want to be at odds with the president's own staff. "He felt that his clout within the administration would be stronger if he did not appear to be usurping power from the president's staff," recalled a White House staff member. Instead, he chose a small office just down the hall.

Along with organizing his personal staff, Mondale lobbied to get loyal staff members placed in sensitive positions in the executive branch. By having people loyal to him in critical positions, Mondale hoped to prevent the president's staff from ever undermining his influence. "He got his people into key positions in the administration," boasted a Mondale staffer. Carter appointed David Aaron, who had served as Mondale's chief foreign policy adviser, as deputy national security adviser. Bert Carp, a close Senate aide, earned an appointment as domestic policy deputy. In perhaps the most dramatic demonstration of his desire to integrate the vice president into the administration, Carter asked Richard Moe, Mondale's chief of staff, to also serve on the president's senior staff.

Once in office, Mondale used his influence to shape a number of administration initiatives. Avoiding specific commitments, he played the role of general adviser and troubleshooter. He helped smooth Carter's rocky relations with Congress and lobbied former Senate colleagues on critical issues, such as the Panama Canal treaties. He played a key role in the Middle East negotiations that produced the Camp David Accords, focused public attention on the plight of the boat people, and tried to mediate conflicts between Secretary of State Vance and National Security Adviser Brzezinski. In June 1978, David Broder concluded that "a close examination of Mondale's workweek leaves no doubt that there is more substance than ceremony in the schedule of the Vice President."

Perhaps no issues absorbed more of Mondale's time than the budget. Carter came to office promising to restore funds to social programs starved from eight years of Republican rule and to use government spending to stimulate economic growth. A growing budget deficit and fears of inflation forced an abrupt change of course. By 1978, Carter had committed his administration to reducing the deficit by cutting expensive social programs. The president, and most of his advisers, believed a more conservative course made both fiscal and political sense. By standing tough against inflation, they believed he would both ensure a healthy economy and impress critical independent voters.

Mondale disagreed both with the policy prescription and with the political strategy that informed it. He believed a few billion dollars of additional social spending would not add substantially to the deficit but would make for much better relations with the traditional wing of the party, which he considered essential to their reelection. "I spent a lot of time trying to keep domestic initiatives adequately funded and to prevent marginal cuts that would do nothing for the economy but would create a firestorm of resentment and opposition," Mondale recalled. "We had lots of fights over these budget decisions."

The irony of the new relationship that Carter created with his vice president was that it institutionalized the division within the administration and prevented the White House from articulating a clear message on the economy. Unlike past presidents, Carter could not ignore his vice president. Mondale played an important role in the budget process, lobbied the president personally during his weekly lunch meeting, and participated in the final budget review process, held each fall in the Oval Office. On many occasions, Mondale convinced the president to reject the recommendation of his budget director and restore funding to programs slated for cuts. The gap between the president's tough fiscal message and his modest budget cuts sent the public mixed signals about the administration's economic program, thus contributing to public perceptions that Carter was a weak and ineffectual leader.

The intense debates over the budget also created deep divisions in the White House. Many of the president's Georgia advisers resented Mondale's influence. "We valued the contacts and experience that Mondale brought to the administration," recalled Jody Powell. "But at the same time we felt a general need to try and keep that perspective in check." They complained that Mondale's outdated political judgment undermined the administration's appeal to moderates. Former attorney general Griffin Bell contended that Mondale, who represented "the liberal bloc of the Democratic party," succeeded in shaping "administration policy to his way of thinking in important areas." The result was "the unclear, all-things-to-all-people voice that the public heard so often from the administration."

Mondale, on the other hand, was troubled by what he perceived as Carter's lack of philosophical conviction. Mondale made his grievances known in his private lunch meetings with the president and in a long October 1978 memo. The vice president complained that Carter had failed to tell the nation where he was going and why it should follow. Because the president lacked a compelling political philosophy or well-grounded assumptions to guide his thought, his policies jumped between liberal and conservative. "I sense you are reluctant to define your own approach and philosophy regarding domestic issues," Mondale observed. The vice president argued that by never establishing a sense of priorities for the administration, Carter had blurred the public's perception of his goals. "If there's one element of your Presidency that cries out for correction, in my judgment, that is it," Mondale stated.

The vice president argued that Carter tried to lead the nation simply through hard work and careful management. The president spent "too much time poring over staff memos" in his office, and "not enough time in public giving speeches and appearing with people," Mondale wrote. "[W]hen we elect a President, we don't want a manager. We can hire them. We want a leader." Carter needed to assert control over the administration by reorganizing the White House, disciplining disloyal cabinet members, and designating Hamilton Jordan as chief of staff.

Along with offering these suggested changes in Carter's style and in the organization of the White House, Mondale made another plea for the president to reconsider his conservative economic policy. "It is my hope that your Administration will demonstrate that we can have both jobs and price stability. If we can, we will have a decisive advantage over the Republican opposition which clearly favors trying to beat inflation at the expense of jobs, a position which I consider to be insensitive."

The divisions in the White House intensified as the economy went into a tailspin and the president's political fortunes declined. By 1979, with inflation and unemployment climbing, Carter's standing in the polls plunged. "You could feel public support evaporating," Mondale recalled. With the administration in virtual paralysis, the specter of Ted Kennedy loomed large in Washington political circles. "Kennedy for President" groups were forming in key primary states, and in every poll Kennedy rated as the overwhelming favorite among Democrats, usually topping the president by two or three to one. More immediately vexing to the president's political fortunes was the gasoline shortage that plagued American consumers in early 1979. By May, gasoline lines in California ran as long as five hundred cars, and prices at the pump climbed above one dollar per gallon for the first time.

As a sense of crisis gripped the White House, Mondale intensified his lobbying efforts, suggesting that by appealing to the party's liberal wing, Carter could undercut support for a potentially fatal Kennedy primary challenge. He renewed his calls for modest increases in spending on key domestic programs and for stronger White House leadership on the energy crisis. By the summer of 1979, as inflation eclipsed unemployment as the administration's top priority, Carter rejected most of his vice president's budget advice. Instead of taking control of the energy issue, the White House floundered.

These were difficult days for the vice president. Fiscal restraint and political realities prevented Mondale from focusing executive power on those issues—unemployment, civil rights, education, and poverty—to which he had devoted his political life. As early as January, he had suggested to his staff "a new relaxation theory," which involved withdrawing from key policy-making roles in the White House, making fewer public appearances on behalf of the administration, and scheduling more vacation time away from Washington. "There was a certain amount of fatalism in the idea," Mondale remembered. "I thought there was not much I could do to change things so why break my health trying." Staff members found him detached and impassive. Eizenstat, after a long lunch with Mondale in June, described him as "very despondent" and "really heartbroken."

Mondale's mood reflected his sense of futility within the administration. He experienced, in all its painful dimensions, the classic dilemma of a vice president: how could he publicly defend policies that he vigorously opposed in private while still maintaining his own identity as an independent leader?

Mondale also worried about his own future. He knew he would be held responsible for the administration's record. He feared that rather than serving as a stepping-stone to the presidency, the vice presidency would be the final resting ground of his public career. "Mondale could see his own political future going down the tubes without the capacity to do much about it because he was not the president," recalled Eizenstat.

Chief of Staff Dick Moe argued that the vice president had been so successful a team player that the public no longer perceived him "to be on the cutting edge of any major issue." Mondale recognized the problem existed, but could think of no solution. A vice president could not assert his independence without alienating the president and forfeiting his influence within the administration. But there was a cost to be paid. Because he defended policies that ran counter to his public record, the public's perception of Mondale's philosophy became blurred. A White House poll in May 1979 showed nearly one-quarter of all Americans did not know enough about Mondale to rate his job performance. Of those who felt they could comment, most found him honest, clean-cut, and sincere, but very few could identify where he stood on substantive issues.

For weeks in the late spring of 1979, Mondale agonized over his predicament. Despite all of his differences with the administration, he had established a close friendship and a strong bond of loyalty with the president. He was a deeply troubled man. Trapped between devotion to the president and commitment to liberal values, he searched for a way out. Mondale's conflict with Carter transcended policy matters. He, like many Washington insiders, believed the president and many of his advisers were politically inept, incapable of understanding the inner workings of Congress, and unable to project a clear and compelling image to the public. It would be impossible for a vice president to announce such strong disagreement and still retain the president's confidence. Circumstances compelled him to choose: loyalty to the president or political independence?

Reluctantly, Mondale began to think that only by resigning could he shock the administration out of its complacency and salvage his own political future. In long, agonizing sessions with his top staff people, Mondale discussed three options: resigning immediately, refusing to run on the ticket with Carter in 1980, or running and winning reelection and then resigning before the beginning of a new term. Mondale spent most of a warm spring afternoon sitting on the lawn of the vice presidential mansion listing the advantages and disadvantages of leaving office. An immediate resignation appeared the least attractive option. Resignation would only add fuel to persistent rumors that he lacked the stomach for tough situations and probably destroy the president's chances of reelection in 1980. Removing himself from the ticket after the 1980 campaign would force him to campaign on the administration's record—something he hoped to avoid.

For Mondale the most attractive way out of his dilemma was to announce at the Democratic convention that for personal reasons he would not seek nomination as Carter's running mate. By withdrawing at the convention, Mondale could have the best of both worlds. By citing personal reasons, he could separate himself from Carter without appearing to insult the president, and, at the same time, he would eliminate the need to campaign on the administration's record.

Ironically, Mondale, who helped pioneer a more influential and effective vice presidency, could not escape its curse. Other vice presidents had faced similar frustrations. Lyndon Johnson had faithfully performed his tasks but felt powerless as Kennedy's legislative team bungled one piece of legislation after another. Franklin Roosevelt's first vice president, John Nance Garner, was so disillusioned with the later New Deal program that he placed his own name in nomination at the 1940 Democratic convention.

Only one vice president, however, had actually resigned from office because of disagreement with the president. In 1832, John C. Calhoun differed with President Andrew Jackson on the burning issue of states' rights. Believing the individual state, as a "sovereign body," superseded the authority of the national government, Calhoun opposed Jackson's attempt to enforce the tariff. Shortly after his native South Carolina declared the federal tariff acts to be void and not "binding upon this State or its citizens," Calhoun resigned.

Unlike Calhoun, Mondale did not have a nullification crisis to justify his resignation. No matter how much he lamented his predicament, he could not bring himself to resign. In part, his decision grew from instinctive caution, a fear of dramatic initiatives whose consequences he could not carefully gauge. In part, it grew from his intense sense of loyalty, especially to those who had helped advance his career. Perhaps the deciding factor was his own intense partisanship. During the summer of 1979, it became clear that Mondale's liberal rival Ted Kennedy would launch a primary challenge to the president. Despite their differences, Carter and Mondale shared a personal disdain for the Massachusetts senator and a belief that a Kennedy candidacy would doom the Democrats in November.

The administration survived the Kennedy challenge, but the combined weight of soaring inflation, a hostage crisis, and the Soviet invasion of Afghanistan was too great a burden. In November, Ronald Reagan scored a decisive victory.

During his final weeks in office, Mondale reflected on his years as vice president. He took great satisfaction in the personal relationship he had established with the president. Throughout four difficult years, they remained steadfastly loyal to one another. A genuine friendship emerged between the two men. At the last White House staff meeting, Carter said he "never had [a] closer relationship than with Fritz." The vice president was, he said, "like a brother and a son." In an obvious reference to the tension that sometimes characterized their relationship, Carter warned his staff: "Don't do anything to hurt him." Mondale shared similar feelings for Carter. "Never before has a Vice President been so generously and so kindly treated by his President," Mondale wrote Carter a few days before leaving office. "On a personal level it was a spectacular relationship," he reflected. "His personal generosity toward me and my staff never wavered during the four years."

That friendship cemented the groundbreaking institutional relationship they had established. Mondale considered the role he played in elevating the stature of the vice president his most important contribution during his four years. It seems likely that the new role that Mondale pioneered will become a model for all future vice presidents. The three immediate successors to the office—George Bush, Dan Quayle, and Al Gore—adopted the Mondale approach. "My conclusion is that the Mondale model is a very good model," Bush told reporters in 1981. "I just think that from the beginning to the end he enjoyed the confidence of the President. He had access to him and could advise him and, when he had a difference, he presented it face to face but without a lot of people around, and thus he kept the confidence of the President." Before assuming office in 1989, Quayle sought Mondale's advice and expressed hope that President Bush would allow the vice president to play a similar role in his administration.

The president deserved much of the credit for that relationship's success. Defying precedent, he readily accepted Mondale's proposals for strengthening the vice presidency. He always solicited Mondale's opinion and carefully weighed his advice. At critical times in the relationship, the president intervened to silence critics and to reassure his vice president. For his part, Mondale, understanding that a vice president's influence depended on his personal relationship with the president, labored to assure Carter of his loyalty. Though he concealed his differences with the president from other administration officials, he rarely refrained from confronting Carter with critical observations.

For Mondale, the vice presidency proved a valuable learning experience, but it failed to propel him into the presidency. In some ways, his term as vice president proved a burden during his 1984 campaign for the presidency. His ties with a failed administration proved a severe political liability. Perhaps more important, the responsibilities of the vice president run counter to the demands of modern media campaigns. A vice president is forced to lose his political identity, to defend policies and programs that are contrary to his own ideology and past positions. The vice presidency requires total loyalty to the president. But public professions of support for all administration initiatives, even those he might have opposed in private, inevitably blurs the vice president's image. Modern campaigns, with their emphasis on sound bites and visuals, require candidates to draw sharp ideological distinctions. Inevitably, the press raises questions about the vice president's character and convictions.

This same problem of definition has plagued Mondale's successors. George Bush and, to a lesser extent, Al Gore have been plagued by questions about their personal convictions. As Richard L. Berke asked in a *New York Times Magazine* article, Gore may be "the strongest No. 2 ever," but, "does he also have what's needed to become No. 1?"

Mondale played a key role in the evolution of the Office of the Vice President. Together, he and President Carter rewrote the rules that have become the standard for all future officeholders. Yet, Mondale's experience also highlights that changing the institutional responsibilities does not alter the political calculus that continues to define and limit the vice president's role.

VI

AT THE PRESIDENT'S SIDE,
1981–1993

It was . . . a special moment in the history of the modern vice presidency when, on January 20, 1989, the booming unseen voice at the inaugural ceremony on the west front of the Capitol reversed the rule of protocol and announced the vice president *after* the president, since on that day he was also the president-elect. Perfectly prepared after eight years in the vice presidency to guide the nation in a time of monumental global change and challenge, George Bush strode forward to become number one at last.

—CHASE UNTERMEYER

The president encouraged me to develop my own model for the vice presidency. And if it can be said that I left an imprint on the vice presidency, it is in the expansion of the vice president's responsibilities and participation in several areas of American public life. . . . The power and influence of the vice president are an extension of the president's power. It would be foolish for a vice president to take new initiatives without the full support of the president.

—DAN QUAYLE

Looking Forward:
George Bush as Vice President
CHASE UNTERMEYER

When, on the evening of July 16, 1980, in the Renaissance Center Plaza Hotel in Detroit, Ronald Reagan telephoned a former rival and asked him to be his vice presidential running mate, the seeds for three great Republican election victories and two presidencies were sown.

The general chatter that night in the convention hall, and especially in the television networks' booths, was that Reagan would ask an even earlier rival, former president Gerald Ford, to join him on the ticket as proof the GOP had healed the wounds that crippled Ford in the 1976 election.

But when Henry Kissinger's earnest effort to repeat past glories in shuttle diplomacy failed to achieve an agreement by which a former chief executive could comfortably serve as vice president to another, Reagan turned to George Bush. This was with great doubt on the part of the nominee and especially his staff that Bush—a "moderate" as opposed to a "movement" conservative and thus almost a liberal in some eyes—would make a comfortable ideological fit. They finally opted for party unity, and the call from Reagan's suite was made.

"It didn't concern me that I hadn't been Reagan's first choice," the ever optimistic and buoyant former congressman, ambassador, party chairman, and CIA director would later write of that night. "What was important, as I saw it," Bush wrote in his autobiography, *Looking Forward*, "was that six weeks, six months, four years from now, he'd know that however he came to make it, he'd made the right choice."

The union of Reagan and Bush was only the third time in twentieth-century political history that a ticket comprised two former foes for the nomination who then went on to victory in the fall. Yet on the previous two occasions—the matching of Franklin D. Roosevelt and John Nance Garner in 1932 and of John F. Kennedy and Lyndon B. Johnson in 1960—the partners had fought only brief intraparty battles before and during the national conventions that nominated them. By contrast, Reagan and

Bush had fought an arduous and sometimes pointed fight across the political map for months, with Bush positioned as a younger, centrist, more experienced alternative to the former California governor.

This fight began with Bush's surprising first-place finish in the Iowa caucuses in January 1980. Reagan surged back to wallop Bush in New Hampshire in February and in Illinois and Wisconsin in March. Bush regrouped and stung Reagan in Massachusetts in March and in Connecticut and Pennsylvania in April, and in early May he almost won the primary in Texas, his adopted home state but for years enthusiastic Reagan country.

Bush would win the Michigan primary later that month, but by then it was clear to his campaign manager, James A. Baker, that no further yardage could be gained without a great deal more money and a divisive donnybrook at the GOP convention reminiscent of 1976, ruining Bush's chance to be Reagan's running mate. Though he said he was not running for vice president, Bush acceded to Baker's advice and dropped out of the race on Memorial Day 1980. Baker clearly had been right: had Bush stayed in the battle all the way to Detroit, he would have only infuriated Reagan and his loyalists, guaranteeing he would not have been even second choice for the second spot.

The campaign provided Bush with the opportunity to assert his loyalty to Reagan and the Republican platform, to the point of altering his position on the issue of abortion (from saying it was not a federal question to supporting a constitutional amendment banning abortion everywhere). It was also a chance to get to know Reagan himself better. They had been acquainted for many years but, coming out of different backgrounds and party traditions, had never been close.

Both George and Barbara Bush were delighted to discover that Ron and Nancy Reagan were also not like some of the hard-right Reagan supporters they had known in Texas, those who in the 1980 primary in the Lone Star State had been whipped up against Bush for his onetime membership in the conspiratorial-seeming Trilateral Commission and the Council on Foreign Relations. (The Reagan operative who did the whipping-up in Texas was a young man named Lee Atwater, who would later guide Bush to his presidential victory in 1988.) In the campaign months in 1980 a true friendship developed between both couples and especially the two partners, which was not a remarkable thing, actually, given the enormous goodwill and lack of bitterness that characterizes both men.

Having won the election by a landslide, Reagan and Bush prepared to govern as a team. They adopted wholesale the historic and well-considered agreement forged by Jimmy Carter and Walter Mondale four years earlier to institutionalize the vice presidency. The agreement appears to deal with trivialities: an office in the west wing of the White House; a standing invitation to the vice president to attend any function on the president's calendar; access to all items in the official "paper flow" going into and out of the Oval Office; and a regular private luncheon every week to ensure that, if they did not have the chance for solitary discussion at any other time, they would have it then. But in fact these are not trivialities in a Washington world that takes extraordinary note of such things and in view of a history in which vice presidents were often cruelly isolated from the business of government.

Mondale, for example, believed so strongly in the axiom "where you sit is where you stand" that he operated only out of his newly won west wing office, going over to his extensive suite of staff offices in the Executive Office Building only for meetings with large groups of people or birthday parties. Because the EOB symbolized the physical isolation of previous VPs, Mondale called it "Baltimore," meaning that if you were over there, you might as well be in Baltimore for proximity to power.

Bush operated easily out of both the west wing and the EOB, liking—and eventually restoring—the huge office there that had once housed secretaries of the Navy and General Pershing. He believed that what determined a vice president's clout was not his office but his personal relationship with the president. With a good relationship, a vice president could almost truly be in Baltimore and succeed. Without one, it would not matter if he had a desk and chair in the Oval Office itself.

This is not to twit Mondale for his attachment to the west wing. It is the place to be in the White House, and he was, after all, pioneering a whole new role for the vice presidency. His overreaction may be likened to that of NASA when it quarantined the first lunar astronauts for fear they might have contracted some otherworldly disease.

If Vice President Bush enjoyed the friendship, trust, and esteem of Ronald Reagan from the outset, this was not necessarily the case with the men and women who had served the new president since his earliest days in Sacramento. To them, Bush was still the man who dared to contest their chief's claim to the mantle of Republican leadership, who had uttered the phrase "voodoo economics" to describe Reagan's plan to promote growth, and who had gathered under his banner the "country-club, elitist moderates" who represented what longtime Reagan supporters despised and rejected. Some still smarted from Reagan's magnanimous and wise selection of Bush's able former campaign manager, Jim Baker, to be White House chief of staff. They saw Baker as a dangerous alien element, if not a wholly subversive force, in the Reagan Revolution.

As the new administration took shape, whenever someone who had backed Bush in the primaries received an appointment, it was to some a sign that Bush was attempting to take over the Reagan government with his own moderate supporters. These appointments were relatively few and largely concentrated in the Commerce Department, headed by the man who had run Bush's successful primary campaign in Connecticut, Malcolm Baldrige. But no one seriously thought that commerce was a major field of battle in 1981. For his part, Bush declined to push for more than a handful of people like Baldrige to receive posts, fully aware that Reagan had won the election and not he.

This chilly atmosphere in the White House at below the presidential–vice presidential level continued into March, when two events beyond Bush's control or instigation occurred to make him a warmly accepted member of the team. The first was Reagan's decision that, whenever he himself could not preside at National Security Council (NSC) meetings, the vice president would do so.

Though this function was given the seemingly new title "crisis manager," it was neither as significant nor as novel a function as the press made it out to be. After all, the vice president had been a member of the NSC since its creation in 1947, in response to Harry Truman's having entered the presidency unaware of the atom bomb and other sensitive matters. It was also logical and obvious that the stand-in for the president should be the vice president.

But it was neither logical nor obvious to one man, Secretary of State Alexander M. Haig, who had let it be known around the capital that he intended to be "the vicar of foreign policy" to the pleasant old man from out west who lacked his own great national and international experience. When announcement of the president's decision was revealed on March 20, while he was testifying on Capitol Hill, Haig was so stunned he mumbled something about resigning. As he considered the matter more, Haig fairly exploded in anger, an ire that quickly found its way into the press.

In contesting Bush's right to be "crisis manager," a role Bush assumed without comment, and certainly without crowing that he now had the keys to the vicarage, Haig instantly did the vice president an immense favor. He demonstrated that *he* was the odd man out in the Reagan administration, not the loyal and silent vice president. From that moment on, Haig was doomed and survived only a little more than fifteen torturous months.

Ten days after the "crisis manager" flap, another far more serious incident sealed Bush's standing among Ronald Reagan's staunchest adherents. Early on the afternoon of March 30, 1981, as Air Force Two gathered speed to take off from Fort Worth to Austin, word was flashed to the vice president via the Secret Service that an attempt had been made on President Reagan's life. Bush canceled the rest of his trip, and after the big plane was refueled in Austin, he headed back to the capital. En route, he received word that Reagan was out of danger and that his vice presidency would not, like Truman's, be cut short.

Bush made some decisions during those dramatic hours that at the time greatly impressed official Washington and especially the shocked and frightened staffers of the wounded president. Even as he took off from Austin, he decreed that he would not take the helicopter waiting for him at Andrews Air Force Base directly to the south lawn of the White House but instead would go (as normal) to the landing ground at the Naval Observatory near the vice president's house.

Bush's military aide and the Secret Service argued that, at a time when it was unknown whether more than one person was involved in the attempted assassination of the president, his going straight to the White House would be more secure. But Bush firmly rejected this argument, saying, "Only the president lands on the South Lawn." He had another, typically sensitive, reason: Mrs. Reagan was back in the White House, trying to rest up from the day's ordeal, and the noise caused by the big U.S. Marine helicopter landing and taking off again would surely disturb her.

The next day, the vice president held meetings with senior government officials in his own west wing office and from his regular chair in the cabinet room. Much was made at the time how this showed admirable modesty and restraint on Bush's part, not using the Oval Office or taking the president's seat at the cabinet table. But doing either of these things was unimaginable for Bush, for the same reason he gave for not putting down his helicopter on the south lawn: they were the president's things, not his. To do otherwise would have been to raise a storm and a justified fury greater than that which had recently hit Secretary Haig.

Bush's demeanor clearly impressed those closest to Reagan. Observed Helene von Damm, Reagan's longtime personal secretary and appointments chief, "Vice President Bush behaved most admirably during this time. He kept a low profile, wouldn't think of taking [the president's] seat at Cabinet meetings, but maintained a reassuring presence nevertheless. Rumor had it that Mrs. Reagan and Mike Deaver insisted upon it. If true, they need not have worried. George Bush is too much of a gentleman to be reminded of how to behave at a time like that."

Also helping Bush with Reagan's prime supporters and wider constituency was his chairmanship of the Task Force on Regulatory Relief, given to him by the president on the first working day after the 1981 inauguration. Mondale had warned Bush against taking an "ongoing assignment" that would seemingly put him in charge of some problem but without the bureaucratic wherewithal to do anything about it other than issuing reports. But Bush instantly accepted the first thing the new president asked him to do out of duty and also out of gratitude.

The assignment gave Bush a chance to play a major role in the primary thrust of the Reagan administration, namely, reducing the involvement of government in the economy. In taking on this job, Bush also had the golden gift of being able to win over those conservative economists and journalists who had never forgiven him for the "voodoo economics" phrase, now a weapon in the rhetorical arsenal of the Democrats and the press.

Reagan's spending and tax cut proposals required (and received) congressional action, but the deregulating of American business and private life could begin immediately through executive order. In this endeavor Bush had the skilled assistance of the man who would be his counsel for the next twelve years, C. Boyden Gray, a Washington attorney who by fortunate coincidence was a regulatory specialist. Gray, working with Office of Management and Budget officials Jim Miller and Christopher deMuth, proceeded to deal with the often maddening minutiae of federal regulations.

As a former businessman who was as staunch a believer in deregulation as anyone else in Reagan's Washington, Bush would review and decide upon the staff's work and advocate it at higher levels. The result was a major decline in federal regulations, to the point that the vice president was able to boast in speeches by how much the *Federal Register* had grown before 1981 and how it had started to shrink afterward. The Task Force on Regulatory Relief, which he headed throughout his vice presidency, was therefore an assignment Bush welcomed and used to great political advantage.

In 1982, Bush took on another major ongoing assignment that would bear political rewards later on. Government and business leaders in Florida had come to him begging the federal government to stop the flow of drugs by air and sea into their state. Thus was born the South Florida Task Force, a consortium of federal officials (including the attorney general and the secretaries of state, defense, and transportation) headed by the vice president to coordinate all national efforts to choke off the importation of drugs.

This would seem a pluperfect example of the sort of chore against which Vice President Mondale had warned, for a vice president could only urge these moguls to work together; he could not force them to do so. Yet the effort was a success, as measured by the vast increase in the numbers of drugs seized and in the decision by drug smugglers to use places other than Florida. This led to the widening of the drug-interdiction campaign to all U.S. borders, not just Florida.

To run the task force on a day-to-day basis, Bush assigned his chief of staff, Daniel Murphy, a retired four-star admiral in the navy who had served as one of his deputies at the CIA. Murphy's experience in the Pentagon enabled him to get a reluctant Department of Defense (DOD) to participate in what it considered mere police work best left to the Coast Guard. With DOD as well as all other agencies, Murphy had another unspoken persuader working in his favor: the fact that in 1989, indeed at any moment, his boss might become president of the United States.

Another arena in which Bush did tireless service for the Reagan administration's domestic policies was on Capitol Hill. As a former member of the House with many friends still in that body and several more in the Senate, the vice president used his intimate knowledge of congressional folkways to be a popular and effective presence. He also used his splendid office just off the Senate lobby, his airplanes, his residence, his appearances at fund-raisers, the telephone, the tennis court, and even the steam bath in the House gym to lobby on key votes. And if at the same time he was winning and keeping friends who might be important supporters another year, then that was an added bonus.

But it was of course in foreign affairs that Bush made his biggest mark in the Reagan administration. Serving as U.S. envoy to the United Nations and to China, followed by his one year's tenure at the CIA, gave him an unequaled knowledge of world affairs and personalities, particularly after the departure of Haig in July 1982. He made numerous foreign trips for both ceremonial and state reasons, where he was received almost as a head of state or a prospective one. Though he would accrue many a joke for attending funerals, Bush had the chance to conduct some solid diplomacy at those functions as well.

His conversation with Chinese leader Deng Xiaoping, whom he had known since his first mission to Beijing, helped secure the agreement with China that governed arms sales to Taiwan, the most sensitive issue in Sino-American relations. His trip to Europe in the winter of 1983 to shore up NATO's commitment to deploy theater-range nuclear weapons was immediately successful. Later, he told the government of El Salvador that human-rights violations by so-called death squads against communist guerrillas were undermining the Reagan administration's efforts to defeat communist forces throughout Central America, after which the abuses stopped.

The funerals and other state occasions abroad, far from being puppet shows, allowed Bush to expand and maintain his contacts with world leaders and sometimes to conduct bilateral business. His most significant necro-diplomatic achievements came in the remarkable twenty-eight-month period in which three leaders of the Soviet Union died: Leonid Brezhnev in November 1982, Yuri Andropov in February 1984, and Konstanin Chernenko in March 1985, leading to the accession of Mikhail Gorbachev. Each time, Bush was dispatched to Moscow to represent the United States, and as soon as all funerary rites were concluded, he held a private meeting with the new boss of the USSR. Ahead of any other world figure, he was thus able to take the measure of the new man, to convey to him what American objectives and attitudes were, and to get the new Soviet leader's views on world issues in return.

In the 1984 campaign, former vice president Mondale, then the Democratic nominee against Reagan, claimed that Reagan's was the first administration since Herbert Hoover's not to have a summit meeting with a Soviet leader. Reagan laughed this off by saying, "Well, they kept dying on me." But in his stead, Vice President Bush had held those summits, and a reelected Reagan would start to hold those of his own with Gorbachev in 1985.

Bush's deep interest and involvement in foreign affairs presented him with a particularly tricky political situation when word broke in November 1986 that the United States had sold arms to Iran and used the funds to supply anticommunist forces, the so-called Contras, in Nicaragua. This episode, which came to be called the Iran-Contra Scandal, was embarrassing to Bush because, while he knew of the approach to Iran, he had been systematically excluded from discussions about arming the Contras. He had also missed two key NSC meetings at which the project was mentioned.

For a vice president known to be a major player in international affairs, who daily received the same if not greater intelligence briefing as did Reagan, the scandal made Bush seem an old-style vice president, one who was, to use his own phrase, kept "out of the loop." Yet he successfully maintained this position, which was verified in inverted fashion by his not being indicted by the Iran-Contra special prosecutor, Judge Lawrence Walsh, who would have dearly liked to do so.

Although there were still some Reaganites (or, as the president's fiercest warriors preferred to call themselves, Reaganauts) who harbored deep doubts that in his heart George Bush truly supported administration policies, there was never any question he would be kept on the 1984 ticket. Reagan coyly kept from announcing his decision until January of that year, leading to speculation right down to the evening of that announcement that he might retire. This kept alive further speculation that Bush would try to succeed him.

Bush was indisputably interested in the presidency—after all, he had run for the job against Reagan in 1980—but he laid down the strictest order to his staff and key supporters not to say anything to stimulate such talk. He knew it would be heard elsewhere only as disloyalty to the president. As a result, vice presidential staffers not only denied the possibility of an opening at the top of the ticket in 1984, they denied there was such a year as 1984 at all. And 1988 did not exist, either.

The 1984 reelection campaign, while a breeze and triumph for Reagan, gave Bush his most difficult time as vice president. Mondale had selected Congresswoman Geraldine Ferraro of New York as his running mate, and as the first woman selected for a major party's national ticket she attracted intense attention from the national media. Much of this was favorable, even adulatory. Bush, who had built and fostered remarkably friendly relations with the national political press starting in the 1970s, suddenly found himself the subject of unflattering stories and characterizations.

These intensified after he and Representative Ferraro met in a nationally televised debate in October. The debate itself was at worst a draw, but the vice president's offhand (but overheard) comment to a friendly supporter that "we kicked a little ass tonight" sparked an outcry from reporters, who had never heard such language before. Even the regal Barbara Bush came in for her own grief when she said the Democratic vice presidential nominee was something that "rhymes with rich." Once again the press was horrified. The 1984 elections mercifully passed, but never again would Bush enjoy the uniformly good press relations he had before the nomination of Ferraro.

As 1985 began, Bush could finally start to act more openly and deliberately in planning his own race for the White House four years later. Despite the stern dictum to his staff during the first term against presidential politicking, Bush clearly had his future in mind as he plotted his travel in those early years. He was frequently in Texas, Florida, and California, that triad of states crucial to any Republican candidate for president, not to forget Iowa and New Hampshire. He valiantly campaigned for GOP candidates in the grim off-year election of 1982 and the better one of 1984, and he raised millions for the coffers of local, state, and national party organizations.

The most important thing he did in 1985, however, was to take as his prime political operative a man the age of his sons who had done much to stir anti-elitist sentiments against him in the 1980 primaries. This was the wiry and wily South Carolinian Lee Atwater, who had been working in the political office of the Reagan White House. Bush had correctly assayed Atwater's talents not only in political tactics, but also in strategy.

It was Atwater who succeeded in getting Bush to make a play for so-called movement conservatives, a group he had spurned throughout his first vice presidential term on the grounds that "they've never been for me and they never will." At the very least, Atwater reasoned, Bush could head off rivals who wanted to run at him from the Right, and he might actually win some support in the process.

And so Bush's schedule began to show a number of appearances before various New Right groups, such as those concerned about abortion, gun control, taxes, and the general conduct of government. Columnist George Will (never a fan of Bush's) was so horrified to see the vice president start to woo those forces that Will confidently thought Bush's breeding would never allow him to touch that he denounced him in January 1986 as a "lapdog" begging for scraps. Yet once Bush became a believer in the Atwater strategy it worked brilliantly, protecting him fairly well against any challenge from the Right in 1988.

At a tactical level, Bush was likewise helped enormously by his mastery of the art of the small gesture. Few citizens, it seemed, escaped receiving one of the famous George Bush personal notes, scribbled on blue-bordered cards beneath a golden vice presidential seal. Often these were only a couple of lines long, saying nothing more than "Great seeing you this morning in Tulsa!" But recipients would frame them proudly, along with a full-color photograph (also inscribed) taken at the "grip and grin" session before a luncheon speech or other event. In addition to these paper souvenirs were meals and drinks at the comfortable vice president's house at the Naval Observatory on Massachusetts Avenue; invitations to the Bush family retreat at Kennebunkport, Maine; rides on Air Force Two or in "the limo"; and a veritable truckload of tie clips, cufflinks, and ladies' stickpins, the prized trinkets dispensed by a young aide or the vice president himself in one of his many offices in Washington.

As a result of all these things, George Bush, who had campaigned so vigorously against Ronald Reagan eight years before, earned the right to wear the Reagan mantle in the campaign of 1988. He wore it first against a field of fellow Republicans in the primaries (most important, Senate Minority Leader Bob Dole of Kansas) and then against the Democratic nominee, Gov. Michael Dukakis of Massachusetts, in the general election. His victory—with 54 percent of the vote and an electoral-college majority of 426 to 111—was both an endorsement of the policies of a Reagan administration in which he had been a major participant and an expression of confidence in his own readiness to be president.

It was also historically significant: as journalists never tired of saying, the only previous time a sitting vice president had managed to win the White House was when Martin van Buren did it in 1836. Indeed, only twice in between van Buren and Bush had sitting VPs even been nominated: Richard Nixon in 1960 and Hubert Humphrey in 1968. Bush's election was also the first time since Herbert Hoover followed Calvin Coolidge in 1929 that a political party succeeded itself after an election.

It was therefore a special moment in the history of the modern vice presidency when, on January 20, 1989, the booming unseen voice at the inaugural ceremony on the west front of the Capitol reversed the rule of protocol and announced the vice president *after* the president, since on that day he was also the president-elect. Perfectly prepared after eight years in the vice presidency to guide the nation in a time of monumental global change and challenge, George Bush strode forward to become number one at last.

Standing Firm: Personal Reflections on being Vice President

DAN QUAYLE

Vice presidents, to borrow a line from the comedian Rodney Dangerfield, "get no respect." America's first vice president, John Adams, described his new job as "the most insignificant office that ever the invention of man contrived." And Franklin D. Roosevelt's first vice president, John Nance Garner of Texas, said that the vice presidency was worth something less than a pitcher of warm "spit"! Not much of a recommendation for ambitious politicians, but few who have been offered the job have ever said no.

It is also fitting that we acknowledge Herbert Hoover's own vice president, Charles P. Curtis. Vice President Curtis was a likable fellow from Kansas who had been the Senate majority leader prior to his nomination and election in 1928. But when Will Rogers heard that Curtis was to be Hoover's running mate, he quipped that "the Republican Party owed Charles Curtis something, but I didn't think the Party would be so low down as to pay him back this way."

In my judgment, and based on my personal experience, the vice presidency can be a rather awkward office. It was not until Vice President John Tyler succeeded President William Henry Harrison after he died in office that it even became clear that a vice president would succeed to the presidency upon the death of the president. That "accident" of succession came more than fifty years after the vice presidency had been created in the Constitution.

It was not until the Twenty-fifth Amendment was passed and implemented in 1967 that the succession of the vice president to the presidency was formally incorporated into the language of the Constitution. It seems that for nearly 180 years, nobody really cared very much about the vice presidency. In that sense, the office could be described as a late bloomer in the history of our federal government.

The fundamental nature of the vice presidency changed, I believe, after Harry S. Truman assumed the presidency on the death of Franklin

Roosevelt. That Truman knew little about Roosevelt's plans and programs at the time he became president is well documented. In his first meeting with White House reporters, he said, "Boys, if you ever pray, pray for me now. I don't know whether you fellows ever had a load of hay fall on you, but when they told me yesterday what had happened, I felt like the moon, the stars, and all the planets had fallen on me." And he was saying that because of his poor preparation for the presidency. In light of Truman's experience, and the reality that we had become the dominant nation in the free world, observers began to realize that both the selection and the preparation of our vice presidents had to be taken seriously.

Since 1940, each candidate for vice president has been selected by a constituency of one: the presidential nominee. At one time, the selection process was open at national political conventions, but that really does not happen anymore. Vice presidents are customarily chosen to fill perceived voids on national tickets, so presidential nominees are very deeply involved in the search for running mates with complementary qualities.

You can see that the national tickets are very well balanced beginning with General Eisenhower's selection of Sen. Richard Nixon in 1952. Clearly, Nixon brought an intense interest in, and understanding of, politics to the Republican ticket. He had served in the House and the Senate; he had traveled in foreign policy circles and would be able to bring President Eisenhower important information. In the same manner, Lyndon Johnson, then a senator from Texas and the majority leader, filled a void for John F. Kennedy in 1960. Kennedy needed to build support among southern voters. These were marriages of convenience.

I will leave it to others to decide what void was filled by President Johnson in 1964 when he selected Sen. Hubert Humphrey. Johnson wanted someone he knew, perhaps also someone he could control. It may surprise you to learn that Johnson did not allow Humphrey to have the desk that has gone to every vice president since Harry Truman. Every vice president has signed the top drawer of the desk except Hubert Humphrey. That was the way Johnson treated Humphrey.

In selecting Spiro Agnew as his running mate in 1968, Richard Nixon put special emphasis on gubernatorial experience. I also believe that Nixon did not care for all the favorable press coverage that his running mate in 1960, former senator Henry Cabot Lodge, had received. Nixon wanted a vice president who would not eclipse him. Clearly, he got what he wanted in the governor of Maryland.

When Gerald Ford assumed the presidency, he gave consideration to three possible vice presidents: Ronald Reagan, George Bush, and Nelson Rockefeller. Ford thought that Reagan was a little too conservative and that Bush needed more experience. Rockefeller was another matter. His political philosophy was acceptable to Ford, and as the governor of New York for many years, Rockefeller brought stature to the vice presidency. At the time, Rockefeller must have seemed the perfect choice, but as we now know, that did not turn out to be the case.

I think Jimmy Carter selected Sen. Walter Mondale because he wanted an "insider," someone who had worked on Capitol Hill, someone who was well connected in the Democratic establishment, and someone from the liberal wing of the party. Carter had none of these attributes; it was a void in the Carter campaign. It is not surprising, therefore, that he chose Mondale. Once again, the two running mates balanced each other.

Ronald Reagan and George Bush were a good fit and had an excellent working relationship. Bush was important to Reagan because he reached out to the moderate wing of the Republican Party. Reagan was the strong conservative, and Bush was the solid moderate. It was a balanced ticket.

George Bush selected me, I think, for three major reasons. The first reason was generational: I belonged to the "baby boomer" generation, an enormous segment of our voting population. The second reason was ideological: I came more from the conservative wing of the party, as did Ronald Reagan. And the third reason was geographical: I was from the Midwest, and that region was going to be a battleground in the election campaign. As was the case with most of the previous tickets of both political parties, I was selected because my credentials complemented and balanced those of the presidential nominee.

Before going on, I do want to say a word or two about Bill Clinton's selection of Sen. Al Gore, because it seems to break the pattern I have talked about. I did not think Clinton would select Gore because they are so much alike: they are the same age, have similar political beliefs, and come from the same part of the country. But Clinton needed to hold the South if he was to win. He needed Arkansas, Tennessee, Kentucky, and some of the other border states that had leaned Republican in recent elections. Clinton also was clever in selling the generational issue as a strength rather than a weakness. Clinton argued that he and Gore represented the passing of the torch to the new generation. It was an effective strategy, to say the least.

Credit for the modern vice presidency should go to Walter Mondale for many reasons, not least his move into an office in the west wing of the White House. It was a simple move, but one with great symbolic importance. It signaled the most significant change in the power and influence of the vice presidency since the position was created. By having an office in the west wing, the vice president was part of the circle of power and influence that surrounded the president. The arrangement also facilitated a close working relationship between the president and the vice president.

Mondale also deserves credit for developing a clear understanding of his responsibilities and for clearly defining the working relationship between the president and the vice president. Mondale had a very solid understanding of which meetings he would participate in and which meetings he would stay out of. Mondale gave the job a definition that it had never had before.

Mondale and the three vice presidents after him all received multiple daily briefings on issues of concern to the president and the nation. For example, every morning during my term as vice president I received an overnight summary of the national and international news from the White House press office. I also received overnight intelligence reports from the Departments of Defense and State. These reports were followed by a daily briefing from the Central Intelligence Agency.

President Bush convened his national-security meetings every morning at eight-fifteen. National Security Adviser Brent Scowcroft, CIA Director Bob Gates, Chief of Staff John Sununu, the president, and I attended the meetings. George Bush paid great attention to foreign policy and matters of national security. It was serious business to him, and it was the first item on the agenda every single day.

There were other important meetings that I never missed. Meetings of the National Security Council and cabinet were high priorities. Meetings with congressional leaders and heads of state also were very important. I did not meet with all heads of state who visited the president, but I did meet with Margaret Thatcher, Mikhail Gorbachev, François Mitterrand, and other leaders of similar stature whenever they came to town.

I generally did not attend interest-group meetings, or the speech- and press-preparation meetings. I went to these meetings only at the president's request because I felt I could best serve him by doing other things.

Going up to Capitol Hill and being accessible to Congress also was important and not to be overlooked.

I will say one last thing about meetings. Decisions are made primarily by a very small group of individuals. Cabinet meetings are a necessity; it is important that the president see his cabinet and offer them a platform from which to speak. National Security Council meetings are important as well. But the meetings of greatest importance are the ones held in the Oval Office with only a few individuals advising the president. That was where we got the most done.

Both George Bush and Ronald Reagan had an open-door policy with their vice presidents. Obviously, if the president was in a one-on-one meeting with John Sununu, Brent Scowcroft, the secretary of state, or the secretary of defense, I would not bother him. But the president told me many times that he wanted me to know everything that was going on in the Oval Office. And I was as involved in presidential decision making as the majority of White House assistants.

George Bush asked only two things from me as vice president: first, to be prepared to address a wide range of national and international issues; second, to be loyal. Those were his two essential requirements. George Bush did not have to ask for my loyalty; he knew he was going to get it. To be prepared to deal with every issue, I had to have the same information that the president had. That required close daily communication with the president and his aides.

I did not spend most of my days in the Oval Office, of course. In fact, I was out of the west wing most of the time. I spent a lot of time on the Hill cultivating our relations with the Congress. I had spent four years in the House and eight years in the Senate, and this experience, I believe, was extremely helpful in passing our legislative programs. I had to do a lot of work with the White House congressional affairs office on Capitol Hill, an assignment I approached with a great deal of energy and dedication.

I also traveled for the president a great deal. The president appreciated the work I did for him in foreign affairs because he had done a lot of it himself during his eight years as Ronald Reagan's vice president. He had been to most of the forty-seven countries that I visited during my time in office, and he was a person who appreciated the importance of solid diplomatic information and understood the importance of good relations around the world. When I returned from an overseas trip, George Bush always wanted a full briefing. He was very interested in the information that I had gained during these trips, and he encouraged me to go to as many countries as possible.

Another assignment given to me by the president was in the political arena. George Bush is a very gifted politician—much better than he thinks he is. He is good at getting up and speaking about his political beliefs in an extemporaneous way. But he was president first and a political party leader second. In truth, he really did not want to deal with politics as much as his staff wanted him to. Well, guess who got to go to all those political fund-raisers! And guess who got to show up at all the state conventions!

When invitations came to the White House, John Sununu brought the stack into our morning meeting with the president. "They really want you in Illinois," Sununu said to the president. Then there was a pause. And Sununu handed the invitation to me. "They really want you in Colorado," he said. Silence again. So Sununu handed me that invitation. And so it went until the stack was gone.

Both the president and his chief of staff knew that I would go to Illinois and Colorado and all the other states and that when I got there I would be the happiest warrior they ever saw. Political events are an important way of getting the president's message to the people. We wanted to participate in these state political conventions, and we were sorry the president could not make them all. Don't get me wrong: the president did his fair share. But the burden of political campaigning falls to the vice president the majority of the time.

Another assignment I had was to serve as the president's liaison with the conservative wing of the Republican Party. George Bush is conservative, but he did not come from that wing of the party. He was not a "movement conservative" as I was. Clearly, I was the logical person to work with this faction, and I had some very tough discussions with my friends about the political philosophy of the Bush presidency.

If I am correct on any one element of George Bush's political philosophy, it is on the matter of his conservatism. He is a family man. He believes in lower taxes, fewer regulations, a strong national defense, and individual liberty. That is what he believes, that is what he practiced, and that was the bedrock of his presidency. As sure as I was in my belief, I had to work hard to retain the loyalty of the movement conservatives.

The president encouraged me to develop my own model for the vice presidency. And if it can be said that I left an imprint on the vice presidency, it is in the expansion of the vice president's responsibilities and participation in several areas of American public life. Let me also say that these new programs were taken on with the president's full support and encouragement. The power and influence of the vice president are an extension of the president's power. It would be foolish for a vice president to take new initiatives without the full support of the president.

I think my most important achievement was the Council on Competitiveness. The Congress, for whatever reason, decided not to confirm the assistant director for regulatory affairs in the Office of Management and Budget. As a result, the Office of the Vice President inherited the responsibility for regulatory affairs. That Democratic Congress did me a real favor, because I had fought my entire political life against excessive government regulation and the overzealous impulses of the federal bureaucracy. I believed then, and believe now, that federal bureaucrats do not understand the disastrous impact of regulations on American commerce and industry.

Of course, the health, safety, and welfare of the nation are the top priorities. But we also must guard against excessive regulation, and thus that task fell to the Competitiveness Council. And we were obviously quite effective. I say that because the very first act of the Clinton administration was to abolish the Competitiveness Council.

My second initiative as vice president was to reinvigorate the work of the National Space Council. Back in the 1960s, Congress passed a law stating that the vice president would be in charge of the Space Council, but most of my predecessors had done little with the job.

I must say that the staff at the National Aeronautics and Space Administration viewed me with suspicion. I had been a member of the Armed Services Committee in the Senate, and I was a very strong advocate for the Strategic Defense Initiative (SDI). Many of those committee votes came down to a choice to add funds for SDI and not fund new NASA programs. Because I had voted for SDI and not NASA, I was something of a persona non grata at NASA, and it took me a while to begin to turn that around.

One of the more difficult situations I faced as chairman of the Space Council was to select new leadership for the agency. Former astronaut Richard Truly had served NASA very well, but we needed a fresher, more innovative administrator. Unfortunately, Admiral Truly had a different view, and his departure from NASA was not as smooth and as graceful as his space flights had been.

Such things happen from time to time, and this was one of the occasions when the president said, "Why are we doing this?" After I explained everything fully, the president expressed his confidence in the plan, and it did turn out to be right. Dan Goldin, who succeeded Admiral Truly, has done a tremendous job. In fact, he has done such a good job that the Clinton people have kept him on. There is no question that he has brought a lot of fresh ideas and needed reforms to NASA.

Another initiative of my vice presidency was legal reform. As you know, I happen to be a lawyer and I am married to a lawyer. I spoke to the American Bar Association in August 1991 at their invitation, but the speech I gave was not well received. In sum, I said that the legal system needed reform because it had grown far too costly, too slow, and too unpredictable.

Most lawyers agree with me on the basic need for legal reform, but the leaders of the American Bar Association thought it was out of place for me to come to their meeting to ask the profession to reform the legal system. The president of the ABA was so incensed by my remarks that he followed me to the microphone and delivered a critique of my speech. He apparently thought I was going to leave, but I stayed there until he finished, then took back the microphone. And as you know, whoever gets the microphone last usually wins.

This incident was one of the few times that we had great press coverage of my activities. It may prove the point that the only people who get less respect than vice presidents are lawyers. Interestingly enough, my call for reform grew to become a very important issue, one that the Bush administration pushed in the Congress; it later became part of the Contract with America.

A final vice presidential initiative worth some discussion is the so-called Murphy Brown speech that I delivered before the Commonwealth Club of California in San Francisco in May 1992. I spoke about the importance of values, and I made the horrendously controversial statement that it would be in the best interests of our children to be born and raised in a traditional two-parent family. I did not say that single parents are bad parents; I did not say that all children of single parents were at risk. What I *did* say was that the two-parent family should be the model. Both mothers and fathers should be involved in raising the children.

Is that a controversial, radical, unprecedented statement? I did not think so in 1992, and I do not think so today. But this speech, with its reference to the television character Murphy Brown, was accused by the Left of being an effort to regulate the American family. Few journalists or pundits read the speech.

Well, what a difference a few years can make! Since that speech, we have seen Republicans and Democrats alike reiterate what I said. Even Bill Clinton has come around to my point of view. And that *is* good; we need to continue that national conversation.

Let me now turn to events that underscore my contributions to the Bush administration. One such contribution came during the budget debate of 1990. In early summer of that year, the administration had put the possibility of a tax increase on the table for discussion, and throughout the summer and part of the fall we got hammered for our tax stance and for going back on a campaign promise. We were continually reminded of the president's campaign pledge of "Read my lips, no new taxes."

The movement conservatives, in particular, were in revolt. They simply were not going to have anything to do with an administration that even considered a tax increase. Not surprisingly, many of the conservatives in Congress voted against us when the bill came to a vote. To this day, I think they were wrong, and I told them so at the time. It was not a pleasant time for me. Coming from the conservative wing of the party as I do, it was difficult to be on Capitol Hill and have my friends say, "If you were up here you would be doing the same thing we are doing." I responded that I would have done no such thing, and I reminded them that I had supported Reagan in 1982 on his tax increase. But as much as I argued, many conservatives would not listen, and they accused me and the president of "selling out" the Republican pledge.

It was not a sellout. I was doing what I considered to be right at the time: helping the president get his budget through the Congress. We were in the transition from Desert Shield to Desert Storm. The president was clearly preoccupied with what was going on overseas. At the same time, he was trying to get some resolution of the budget. Once again, I was on the point in trying to rally the conservatives. I am sure that all my lobbying and arm-twisting made a difference on the vote, but not as much as I had hoped.

The second event in which I played a major part was the 1992 reelection campaign. There is no single reason that the Bush/Quayle ticket lost in 1992—there are a number of reasons. Perhaps the most important one was that we did not have a good strategy for communicating the accomplishments of the Bush administration and our vision for the next four years.

We foolishly allowed Clinton and Gore to define the issues. Remember the slogan, "It's the economy, stupid"? If your opponent defines the issues to be debated before the American people, your opponent is going to win. It was a terrible political mistake and a grave miscalculation on our side to buy into their agenda. And every time you do that you are going to lose. That is the bottom line.

On an ironic note, the 1988 campaign was not pleasant for me. Even though I was elected vice president, the battering I took during the campaign was, in a way, a personal defeat. But the 1992 campaign was almost a reverse experience. I had some terrific personal achievements on the campaign trail, only to have them followed by the biggest political defeat of my life. It was the first time that I had been on the losing side in an election.

But in looking back over the preceding four years, I was pleased with what I was able to accomplish as vice president, satisfied that I had succeeded in the debate with Al Gore, and grateful for the experience of serving in the second highest office in the land. For me, at least, the 1988 and 1992 campaigns are bookends in more ways than one.

As I stated earlier, the vice presidency is an awkward office because the vice president is both the president of the Senate and a White House adviser who will carry out the president's agenda on Capitol Hill. Like all recent vice presidents, I was caught between two branches of government, which at times can be very frustrating.

But I do not regret a minute of my vice presidency—not even the attacks and character assassinations by the press. My satisfaction with the job came from serving the American people in general and in serving with George Bush in particular.

I am sure that all of you know of my deep and genuine affection for George Bush. He may well be the most decent individual I have ever met. He is a man of enormous integrity and extraordinary character— someone who, I believe, will go down in history as a great president. Many of the changes that we see today are because of his foresight, his ideas, his agenda, and his strategies. I was fortunate to be able to serve with him. He made being vice president a much easier task for me than it had been for others.

The title of this book is *At the President's Side*, and I like to think of myself standing with George Bush, both literally and figuratively. I am pleased that we are still very close and that both George and Barbara have always made Marilyn, our children, and me feel like part of their family. I learned much from both of them during our time together in Washington. As a vice president and as an American, I could not ask for better friends.

VII

PROXIMITY AND POWER

All in all, the Office of Vice President has been made better than it was for its incumbents, generally, and even for our presidents, who surely get more staff work and more loyalty out of them, on average, than FDR could ever have expected or received even from Henry Wallace, to say nothing further of Garner. Looking ahead, I see no major ways to make it better still.

—RICHARD E. NEUSTADT

It seems to me that we ought to give the vice president an assignment that will prepare him for the presidency if that becomes necessary. . . . Simply stated, I believe the vice president should be the White House chief of staff, that he should be the chief operating officer, with the president of course as the chief executive officer. As chief of staff, the vice president would be the president's deputy in fact as well as in title.

—JAMES CANNON

Vice Presidents as National Leaders: Reflections Past, Present, and Future

RICHARD E. NEUSTADT

At about the time that Franklin D. Roosevelt won his first election to the presidency, there appeared on Broadway a lighthearted spoof of elections, a musical comedy titled *Of Thee I Sing*, with words and music by George and Ira Gershwin. The plot, such as it was, owed more to the political culture of the twenties than to the seriousness of the Great Depression, or the New Deal yet to come, but one charming song included the deathless couplet: "Who cares if banks fail in Yonkers, as long as you've got a kiss that conquers?"

The show also included a vice presidential candidate, played by Victor Moore, for every laugh you can imagine, with the evocative name of "Throttlebottom." He embodied every cliché ever written since the Civil War about the general uselessness and ineffectuality of the vice presidency (that is, while the president drew breath).

In one splendid scene—which actually may have been in the sequel, *Let 'Em Eat Cake* (since I saw both and tend to mix them up)—Throttlebottom is the last person in a line of tourists being guided through the Oval Office. He asks, a bit plaintively, where the president sits. When he eventually identifies himself, no fellow tourist recognizes him; they ask him where he lives, and what he does, but cannot keep their minds on his answers.

With only a bit of literary exaggeration, this represents the prevalent view of vice presidents, and indeed their view of themselves, some sixty years ago. Their position was profoundly ambiguous. While the president lived, they had no role in the executive branch—nor staff, nor office, either. Rather, they subsisted on the margin of the legislative branch, with a constitutional duty to preside over the Senate and decide tie votes, of which there were few.

In the heyday of the nineteenth-century two-party system, they sometimes had good access downtown, commensurate with sectional strength at the level of state parties, needed for the president's last nomination, useful for his next. But John Nance Garner of Texas, FDR's running mate, was almost the last of that breed (and once Roosevelt got rid of the two-thirds rule for nomination in a Democratic convention, he made haste to get rid of Garner).

Yet on the other side of the ambiguity was the unquestioned fact, settled since 1841, that let the president but die, no matter how, of what, or when, and the vice president would be everything the presidency could make him, for the balance of the unexpired term. Throttlebottom at 5:00 P.M., sworn in as president at 7:00, with the Oval Office his thereafter. That had been Harry S. Truman's experience, and Calvin Coolidge's and Theodore Roosevelt's before him, just in the first half of this century. An ambiguity indeed, at least from the perspective of a Throttlebottom! Until the moment he succeeded, to call someone like him a "national leader" would have been regarded as ridiculous.

Since Truman's brief vice presidency—and in large part because of it— the privileges and duties, staffs and offices, prestige, and even methods for selection of vice presidents have been transformed. The high points of that transformation came in Truman's own administration, and in Eisenhower's, in Ford's, in Carter's, and in Clinton's, with more continuation in between than slippage. As a generalization, let me state that the change has made most vice presidents genuinely useful to the country, to their presidents, even to themselves, and much better prepared for succession, whether by death or otherwise—a laughingstock no longer, in any of these terms.

Having said that, let me assert, first, that in a new guise the ambiguity is with us yet, altered in particulars, almost out of recognition, but not in its essentials, except to be frustrating to vice presidents in fresh and direful ways. For the very things that strengthen the vice presidency most are free gifts of the sitting president, almost as readily subverted as bestowed, thus rendering vice presidential influence, in most respects, contingent upon presidential friendship and generosity.

Second, the public attitude toward vice presidents has certainly altered, along with their perks and their propinquity to presidents. Their national name recognition now is high. They are numbered among those the public thinks of as its "leaders" (often, nowadays, with gnashed teeth). And they are thought to have presumptive rights to be considered for the next presidential nomination. Yet their positions are so contingent on the favor of their president that until late in his term, at least, they dare not be seen fighting him. In this they are more weakly placed than any other senior officer at either end of Pennsylvania Avenue.

Third, what can be done about this has been done, or indeed overdone, from a systemic standpoint, organizationally and procedurally. Precisely what has made vice presidents useful to their presidents—as certainly the last four have been—is their ability to advise from a position at once equally political (yet with a longer future), and reliably dependent, hence reasonably to be trusted. So the ambiguity is part and parcel of the dependency making for trust, and the dependency is the underside of gifts that can be subverted. It all fits. Therefore, we might best do what I once heard Clinton Rossiter advise Sen. Birch Bayh (unsuccessfully), with respect to the higher office, "Leave your Constitution alone." So with the vice presidency.

But fourth, if one does wish to contemplate substantial change, regardless of such advice, I think it the beginning of wisdom to remember what my old boss Mr. Truman used to say, from time to time, namely that given our Constitution and traditions, "This country can only have one president at a time." That, of course, is what keeps the ambiguity alive and well.

Let me elaborate a little on those four points. The plight of Mr. Truman, taking over in the midst of war—wholly uninformed by FDR regarding foreign relations—with decisions on atomic weapons looming up to keep the issue of his ignorance alive in future years, was the proximate cause of what has been a revolution in the vice presidency. This turned Throttlebottom into an anachronism, when *Of Thee I Sing* was revived some years ago. The need to know in case of sudden elevation has been attended to, insofar as seems humanly possible. This has happened in familiar stages.

To recapitulate briefly: In 1949, the vice president was named by statute to membership on the National Security Council (NSC). In 1953, he was given office space and staff in the Old Executive Office Building, and was regularly included in all cabinet gatherings. In 1961, he became chair of the Space Council (more staff). In 1975, he chaired the Domestic Council—not a happy or long-lived addition—and received an official residence with the best view in town: Admiral House, seized from the Chief of Naval Operations. In 1977, the vice president acquired another office, this one in the west wing itself, close to the president's own, along with the promise of a private lunch between them every week. This enhanced the opportunity to test George Ball's dictum that "nothing propinks like propinquity." While the intimacy with their presidents has varied among successive vice presidents, each, I am told, has urged upon the next the importance of retaining that office and those lunches.

To conclude this summary, in 1989 Vice President Dan Quayle took over the leadership of regulatory review from the Office of Management and Budget, which in the next administration was turned back with a sort of trade for government reorganization. In 1993, Vice President Albert Gore, who, breaching precedent, had campaigned with the presidential candidate to their undoubted advantage, breached another precedent, it seems, by differing with the president as often as he pleased, in any audience that was not public—not, of course, in one that was, an ultimate constraint. So, at least, I am told by friends in Washington. They also say that, in result, department heads and White House aides seek Gore's ear, and support, with equally unprecedented enthusiasm, even in Mr. Clinton's presence. If so, these things say more about Clinton than about Gore. Future VPs ought not to count on them!

Incidentally, while Al Gore was my student, and a good one, with whom I keep in distant touch, I have not sought his views on this essay, not wishing to commit him in any way. My contemporary sources are less intimate than that (hence less reliable!).

In this recapitulation, I promised to be brief. So I leave to others the details, and nuances. Of the latter there are many.

At the start of this sequence, Mr. Truman himself made sure that Alben Barkley was invited to cabinet meetings and became a statutory member of the National Security Council. This statutory cabinet committee was established in 1947; it began to come alive for presidential purposes after the National Security Act amendments of 1949. Truman and Barkley were both aware, I think, that cabinet sessions usually amounted to mere show-and-tell affairs, by others than the president. They had become so, in that Democratic era, when FDR caught Garner (or thought he did) peddling White House intentions to its enemies on the Hill. Not much was to be learned, therefore, from cabinet meetings, but maybe something—who could tell?

As for the NSC, in the more titillating and more secret realms of defense and diplomacy, statutory membership offered the VP a lot to learn, provided only two things: that he went to almost every meeting, after being briefed by his own people on all papers, and that if the president preferred informal meetings as substitutes for formal ones (where statutory members had a formal claim), the vice president was invited to those too.

As I recall, Mr. Barkley was less concerned with learning than Truman was on his behalf. Reportedly, the vice president was bored by cabinet meetings, and his attendance at the meetings was sporadic. As for the NSC, he absented himself on constitutional grounds. A member of the legislative branch, as he still viewed it, following long tradition, he ought not to participate in quintessentially executive functions such as formulating foreign and military policy. That, at least, is what the White House staff was told to explain his usual absences. So far as I know, such inhibitions vanished with Mr. Barkley.

For this, I think President Dwight D. Eisenhower is chiefly responsible, with an eager assist from Vice President Richard M. Nixon, no traditional attitude there, no hanging back. Ike created two vital precedents. First, he gave Nixon office space—and staff, actual warm bodies—in the Old State Building (or, as we now would say, the Old Executive Office Building). Second, Eisenhower regularized procedures for cabinet and NSC meetings and for preparatory staff work to ensure all parties received a hearing, and a sense of due process, even if excluded from intimate—often more decisive—conversations with small groups along the way. (This reflects the "hidden hand" methodology that Fred Greenstein has written about.) Nixon, institutionally the weakest of participants, could not help but benefit, especially in terms of just the sort of learning that Truman, as vice president, had no chance to do. By 1960, the VP not only was, in fact, but also saw himself to be an officer of the executive branch.

John F. Kennedy, when he came in, made haste to shore up that impression, as best he could, in the mind of his volcanic, larger-than-life vice president, the former Senate leader Lyndon B. Johnson. He was given even better office space in the same building, and still more staff to occupy it. While Kennedy could not assure LBJ of the procedural regularities Nixon had enjoyed, since Kennedy himself destroyed them early on, he endeavored to be scrupulous about inviting the vice president to attend every meeting where decisions might be made about which he might later need to know. This had reasonably good results, so far as it went. As an observer of decision making, LBJ was certainly far better off than Truman had been, when both succeeded on their president's death, though there were numbers of nuances even Johnson had not known, or caught, in the interstices of foreign policy.

But there was just the rub. Executive official he might be, but save for space programs (a sop that Kennedy had lent him), LBJ, in his own understanding, was a mere observer. In theory, he was free to speak his mind, and to do all he could with reasoned argument. Reportedly, Johnson never thought he had such freedom. He was the author—and certainly a practitioner—of the advice that Walter Mondale once informed me he had been given by Hubert H. Humphrey, LBJ's vice presidential successor: "Never be seen by a third party to be differing with the president, unless, indeed, he's sanctioned it in advance." (Why not? Because the third might tell a fourth, the fourth a fifth, etcetera, and into the press.)

Learning is all very well, especially if someone has been so far out of the loop as Truman; but for persons of experience, ambition, and drive, satisfaction of the need to know leads promptly to a passionate wish for influence. Nixon surely felt this, as did Humphrey. But they, at least, were tied to older and more experienced presidents. How much more passionately must LBJ have felt it in a White House headed by a man substantially his junior in both age and experience, and possessed of a brother, the redoubtable Bobby, who barely bothered to be civil to the vice president of the United States!

For someone of experience, ambition, and drive, the vice presidency can become a horror, and so it was, by all accounts, for LBJ. Apparently, he had taken to drink in a serious way by the time Kennedy died. Having experienced the office so, Johnson made sure his vice president, poor Humphrey, had a comparable experience. In the process, LBJ displayed what remains fundamental, the source of continued ambiguity. Revolutionized or not, the vice president's enhanced role and status are contingent on the pleasure of the president. Without that, they are rendered irrelevant, even the statutory ones.

To exemplify, in early 1965, months before the critical decisions, Humphrey wrote Johnson a long private memorandum, politically cogent, reading well in retrospect, opposing Americanization of the Vietnam War. You can find this in Humphrey's memoirs, along with a sanitized version of what followed. The unsanitized version I had from sympathetic White House aides, much nearer to the time. By their account, LBJ immediately banned Humphrey from all further substantive meetings on Vietnam for almost a year, then sent him to Saigon to deliver a speech of extravagant praise for the South Vietnamese leaders. After that, publicly committed as it made him, the vice president was allowed back in the room.

But what of Mr. Humphrey's statutory membership on the National Security Council? President Johnson handled that, evidently, either by labeling meetings as other than formal sessions or by simply ignoring Humphrey's formal rights. The same occurred with NSC papers. What was the vice president to do? Sue?

When asked for Johnson's motives, the same sources speculated that the president had read Humphrey's memo and said to himself, "Why did he put it in writing?" Which instantly led to the question: "To whom does he mean to leak it?" That could have sufficed. Having seen Johnson a little, at just about that time, I find the speculation quite believable. The decisions lying just ahead had put him on the rack. He recalled Roosevelt's too cute "court-packing," which sank his great majority in 1937, and Truman after "losing" China, and "Truman's War" in Korea, and General McArthur's defiance. Whichever way Johnson chose to go in Vietnam threatened (in his own mind) his congressional majorities for Great Society reforms, also threatening his pledge of 1963 to "let us continue." All this with Bobby sitting in the Senate, darling of the media. Now Humphrey, on whom LBJ had thought he could rely, a pet on his leash, evidently contemplated something uncontrollable!

Granting that no president since has had paranoid reactions, or a lack of manners toward his intimates to match Johnson—except Nixon— Humphrey's case poses a critical question. Has the vice presidency so evolved in the interim as to render this example inapplicable? At present? In the future? I believe not. Why not? Consider a few thought experiments.

Suppose Clinton sought to discipline Gore more politely, without breaching the spirit of the latter's statutes: Could perquisites be used instead? Could a vice president be deprived of office space? Try drafting the press release: "Since the chief of staff deems it essential to expand, the vice president has graciously agreed to use his office at the Capitol." No. Or what about staff? "The vice president has graciously agreed that, mindful of the budget deficit, he will dispense with his own staff and henceforth depend on mine." Again, no. The trouble is that since predictable news stories before the inauguration had told what the vice president would get, by way of perks (a follow-up, indeed, to the news stories after his selection), the White House press corps would be instantly alerted by a downward alteration—even if better phrased—would smell controversy, and would go for it.

That might not matter if the president were prepared to withstand the publicity until it died away. Perhaps four days, in Quayle's case? Up to a week in Bush's? Maybe a month in Humphrey's or Gore's, if Congress were in session to comment on the story? Surely not more. But in the electronic age of multiple channels, compounded by talk shows, the price would seem too high, I think, if not at first to an angry president, then to his appalled communications staff. For presidents ought never to look churlish in a petty way on national television, and even those who forget tend to know that, if reminded.

Now, suppose Clinton sought to discipline Gore, but saw, or was reminded, that he should exempt Gore's perquisites. Would our contemporary president be likely to adopt the Johnson treatment? With respect to interrupting formal functions, I rather doubt it. This is not because I think President Clinton is too nice to conceive such a thing. Under pressure I expect he probably could. But in his White House almost every policy argument seems to leak—which may, from now on, be endemic—and, once leaked, attracts that same array of media as swarm over changes in perks. Moreover, journalistic standards have so changed, to say nothing of the world situation, that "national security affairs" no longer have the cachet, or the shielding from reporters, of the old days before Johnson made those Vietnam decisions.

Furthermore, in the case of Messrs. Clinton and Gore, their joint campaigning, followed by two years and more of relative freedom in the White House for an activist vice president, would make his sudden, sustained absence from an area of policy where he had generally acknowledged a need to know, a major sustained story, print as well as electronic, and a major matter for the opposition on the Hill. If I am right in this, then the vice presidency has gained something in thirty years, courtesy not only of the National Security Act, as tradition has evolved, but also of the changes in the world, the media, and politics.

Yet, even so, is our hypothetical Gore secured from the effects, if not the form, of what befell the actual Humphrey: exile, followed by humiliation? Again, I conclude that the answer is no, for now that the vice president is an executive official, in the west wing of the White House to boot, his schedule can be almost at the president's disposal, for good or ill. A president bent on disciplining his vice president will scarcely fail to notice. And here's a weapon that can be applied with scarcely a blow to be seen by the press!

In short, what Johnson did to Humphrey about the National Security Council may be outmoded; what he did in sending him to Saigon seems as relevant as ever, and as usable.

We recently have witnessed a perfectly benign example of presidential power to constrain and shape vice presidential schedules. To the best of my knowledge, nothing disciplinary was involved; quite the contrary. But it does suggest the range of possibilities in scheduling, were discipline intended, without touching statutory rights, or office space, or staff.

I expect everyone recalls the joint campaigning of Clinton and Gore. You may also recall their joint appearances thereafter. Every time Clinton was seen on television, or in print media, there also was Gore, perhaps a pace behind, standing stiffly at semiattention, with scarcely a word to say. No doubt this made some points at the beginning, both for Clinton nationally and for Gore in Washington. But gradually it began to make the latter a raw joke on late-night television, then not-so-late. Gore was about to be Quayle-ized. The practice then tapered off.

Alongside the public-relations risk, consider the consequences for Gore's schedule. That practice put his daily doings wholly at the mercy of the president's. Since Clinton, by all accounts, liked to change his schedule frequently, on impulse, and used to feel no compunction about it, the vice president's, being derivative, was changed or torn up on no notice. For a while, his scheduler was in despair, the rest of his staff in distress: so, at least, some White House aides have told me.

It follows that the inevitable subordination of the vice presidential schedule to the president's, and to the latter's wish or whim, is a weapon he can always use against his own vice president, with the advantage that, skillfully wielded, it can leave no visible marks on the body. I do not suggest for a moment that Clinton has so used it against Gore. But the option is there, for another Johnson to use against another Humphrey. And if public relations militates against keeping him out of meetings, schedule him so that he is kept out of town! His schedule is, at any rate, a key to his dependency.

In the real world, setting such speculations aside, Mr. Gore seems to have been treated with genuine liking, rare consideration, and strikingly unusual autonomy. If it is true, as former White House aides allege, that Gore decided, in the fall of 1993, to debate Ross Perot without consulting anyone, from Clinton down, then the term *autonomy* scarcely suffices. *Vice principal* appears more like it. (Of the vice presidents I have previously known, none, I believe, would have dared to decide on their own.)

Yet another key to the vice president's dependency must be presumed to remain at hand. Mr. Clinton may let him decide on his own risks, but there is no sign that he has delegated ultimate decision on the president's risks. And those include the substance, personnel, and processes of policy in his administration! Some presidents have delegated vastly to their chiefs of staff, but never, in anything like the same degree, to their elected colleagues. It is easy to grasp why: malfeasance aside, the elected vice president cannot be fired until the next quadrennial party convention, if then—our version of the crown-prince problem.

There also is no sign that Mr. Gore perceives his situation as a horror. But that is a tribute mainly to his president. For the future, there are no guarantees. And as a person of experience, ambition, drive—which I presume him to remain—Vice President Gore would be unlike most predecessors if he did not feel some pain each time his arguments fail to be followed. That could accumulate into a lot of pain, the ache of recurrent frustration. Yet, unlike a member of Congress, or even, to some degree, a member of the cabinet, no vice president in his right mind complains to anyone within reach of the media, not unless he is courting Garner's fate (as Garner himself might have done). Thus, this again is speculative. We will not know about Gore, with assurance, until his memoirs (if then).

So even in the ideal case, which perhaps we see before us now, we must presume the vice presidency to have some awful aspects for anybody with the qualities we are bound to wish the vice president had, the moment the president dies! The ambiguity a Throttlebottom faced has been dolled up with real estate, assistance, name recognition (and the hazards now common to celebrity). But the essentials remain: the other person has all the authority, and if he does not happen to approve what you are doing with such driblets as he hands you, he can render your life miserable, your future cloudy. Indeed, he may do that to you unintentionally, regardless, as Bush, with the best will in the world, did to Quayle.

Mr. Quayle's case, somewhat like Mr. Nixon's under President Eisenhower, highlights an aspect of the latter-day vice presidency that is all to the good—and indeed contrasts sharply with Throttlebottom's day—but does not stand out equally in Gore's instance, or Humphrey's. Quayle had been plucked out of the Senate early, had much to learn in foreign policy, encountered the executive establishment for the first time, also the national media—where his initial meeting almost sank him. Learning, therefore, and experimentation in all these realms, looking with hope, I suspect, toward 1996, may have been for him a sturdy shield against frustration, of a sort unavailable to Johnson as vice president, or to Humphrey, or even perhaps (it is all relative) to Gore. If so, though ambiguity remains in its fresh character, to be vice president now, especially if new to national politics, has compensations far beyond the dreams of those who held the office sixty years ago—that is, all dreams but one!

All in all, the Office of Vice President has been made better than it was for its incumbents, generally, and even for our presidents, who surely get more staff work and more loyalty out of them, on average, than FDR could ever have expected or received even from Henry Wallace, to say nothing further of Garner. Looking ahead, I see no major ways to make it better still. On the other hand, I see two tendencies and hear of two proposals that I think could make it worse. Let me identify these and close.

First come dubious tendencies. They affect the presidency and vice presidency alike. One is technological, and societal. It derives from the onrush of communications technology, which threatens to divide a president's national constituency—and a vice president's prospective one—into a myriad of "narrow-cast" subgroups, out of sympathy or even touch with one another.

Other social factors are contributing to this as well. Unless offset by personalities or national crises, widely and directly felt, or by some possibly disastrous combination of the two, I foresee the decline of the twentieth-century presidency, which began to take shape with Teddy Roosevelt's brilliant "management" of the first electronic medium, the wire services. Those services helped him make the White House a unique national source, alike of ideas and of entertainment, his "bully pulpit." It served as such, from time to time, well into the 1980s.

But as the pictures multiply, the variety increases, the viewer options rise, and with them the noise level, that pulpit becomes hard to see, its user hard to hear. Without it in the background of everybody else's calculations, Teddy Roosevelt's presidency shrinks back toward the size of Grover Cleveland's. If so, the vice presidency shrinks with it.

Someday, Throttlebottom's anonymity may look good by comparison with the future vice presidents' mishmash of diverse and contradictory images, flickering amid the disarray of more beguiling pictures.

The second tendency is administrative or organizational. It has to do with the continuing existence, deepening into tradition, of two gradually enlarging staffs, located cheek by jowl, work intertwined, each motivated to be holier than the pope, more royalist than the king, with regard to their separate principals, the president and vice president. Reassuringly, it can be said, and often is, that this condition is forty years old, and open warfare has not broken out yet, the Republic still stands, the vice president—and his staff—is still properly subordinate. But what is rarely spoken of, or in most quarters even understood, is the amount of effort it has taken in the past—and I do not doubt at present—to achieve this benign result. And as the staffs enlarge, which on a secular trend, thus far, they still show signs of doing, what then? That is a rhetorical question. I leave it with you.

Finally, let me mention two proposals that give me pause. There are also others, but I will spare you. The first consists of ideas from various sources about making the vice presidency more "democratic," by removing the selection of elective incumbents from the sole discretion of the winning presidential candidate, where by common consent it now rests in quadrennial elections. So it has done since state party leaders lost their place in nomination politics. To my mind, removing the discretion of the presidential candidates is a bad idea. It is a product of false populism. Not all of it is "false" (some of it could be better described as "Gucci" populism; I'm not sure in which category this stands). Regardless, the whole process of channeling the ambiguity of the vice president's position into its new guise—of rendering the office educative, also useful, even if not fun— is put at risk by every increment of personal and intellectual distance between him and his president.

Messrs. Eisenhower and Nixon were, in fact, the last vice presidents selected more by party than by president. So are Kennedy and Johnson, for the latter was selected by the former, but on old-style party grounds, as indeed was Bush by Reagan. Congressional confirmation complicated naming Ford and Rockefeller, but these, I presume, are rare cases.

The new selection style has been exemplified, thus far, by Messrs. Humphrey, Mondale, Quayle, and Gore. I omit the sheer mistake of 1968, which in the circumstances could have tripped up party managers as readily as it did Nixon. From any standpoint, those four compare well with the products of earlier party selection. This is partly because presidential nominees have become well aware that journalists will comment on their choice of running mate as a first test of their performance in the White House. Well and good. Let us leave it just there!

The second proposal that troubles me would modify the Twenty-fifth Amendment to insert private physicians into political decisions. Let me be plain: I never liked that amendment in the first place. I sided with Clinton Rossiter, and pleaded with Bayh—to no avail. Eisenhower and Nixon had made a sensible personal agreement—two men confronting their personal problem—on what to do if the president were temporarily disabled, and also when he recovered: Nixon should reverse the Tyler precedent and serve as acting president, until Ike found that he had gotten well enough to resume and, by implication, that the White House physician agreed with him. Kennedy and Johnson chose to follow suit. So did Johnson and Humphrey.

Then the amendment took those matters out of their hands. It also provided what to do if the president asserted he had recovered, while the acting president, backed by a majority in the cabinet, thought he had not: the latter stays in office until Congress decides between them by a two-thirds vote. This violates Truman's dictum: one president at a time. I shudder to think what might happen if it ever were invoked.

Fortunately, in the 1980s the Reagan and Bush administrations elaborated contingency plans. They reportedly eased the problem by providing both the president and the vice president the same source of advice, namely the White House physician, selected by the president at the outset of a term, or carried over from the previous administration, consulting with whatever specialists he or she chose to bring into the case. So matters seem to stand: those contingency plans being still in effect, as I hear it, approved by Clinton and Gore.

Unfortunately, in my view, this arrangement is now being challenged by a group of private doctors, cheered on by Arthur Link, who has obvious reasons for concern as the biographer of Woodrow Wilson. In their view, no White House physician is to be trusted, just because of his selection or continuation by the president. The latter might overawe or dominate his own appointee. Therefore, the determination should be made by an ongoing panel of private physicians, selected by the profession itself, confirmed by Congress, periodically examining the president, publicizing the results, while preempting advice to the vice president and cabinet, with authority to do so embedded in the Constitution itself, through revision of the Twenty-fifth Amendment.

Granting that the worries behind this proposal are serious, and the proposal itself well meant, it is expressive of that great American urge, rampant in many professions, to mistrust the patriotism and good sense of people living in the future, especially if they are politicians, not good professionals, not experts. If we were now in ordinary times, we could assume that nothing much would come of this, and treat it as a historical curiosity, alongside similar assertions in the past, from engineers, physi-cists, and economists. But these may not be ordinary times! Witness all those populists out there—Gucci and otherwise. I offer, therefore, one last piece of keynoter's advice. Echoing Clinton Rossiter: Let us leave our Constitution alone! Let those who have to face exceptional problems deal with them in their own terms and time.

Defining a Public Role for Vice Presidents:
A Symposium
HUGH SIDEY, JAMES CANNON,
ROBERT H. FERRELL, CHASE UNTERMEYER,
R. W. APPLE JR., AND RICHARD E. NEUSTADT

Hugh Sidey:

My measure of the vice presidency is a bit unusual, or at least it has been in recent years. I live in Potomac, Maryland, about a twelve-mile drive from the White House, and I travel to my office along Massachusetts Avenue. The entrance to the vice president's house is on Massachusetts Avenue, and I gauge the activity of the vice president—his worthiness—by the number of traffic jams that I encounter as I pass by his house!

A new measure of congestion was established by Mr. Bush, increased with Mr. Quayle, and we are now at maximum gridlock! Massachusetts Avenue is tied up at all times of the day and night. Diplomats and journalists go in and out constantly. All manner of events of high and low culture take place at the vice president's house. On Halloween, the "Great Pumpkin" rises on the lawn and gives pumpkins to the little people. At Christmas, the vice president hosts a moth-eaten Santa Claus and, if you lean close enough, you can smell a bit of bourbon on the old fellow's breath. But if you were a Santa Claus in that situation, you would take a nip too, I think!

It seems to me, after observing nine presidential administrations, that there is a rare harmony between the offices of the vice president and the president in recent years. It is not guaranteed, of course. It depends too much on the people who are elected, their personalities, how mercurial they are, how difficult, how bright, how graceful, and how sensitive they are. But for the moment it is a truly remarkable relationship.

Now let me sketch a little background. I want to share my thoughts on how this special relationship came about. In my time, Richard Nixon, Lyndon Johnson, Hubert Humphrey, and Spiro Agnew all had grave difficulties with the presidents they served. But then it changed with Gerald Ford, Nelson Rockefeller, Walter Mondale, George Bush, and Dan Quayle. I will not comment on the political fallout or the image problems these men had. But the serving of the president was different for this latter group. It was kind of a threshold; the relationship had changed.

I have been around the White House for the past forty years, and the public interest in the presidency has changed dramatically in that time. I give some of the credit for this change to my academic colleagues who have thought about the presidency and written about it extensively. And I also give some credit to the much maligned media, of which I am a member.

I watched the press coverage of the White House evolve and expand over four decades. It has been an amazing transformation! When I first started covering the White House during the Eisenhower administration with Press Secretary Jim Haggerty, there were only about twenty regular White House reporters. We would all shuffle into the pressroom once a day, and, more times than not, Haggerty would come down from his office, yawn, scratch himself, and say, "Sorry boys, no news today." And then we would all go off and have lunch, take a nap, and forget the White House!

That environment has changed dramatically in forty years. Today, you have up to two hundred reporters covering the White House regularly, and some of them need fifteen-minute updates and new leads every day. A soap opera has been created in the White House! There you have it. The first family and all the family's aides have become important to the press. The chief of staff has been made a god. Even the social secretary has become important. On some days, the national-security adviser and even cabinet secretaries achieve a status more prominent than celebrities!

We now have an environment in which White House dogs write books and where cats are chronicled through the day. And swept into this environment is the vice president. He had been absent. He had been left to his own devices on Capitol Hill.

The first vice president I met was Richard Nixon, and he was a lonely man back during his tenure. When I saw him in 1957, my first year in Washington, he drifted at the edges of the administration. It was not until Ike had his heart attack that Nixon was drawn into the administration and given foreign missions and substantive domestic tasks to accomplish.

Yet there was a strangeness about Nixon. I flew with him in the election campaign of 1958—six weeks on a little Convair airplane. To the best of my knowledge, there was no White House operative on the airplane. If we went into a city like Grand Rapids and there was someone on the plane from the White House, that person went out the other door from Nixon. Somehow, no one in the White House wanted to be associated with Richard Nixon except by necessity.

Lyndon Johnson had similar problems: it was not his relationship with the president, but rather with the Kennedy family. Johnson was kept at a distance, socially and culturally. He was excluded from the inner circle of the so-called new frontier.

But the relationship between the president and his vice president changed dramatically in the 1970s, especially when Vice President Mondale received an office in the west wing of the White House. If you have two hundred underemployed journalists covering the White House, you cannot see the president or the national-security adviser every day. The vice president is an obvious man to probe.

So I think the changes in the media and in the proximity of the vice president to the president have had a profound effect on the kind of person who is chosen to serve in that office. Out of this media attention and the academic study has come a very good working relationship between our presidents and vice presidents. And that is all to the good.

James Cannon:
I have two comments to make on Richard Neustadt's essay before I go on to make some general comments. First, not everyone will agree that the vice president's residence offers the best view in Washington! The best view is from the Oval Office, across the south lawn of the White House. And for second place, it is a tie between the view from the Capitol office of the Senate majority leader and the view from the office of the Speaker of the House of Representatives. The latter view is spectacular, sweeping down Capitol Hill across the weathered bronze of Ulysses Grant and west across the mall to the Washington Monument and the Lincoln Memorial!

My second comment has to do with the Twenty-fifth Amendment. *Fortuitous* is the word for that amendment, and without Sen. Birch Bayh we might not have it. The Twenty-fifth Amendment was critical in 1973, when Spiro Agnew was forced to resign the vice presidency. Without that amendment, Speaker of the House Carl Albert would have become president upon the resignation of President Nixon. Speaker Albert himself has said and written that the very *legitimacy* of the United States government would have been called into question had he or any other nonelected Democrat taken over after a Republican president—elected two years earlier by a landslide—had been forced out of office. So I disagree with Professor Neustadt on this amendment. I think its value is self-evident in the events of 1973 and 1974.

I also have some general comments on the vice presidency, views culled from my years of government service. Every schoolchild knows that the only reason we have a vice president is to take over if something happens to the president. That being the reality, it seems to me that we ought to give the vice president an assignment that will prepare him for the presidency if that becomes necessary.

He, or she, needs to be in the mainstream of presidential information, decisions, and execution. The office that best fits is the office of the chief of staff. Simply stated, I believe the vice president should be the White House chief of staff, that he should be the chief operating officer, with the president of course as the chief executive officer. As chief of staff, the vice president would be the president's deputy in fact as well as in title.

I propose that every nominee for president choose the vice president for qualities and experience that would make him or her a good executive manager. And if the nominee is elected, the president should put the vice president to work as chief of staff, responsible for managing all the affairs of government under the president's direction. He should be the chief operating officer, overseeing all the executive branch of the government.

Ideally, the vice president should be chosen because he is qualified to be president, so let's give him a job that will make him more qualified. Nothing is hidden from a good chief of staff; and nothing should be hidden from a vice president. If he, or she, works for the president in that capacity, the vice president would not need a separate staff, except for a knowledgeable assistant to follow the Senate and let him know when he or she needs to come in for a tiebreaker.

As White House chief of staff, the vice president would command the respect of the cabinet and the presidential assistants. He or she would have real executive and political power, not the power of an understudy, a performer waiting in the wings.

I cannot tell you why, but all presidential assistants, if not arrogant when they enter the White House, soon become so, and all of them quickly come to disdain and diminish the vice president. That would be less likely if the vice president had a real job, and if he or she were known to be and seen to be carrying out the president's decisions. So I say, put the vice president to work. I also suggest that the vice president's political assignments be kept to a minimum, and, please, let us not send the vice president to any more funerals for foreign leaders!

Now suppose that the vice president turns out to be incapable of handling the job of chief of staff. My answer to that is, the sooner the president finds that out, and the sooner the press and the American people realize that, the better off the country will be. If a vice president cannot manage for a president, then we will know early on that he should not be president!

Let us consider the idea in terms of people we know. Would Al Gore make a good White House chief of staff? Yes, I think he would probably be better than anyone President Clinton has had yet. What about Dan Quayle? I watched Quayle come into the Senate, and he was a very effective young senator. He would have been a far, far better White House chief of staff than, say, John Sununu. Consider this: Jim Baker and Howard Baker served President Reagan well in the office of chief of staff; either would have been an outstanding vice president. Fritz Mondale would have been a far better chief of staff for President Carter than Hamilton Jordan.

Could Nelson Rockefeller have been President Ford's chief of staff? It was not easy for Rockefeller to be subordinate in anything, but he knew political management; he had done it for twenty years in Albany. Ford picked Rockefeller because of his experience in governing, and it created difficulties for both when such a high-powered vice president ended up with too little to do.

In brief, every president needs all the quality help he can find. Why let a good vice president sit idle when there is so much to do?

Robert H. Ferrell:

Richard Neustadt has written of vice presidents during the past fifty years, and the rest of the essays in this book consider holders of the office beginning with Theodore Roosevelt in 1901. I want to go back earlier and tell a few stories about our nineteenth-century vice presidents.

The purpose of my drill is to show that under the Constitution the initial century's vice presidents were a pretty sorry lot. Whatever the limitations of later holders of the office, and contrary to Richard Neustadt and Clinton Rossiter's advice not to tinker with the Constitution, the nineteenth-century vice presidents needed, I think, a constitutional amendment requiring much more of them, perhaps even eliminating them.

Consider the case of Aaron Burr, who was vice president during Thomas Jefferson's first administration, 1801–1805. He, of course, shot and killed Alexander Hamilton in 1804. Thereafter, if not before, he was capable of just about anything. Even into his old age.

As is sometimes related, at age seventy-seven he married the most admired woman in New York City, Madam Jumel. After a year she sued for divorce, charging infidelity! Burr contested the suit and the whole city laughed at their mutual protestations. Burr eventually suffered a stroke, and made a will in which he designated two illegitimate daughters as heirs; one was two years old, the other six. Questioned about this impossibility, he explained, "When a lady sees fit to name me as the father of her children, why should I deny that honor?"

I pass to Jefferson's second vice president, George Clinton, who was beset by what a later generation would call Alzheimer's disease. A senator of the time said he had "no intellect or memory." He would forget questions, miscount votes, or declare votes before they were taken.

A question not of incompetence but perhaps ineligibility might have been asked of Madison's second vice president, Elbridge Gerry, who years earlier had signed the Declaration of Independence but then refused to sign the Constitution because of certain "details of the instrument."

The qualifications for the vice presidency during the administration of Martin Van Buren were strange. Richard M. Johnson became eligible, and received the august office, mainly because he had killed the Indian chief Tecumseh. His campaign slogan was "Rumpsey Dumpsey, Rumpsey Dumpsey, Colonel Johnson killed Tecumseh." Johnson's other attraction was his advocacy of regular Sunday delivery of mail, for he believed in separation of church and state.

William Rufus King became vice president in 1853, under Franklin Pierce, because the latter's managers invented a wondrous campaign slogan comparing Pierce with his Democratic predecessor elected in 1844: "We Polked you in 1844, and we shall Pierce you in 1852!" King died shortly after taking office. He was known, when nominated, to be terminally ill with tuberculosis. He went to Cuba for medical treatment, and received special permission from Congress to take the oath of office in Havana. He was so weak he had to be propped up by aides for the swearing-in. He thereupon managed to return to Alabama, his home, where he died.

Hannibal Hamlin, Lincoln's first vice president, was brought on the ticket because of geography: he was from Maine, and hence balanced

Illinois. He once described himself as "the most unimportant man in Washington." His single distinction was that like two earlier vice presidents, Jefferson and Adams, he died on the Fourth of July, in 1891.

Andrew Johnson was ill prior to his inauguration, and ill-advisedly drank several glasses of brandy, and delivered a rambling, drunken tirade at his inaugural ceremony.

Grant's vice president, Schuyler Colfax, was known as "Smiler," because he smiled so much. He also received twenty shares of Credit Mobilier stock, and this forced him, perhaps with a smile, to explain how money came to him in odd ways, as when at the breakfast table a thousand-dollar bill fell out of an unmarked envelope. His stock purchases, or gifts, forced him out of the vice presidency, into the lecture circuit, and he died in Minnesota while switching trains in subzero weather. Smiler, it was said, died with a grin frozen on his face.

Cleveland's first vice president, Thomas A. Hendricks of Indiana, held office for thirty years prior to becoming vice president. This may not have been a recommendation, by his own admission. Among other positions he had been governor of Indiana, and he allowed as to how the requirements of that office were no more than those of a notary public. His qualities were difficult to count and, in the words of the periodical *The Nation*, "We must take the liberty of warning the Democrats that Mr. Hendricks, already a heavy load to carry, may readily become heavier by making speeches. He is in some respects a ridiculous nomination and would be worse than ridiculous if he were to have any political duties." Fortunately or unfortunately, he was an ill man, having suffered two strokes before the convention that nominated him. Nine months after his inauguration, another stroke took him off.

My conclusion after reviewing this motley crew is that the nation would have been better had it had a constitutional amendment that more clearly defined the qualifications for the second highest office in the land. Perhaps if we had such an amendment we would have had better vice presidents.

I also would like to comment on a recent proposal by Arthur Link of Princeton University, the biographer of Woodrow Wilson, that there should be a change in the Twenty-fifth Amendment. Dick Neustadt mentions this proposal in his essay, and I believe that it deserves further attention.

Link and a large group of physicians interested in presidential health met recently and concluded that the physicians of the country should appoint a group that then would examine a president periodically and report to the country on the result. If a report of such a group was that the president was in straits, then he, the president, would be replaced by the vice president.

Dick is against this proposal by Professor Link and the physicians. In the last piece of advice in his address he says, taking a point from the late Clinton Rossiter, that we should not tinker with the Constitution.

Five years ago I published a book on presidential health that did not get much notice because three other books came out at about the same time. The other books were more general than mine, one of them covering ill heads of state from time almost immemorial. I began with Grover Cleveland, and went up to George Bush, but concentrated on the illnesses of President Dwight D. Eisenhower, especially his heart attack of 1955.

Let me offer just a few details about Eisenhower's heart attack, how it was handled, and how, I think, badly it was done. It was a case akin to that of Wilson in 1919. The year 1955 is not so far back into history. Many of us in this room remember the occasion very well.

Suffice to say that what happened with Eisenhower's major heart attack—it was a three on a scale of five, and could have been easily described as a four—was that everything seemed above board, decisions of the physicians taken with propriety, and the most important medical decision of all, which led to the political decision that Eisenhower could run again in 1956, taken with complete neutrality. But it was not proper, nor neutral, that last so-called medical decision.

In the Eisenhower Library in Abilene there are the papers of Brig. Gen. Thomas W. Mattingly, who was Eisenhower's cardiologist. Tom Mattingly is alive and well at the present time, in retirement in Davidson, North Carolina. His detailed account of what happened in 1955 is much worth attention. It is perfectly clear that the president was in real trouble. Tom thought he had suffered a left-ventricular aneurysm, which in the statistics of the time meant 80 percent chance of death within five years.

What happened was that Eisenhower and the administration put the issue of 1956 in the hands of a panel consisting of the president's personal physician, who was a medical corps major general, together with Tom and the world-famous cardiologist Paul Dudley White. The vote was two to one, although this was not known publicly.

Then a grand press conference occurred on February 14, 1956, with the physicians arrayed at a table. White was in the middle. I went out to the Harvard Medical School where White's papers are in the library, and there saw how he had tried draft after draft of what he wanted to say at the medical press conference. White was an ardent Republican. Finally, at the conference, and to Tom Mattingly's amazement, White said that he thought Eisenhower could hold a position of very high responsibility, which meant the presidency, for a period of from five to ten years.

What White said in February 1956 was a wild guess. Actually, he guessed right, for Eisenhower's next heart attack was in 1965. But it was a terrible situation, a bad one, in our own time, equal to what happened with Wilson in 1919, and to prevent such decisions I think we need to tinker with the Twenty-fifth Amendment.

Chase Untermeyer:

I would like to focus a bit on the transition of the Office of Vice President from one administration to another and then add a few personal reflections on the vice presidency based on my service with Vice President Bush.

I regret that Richard Moe could not comment on Professor Neustadt's paper. I say this because those of us selected by Vice President-elect Bush for his future White House staff in the winter of 1980–1981 owe a special debt to Dick Moe and all his colleagues on the staff of Vice President Mondale.

Proud of their historical achievement of helping mold the modern vice presidency, the Mondale staff were intent on doing everything they could to see that infant institution preserved in the new Reagan-Bush administration. They totally submerged whatever feelings of regret or bitterness they had about the results of the election to teach us Bush staffers, often with the zeal of missionaries, how their office worked and how best to get along with a presidential staff.

Dick Moe, Jim Johnson, Mike Berman, Al Eisele, Maxine Isaacs, and other Mondale staffers suspected that in an administration in which the vice president had been the rival of the president not very long before, George Bush and his staff might be quarantined in the Old Executive Office Building with what might be called "throttle-botulism."

How this did not in fact come to pass will be described in my essay on the Bush vice presidency found elsewhere in this volume. But these concerns had valid historical precedents, so Moe and Company were right to alert us to the danger when they began the extensive and complete briefings that commenced soon after the 1980 election. Dick and his cohorts on the Mondale staff, therefore, deserve a tribute for passing on a torch they helped light.

From my close observation from 1981 to 1983, it became clear that there are two great roles a vice president may perform if he or she has the experience and weight to do so. The first is to be the highest ranking and most respected adviser to the president, the one whose advice matters most, who can almost literally have the last word. This is something the president clearly must want and something he must express in the strongest terms to his staff. Once this message is delivered, then all the elements of the Carter-Mondale agreement of 1976—the west wing office, full participation in any or all of the president's meetings, and access to all state papers sent to the Oval Office—merely serve to guarantee the vice president's status as privy counselor.

The second prime role is that of senior-most ambassador of the administration to Capitol Hill. In all the effort to move the vice presidency closer to and deeper into the executive branch since World War II, sight cannot be lost of the unique benefits the vice president can bring the president by virtue of his ancient constitutional status as an officer of the legislative branch.

These benefits begin with one of the most remarkable pieces of real estate in Washington: S-212. This is the vice president's staff office in the Capitol building, not to be confused with his personal office just off the Senate lobby or the extra staff quarters in the Dirksen Building or the one back home in Indiana, or Tennessee, or Texas, or the vice president's elegant offices downtown in the west wing and in the Old Executive Office Building. It can almost be said that the sun never sets on all the offices a modern vice president has to knock around in!

But S-212 is special. As tourists and lobbyists crowd the ornate Senate Reception Room in eager anticipation of shaking hands with The Senator, few are aware they are standing mere feet away from the single toehold of the executive branch in the Capitol. Just inside the polished door are the offices of the vice president's Senate liaison, the man or woman who monitors action on the floor and makes those dreaded phone calls to the vice president's house at midnight to say that a vote crucial to the administration might end in a tie.

What really makes S-212 special is that its two fairly tiny rooms are the only place an administration has for the White House staff, for cabinet secretaries and their various assistant secretaries for legislative affairs to plot their tactics and make their phone calls while working on hot legislation.

As president of the Senate and doyen of all his castle keeps on the Hill, the vice president may approach senators in a casual, collegial, yet majestic way as no single-shot emissary from the White House or a cabinet department ever can. If the vice president is a former senator, as has frequently been the case, he can bring a vast inventory of personal relationships to bear in the president's cause.

A former House member who never served in the Senate before becoming vice president, like Gerald Ford and George Bush, also carries valuable assets into the job. If the Senate is often deemed a club, then the House is a fraternity, a place where being one of the guys—a regular participant in the gym or a good fellow in one of the societies like Chowder and Marching—carries lifelong benefits. Of course, a large number of senators also served in the House, and Vice Presidents Quayle and Gore had the advantage of serving in both bodies.

Because of the tremendous extra reach a vice president with prior service in Congress can bring an administration, I am bold to say that the job description of the modern vice president should read "Hill Experience Required." This should especially be the case with presidents who lack such experience themselves, as former governors Carter, Reagan, and Clinton found to their benefit. This is not to say that it would be unwise for a presidential nominee who is a sitting senator to select a governor without previous congressional service for the ticket. There may be eminently sound personal and political reasons to do so. It is just that such a running mate would be less likely to succeed in the high-level lobbying function of a vice president than would one who had served on the Hill.

A few further miscellaneous thoughts on the vice presidency: historical evidence seems split on the wisdom of a vice president's assuming a so-called ongoing assignment. Walter Mondale, having observed the agony of his mentor Hubert Humphrey as head of the Space Council and of Nelson Rockefeller as head of the Domestic Policy Council, strongly advised his successor to scorn them, as he had done under Jimmy Carter. He said this because such jobs appear to give the vice president a responsibility without the bureaucratic power to compel anyone to see it through to success.

Yet it took only a moment for George Bush to agree to Ronald Reagan's request that he head the new administration's efforts to deregulate the nation's economy. It is hard, after all, for vice presidents to say no to presidents on anything. But in Bush's case, the Task Force on Regulatory Relief was a special opportunity. For one thing, it was no sideshow to the administration but a major policy focus. People tend to forget that "Reaganomics" was not just about cutting taxes and spending but also about reducing the size of the *Federal Register.*

Bush instantly recognized he had the chance to gain standing and respect with the conservative intellectuals and Reagan loyalists who cursed his name whenever the press gaily tossed about the deathless phrase *voodoo economics* that he had deployed against Reagan in the Pennsylvania primary just nine months earlier. In my essay on the Bush vice presidency I talk about Bush's other major assignment, that of chief of all drug-interdiction efforts. In short, an ongoing vice presidential assignment can be desirable if the subject is important to the president and a torment if it is not.

Here I inject "Untermeyer's Axiom on the Vice Presidency": the only valuable commodity a vice president has is his time. The time of presidents is valuable, too, but presidents can sign or veto bills, appoint judges, send the marines, summon the networks, and do various other deeds their veeps cannot. Everything that has or will be said in this conference on the vice presidency boils down to decisions on how a vice president spends his time: whether to stay in the west wing and participate in meetings; to travel the nation to stir up support for administration policies and for the party; to roam the world in search of friendship for America; to lobby or merely preside on Capitol Hill; to play golf or basketball; and so forth.

There is nothing a vice president can give anyone but a slice of his calendar, and it is for this reason that Professor Neustadt told us that a devastating ploy a president could pull on his number-two is to take charge of that calendar and deprive its holder of even this prerogative.

A final word about final rites, meaning funerals. Much late-night laughter has gusted forth in recent years about vice presidents going to foreign funerals as the nation's official mourner. George Bush, who bore most of these guffaws, added to the joke book by claiming his motto as vice president was "You die; I fly."

By contrast, the first indignity visited upon Vice President Hubert Humphrey by Lyndon Johnson was in not being sent to represent the

United States at Winston Churchill's funeral about two weeks after the 1965 inauguration. All Washington buzzed about what this meant, but Art Buchwald had the best explanation: "Hubert can't look sad."

In the *New York Times* of February 19, 1995, Vice President Gore denied he ever said "I don't do funerals," but in fact he seldom does, preferring to involve himself in such larger world issues as population control and denuclearization. All this is admirable, but it overlooks a simple reality: a funeral for a departed head of state is no different from one for your Great-Aunt Beatrice; it is not for the dead but for the living. The most frenzied diplomatic activity before and during such events is not in determining who will stand where at the ceremony but in holding what are known as "bilaterals"—meetings between two foreign leaders.

Sometimes a funeral, inauguration, or other great national observance will draw a dozen or more presidents, prime ministers, and foreign ministers. They are thus golden opportunities for an American vice president (usually accorded a rank somewhere between a head of state and a prime minister) to discuss all manner of important issues with key people from other lands in one morning.

This is why Vice President Bush attended so many foreign funerals: to get to know world leaders and to try to resolve disputes between the United States and other countries that would be much harder to do at lower levels in one or the other's capital. A CIA officer I know may have overstated matters a bit—but in spirit not at all—in saying, "George Bush put together the coalition that fought Desert Storm at all the funerals he attended as vice president."

So, funerals can be real diplomatic business, at the very least a grand chance to learn, and a vice president is wise to take advantage of the opportunities that the Grim Reaper will give him from time to time.

R. W. Apple Jr.:
It is a great honor to be here with Professor Neustadt. Believe me when I tell you that his book on presidential power is on the desk or in the briefcase of every political and presidential reporter in Washington, and it has been there for a long time. He does not get quoted as much as he did in the past. It is a little bit embarrassing; it is not as if his is the only book on the subject, so we journalists go looking around for other scholars to quote. But none of their books are as good as *Presidential Power*.

I would like to take issue very briefly with Chase Untermeyer and say that Hubert Humphrey could look sad. And indeed, I think that my formative experience with the appalling nature of the vice presidency came one day in Seattle in the 1968 presidential campaign when Hubert Humphrey, desperately trying to defend a completely insane Vietnam policy concocted by the totally misguided Lyndon Johnson, was heckled and had things thrown at him. I happened to be in the greenroom when Humphrey came offstage, practically crying and wringing his hands.

He grabbed me and said: "Now you're going to write a story about how they hate me, aren't you?"

"I wouldn't describe it as one of the great receptions of your career," I said, "but I will try to tone it down."

"What you don't know, and what you can't write, and what I can't say but I am going to say because I am Hubert Humphrey, is that I have a plan to end the war and for eleven days Johnson has had me on a string and he won't let me say anything about it. I feel completely castrated and I am really furious I ever took this job."

The plan finally emerged in the famous Salt Lake City speech, which, as I recall, came three days after Seattle and began to turn the election around. I, for one, believe that Hubert Humphrey would have had a good chance of being elected president if Johnson could have gotten his ego out of the way, which is a big "if."

The point of the story is that no matter how things have improved, vice presidents do not have any power. As Professor Neustadt has said, the so-called power of the vice presidency is all derivative from the president. The vice president is never going to have any power, and that is where the "chief executive officer/chief operating officer" analogy breaks down.

In a corporation, both of those officers have a responsibility to a board of directors that, in turn, has a responsibility to the shareholders. In our federal system, the president is responsible to the electorate, and the vice president is responsible to the president. It is an entirely different arrangement.

Nevertheless, no one ever says no to the vice presidency. They all say they are going to say no, but they don't. Nelson Rockefeller always said he was going to say no to the vice presidency. He had a phrase for it: "I'm not stand-by equipment." One time, we were on his plane—and in Rockefeller's case, it was his plane, not the government's—and he said:

"You know, I would rather be an ambassador or a senator. I would even rather be a banker like my brother than be vice president." But when he was asked, Rockefeller said yes. Even Lyndon Johnson, obviously the most powerful Senate majority leader of the modern era, succumbed to the wiles of the Kennedys and the late Phil Graham of the *Washington Post*.

I would like to differ with my colleagues in saying that there is considerable danger in the way we choose our vice presidents. I certainly would not advocate any changes in the Constitution. But I think that all of us—as journalists, academics, and practitioners—should bring all the pressure we can on presidential nominees to proceed in an orderly way in choosing their running mates.

What do I mean by "an orderly way"? Well, in the old days, the party played a role; the party did some vetting of vice presidential candidates. Now, as in so many other things, the vetting has fallen to the presidential staff and the media, and both in different ways are unqualified for this job.

If there is no advance publicity on the group from which the vice presidential candidate might be drawn, then there is no possibility of any useful news-media scrutiny. That is to say, once the person is chosen and announced, he is not going to be unchosen and unannounced except in the most extreme circumstances. So the news media can bash the person, but to no good end.

I advocate a change of procedures. Who have been the vice presidential candidates who have gotten in trouble? Well, there was Mr. Eagleton. He was chosen in the dead of night after Senator McGovern had achieved the notable first of running such a totally screwed-up convention that he gave his acceptance speech at two o'clock in the morning, when sane people had gone to bed. There was Spiro Agnew, who was chosen after a fairly surreptitious process. There was Dan Quayle, whom George Bush sprang on us at a New Orleans boat dock. All of these selections should have received a more thorough vetting prior to the naming of the vice presidential candidate.

I think it is worthwhile for a presidential candidate to name the four or five candidates he is considering for his running mate. I know that presidential candidates are like little boys and like to keep secrets. But this is a serious business. These vice presidents are far more likely than anyone else in the country to become president once they are chosen as vice presidential nominees.

I think it is worth having other politicians in the party look at the nominee's list of possible running mates. I also think that it is useful for the news media to have a serious look at the names on the list.

I want to make two more points. The first has to do with the news media. Basically, the media are interested in only two things about vice presidents. Of course, we do our civic duty and write about the operational arrangements, but what we are really interested in is: will he tell us who is getting to the president and on what? And is there daylight between the president and the vice president on an issue? In other words, is there a leak or is there a split? Successful vice presidents do not leak and conceal splits, and that is why successful vice presidents disappear from the news.

My second point is to pitch this symposium forward just a bit. There are some interesting experiments being discussed. If they would just let us write what we hear at dinner parties, it would be so much more interesting! You will remember that Ronald Reagan proposed running with Sen. Richard Schweikert, a moderate, in 1976 as a means for getting a little bit of middle ground in his campaign against President Ford. It is not clear whether such a tactic would succeed in securing a nomination. This tactic shows, nonetheless, that the vice presidency remains a powerful bargaining chip.

Finally, I want to compare first ladies—Hillary Clinton in particular—to vice presidents. I know that the very thought is controversial, but it seems to me that Hillary Clinton is in a similar position to the vice president. Her power, too, is derivative. And when she has exerted it to the maximum, as she did when she was put in charge of the attempt to reform our medical care system, she has attracted a kind of lightning that vice presidents attract in the same situation.

In some ways, it is easier for presidents to turn to relatives for advice and counsel than it is to depend on their vice presidents. Bob Kennedy is the most prominent example. Relatives, presumably, are more trustworthy. The problem for relatives is that in political terms, they have even less legitimacy in terms of electoral support than vice presidents.

We have now a new model of the presidency and decision making in the White House with polycentric power structures. It is sometimes very difficult to figure out who is in charge. I would say as a final thought that one of the problems of strengthening the vice presidency is that it could become embedded in that kind of ambiguous power structure. And that, my friends, would not be a good thing for the nation in general or the presidency in particular.

Richard E. Neustadt:
I want to make just a few comments in response to what my colleagues have said. In particular, I want to emphasize one of Johnny Apple's points, and you need to remember it by the code word *Hillary.*

It is a very serious point. A one-time member of the Clinton administration, a fellow who had experience in previous administrations, said to me: "I pity the chief of staff. I have never seen anything like this before. He has three principals independently telling him what to do." Say "Hillary" to yourself!

On another of Johnny's points let me underscore that I think Al Gore has been a successful vice president in part because he refuses to allow any of that daylight, as Johnny calls it, to show between his own views and those of the president.

I once asked a member of Gore's staff what the staff did about getting debriefed on vice presidential/presidential meetings and vice presidential/presidential decisions. The answer was that the vice president was very good about debriefing his staff on the president's position on any particular issue. So I asked about the vice president's position. The staff member responded of Gore: "He will never say a word; we have to watch his eyebrows."

Just for the record, Johnny Apple's suggestion about a vice presidential selection process was followed, in fact, by Mr. Carter. He gave the press and politicians an opportunity to review the potential candidates by calling these men and their wives down to his home in Plains, Georgia, to be interviewed on successive weekends. So this process has been used in a sort of way to some success.

I do not want to belabor the disability issue raised by Bob Ferrell, but let me make two observations on it because I do take it seriously. Mr. Eisenhower's choice to run for president a second time was a political decision that he himself made in light of his understanding of his risks and the country's concerns if he did not survive his second term. It was his decision. He was the president. He put himself forward for reelection.

It was a political decision, not a medical decision, and I regard that distinction as fundamental. And it turned out to be a good decision. He was able to carry on, and he could have run for a third term if the

Republicans had not been so incautious in pushing through the two-term amendment, and he would have made it. Eisenhower would have lasted through 1964.

The other point I want to make on the disability issue is to consider, in this day and age, the selection and work of any eminent panel of physicians. There would have to be representation among the major groups of physicians. The cardiac experts would want two people; the cancer people would want three; the psychiatrists, if you will excuse the pun, would lobby like crazy for a place on the panel. And there would have to be equal representation of minorities and women on the panel. And if the medical panel was not careful in its presentations, you could be damn sure that the Congress would intervene.

So we would end up transferring what is a political decision to a motley crew of physicians! Would this really improve the presidential succession process? We have got to leave some things to the judgment of responsible people. And if they make mistakes, so be it. The kinds of mistakes presidents can make are endless. I think they ought to be allowed to make mistakes, after medical advice, on their own futures as well.

Finally, let me say just a word about Hugh Sidey's "soap opera." It is a wonderful image! I had not previously had the wit to think of it, but I will use it with or without attribution from now on! Decision making in the White House has become an extraordinary phenomenon. My own guess is that Sidey is correct. The soap opera at 1600 Pennsylvania Avenue provides the vice president with a continuing utility and a continuing access to the media because the media has access to him. That has not happened before. I did not mention it, but it is certainly one of the frail strengths of the office, and I will work it into my next essay on the subject.

Guide to Further Reading

Historians and political scientists have largely neglected the vice presidency. That there are only five serious studies of that office in recent years is an indication of how little work has been done on this subject. Were it not for Joel Goldstein's *The Modern American Vice Presidency: The Transformation of a Political Institution* (Princeton: Princeton University Press, 1982), Paul Light's *Vice Presidential Power: Advice and Influence in the White House* (Baltimore: Johns Hopkins University Press, 1984), Marie D. Natoli's *American Prince, American Pauper: The Contemporary Vice Presidency in Perspective* (Westport, Conn.: Greenwood Press, 1985), Jules Witcover's *Crapshoot: Rolling the Dice on the Vice Presidency* (New York: Crown, 1994), and Mark O. Hatfield's *Vice Presidents of the United States, 1789–1993* (Washington, D.C.: U.S. Government Printing Office, 1997), we would have no recently published book-length studies of this important office.

For the rest of it, accounts of individuals who served in the vice presidency have bordered on the ridiculous. Books with titles such as Sol Barzman's *Madmen and Geniuses: The Vice Presidents of the United States* (Chicago: Follet Publishing, 1974) and Steve Tally's *Bland Ambition: From Adams to Quayle—The Cranks, Criminals, Tax Cheats, and Golfers Who Made It to Vice President* (New York: Harcourt Brace Jovanovich, 1992) show little respect for the vice presidency or the men who served in that office.

Even if they have produced only a handful of extended studies of the vice presidency, scholars, of course, have not ignored the presidency itself. Readers will benefit from another reading of Richard Neustadt's *Presidential Power*, rev. ed. (New York: Free Press, 1990), James David Barber's *The Presidential Character*, 2nd ed. (Englewood Cliffs, N.J.: Prentice-Hall, 1977), Thomas E. Cronin's *The State of the American Presidency* (Boston: Little, Brown, 1975) and *Rethinking the Presidency* (Boston: Little, Brown, 1982), Stephen Hess's *Organizing the Presidency* (Washington, D.C.: Brookings Institution, 1976), and Clinton Rossiter's dated but useful *The American Presidency*, 2nd ed. (New York: Harcourt, Brace, 1960).

Leonard Levy and Louis Fisher, in concert with many of the nation's best presidential scholars, recently published *Encyclopedia of the American Presidency*, 4 vols. (New York: Simon and Schuster, 1994). This work includes brief but useful essays on all the twentieth-century vice presidents. Of particular note is Joel Goldstein's excellent essay, "Vice President" (1556–63).

But the vice presidency requires our attention if only because the office sometimes leads to the presidency. In this respect, an issue of continuing interest and controversy is the Twenty-fifth Amendment. The amendment provides for the vice president to temporarily assume the powers of the presidency if the president should suffer a debilitating illness and be unable to perform the duties of his office. Former senator Birch Bayh, the leading advocate of the amendment, recorded his views in *One Heartbeat Away: Presidential Disability and Succession* (Indianapolis: Bobbs-Merrill, 1968). John D. Feerick has written extensively on the amendment. See his *From Failing Hands* (New York: Fordham University Press, 1965) and *The Twenty-fifth Amendment* (New York: Fordham University Press, 1976). A well-written and passionate study of the overall issue is Robert H. Ferrell's *Ill-Advised: Presidential Health and Public Trust* (Columbia: University of Missouri Press, 1992).

Turning to the vice presidency, historians have mixed views on the office in this century. John Milton Cooper refers to the vice presidency in the first two decades of the twentieth century as a "shadowed office." Cooper's description is apt because the office and the men who held it were mere shadows within their administrations. This is not to say that these men were not able individuals, just that there seemed to be no place for them within the political process other than to preside over the Senate and break the occasional tie vote.

Cooper's analogy might easily be extended to the history of the vice presidency during the entire first half of the century. Little changed in the office from the time that Theodore Roosevelt took the oath in March 1901 until Alben Barkley stepped down in January 1953. Three of the eleven men to hold the office during the first half century went on to become president through the deaths of their predecessors, but it is debatable whether or not any of these three—Roosevelt, Coolidge, and Truman— would have been nominated or elected president had they not been president already.

It is not surprising, therefore, that many of these "shadowed men" have yet to find biographers. In fact, even the many biographers of Roosevelt, Coolidge, and Truman give short shrift to their vice presidencies.

Theodore Roosevelt is an excellent example. In his masterful biography, *The Rise of Theodore Roosevelt* (New York: Coward, McCann, and Geoghegan, 1979), Edmund Morris devotes only 12 pages to TR's vice presidential nomination, 4 to his campaign, and 4 to his vice presidency—in a book of nearly 750 text pages. "Theodore Roosevelt's formal service to the nation as Vice President lasted exactly four days," wrote Morris in the opening sentence of the epilogue to the book, "from March 4 to March 8, 1901."

Morris was following the pattern established by Roosevelt himself. In his *Autobiography of Theodore Roosevelt* (New York: Macmillan, 1913), TR devoted only 3 pages to his vice presidency, the substance of which was that Boss Thomas Platt forced him to take the nomination! Other accounts of his vice presidency can be found in Henry F. Pringle's *Theodore Roosevelt* (New York: Harcourt, Brace, 1931) and in William H. Harbaugh's *Power and Responsibility: The Life and Times of Theodore Roosevelt* (New York: Harcourt, Brace, 1961).

Roosevelt chose as his vice president the able senator from Indiana, Charles King Fairbanks. Sad to say, the best source of biographical information on Fairbanks remains the brief entry by John D. Hicks, "Fairbanks, Charles Warren," in vol. 3 of *Dictionary of American Biography* (New York: Scribners, 1932), 248–49. In addition, there is passing mention of Fairbanks in Pringle's *Theodore Roosevelt* and in Lewis L. Gould's excellent study, *The Presidency of Theodore Roosevelt* (Lawrence: University Press of Kansas, 1991).

William Howard Taft's vice president, James "Sunny Jim" Sherman of New York, has fared no better than Fairbanks. As with his predecessor, the best source of information on Sherman is Edward Conrad Smith, "Sherman, James Schoolcraft," in vol. 9 of *Dictionary of American Biography* (New York: Scribners, 1935), 82–83. Sherman is mentioned on scattered pages in Pringle's *The Life and Times of William Howard Taft*, 2 vols. (New York: Farrar, Rinehart, 1939), in Donald F. Anderson's *William Howard Taft: A Conservative's Conception of the Presidency* (Ithaca: Cornell University Press, 1973), and in Paolo E. Coletta's *The Presidency of William Howard Taft* (Lawrence: University Press of Kansas, 1973).

Thomas Riley Marshall of Indiana served two terms as vice president in the administration of Woodrow Wilson and fared better among historians than his two immediate predecessors. He published his memoirs under the folksy title *Recollections of Thomas Riley Marshall, A Hoosier Salad* (Indianapolis: Bobbs-Merrill, 1925) and was fortunate to have a biographer, Charles M. Thomas, who wrote *Thomas Riley Marshall: Hoosier Statesman* (Oxford, Ohio: Mississippi Valley Press, 1939). Also of value is John D. Hicks, "Marshall, Thomas Riley," in vol. 6 of *Dictionary of American Biography* (New York: Scribners 1933), 330–31, and three of Arthur Link's masterful studies: *Wilson: The Road to the White House* (Princeton: Princeton University Press, 1947), *Wilson: Confusion and Crisis, 1915–16* (Princeton: Princeton University Press, 1964), and *Wilson: Campaign for Progress and Peace, 1916–1917* (Princeton: Princeton University Press, 1965). Also see Arthur Walworth's *Woodrow Wilson,* 2 vols. (New York: Longmans, Green, 1958), and August Hecksher's *Woodrow Wilson* (New York: Macmillan, 1991).

The three men who served during the so-called Republican ascendancy during the 1920s all achieved the distinction of biographies. Of the three—Calvin Coolidge, Charles Gates Dawes, and Charles Curtis—only Coolidge is remembered, and his image is that of a parsimonious, do-nothing president. These men remain in the shadows as vice presidents.

The vice presidency of Calvin Coolidge received a significant amount of attention largely because it was seen as a preface to his presidency. The earliest account can be found in a 1924 campaign biography by Robert A. Woods, *The Preparation of Calvin Coolidge: An Interpretation* (Boston: Houghton Mifflin, 1924). Coolidge offered his own views in his *Autobiography of Calvin Coolidge* (New York: Cosmopolitan Book Company, 1929). Two dated accounts are William Allen White's *A Puritan in Babylon: The Story of Calvin Coolidge* (New York: Macmillan, 1938) and Claude M. Fuess's *Calvin Coolidge: The Man from Vermont* (Boston: Little, Brown, 1940). The best historical account is Donald R. McCoy's *Calvin Coolidge: The Quiet President* (1967; reprint, Lawrence: University Press of Kansas, 1988).

Dawes was the subject of an early biography published after his vice presidency. Paul R. Leach's *That Man Dawes* (Chicago: Reilly and Lee, 1930) offers a sympathetic and popular account of his rather extraordinary career up through 1929. Dawes himself offered the next commentary on his vice presidency in 1935 when he published *Notes as Vice President, 1928–1929* (Boston: Little, Brown, 1935). Another journalistic account was published by Bascom N. Timmons in *Portrait of an American: Charles G. Dawes* (New York: Henry Holt, 1953).

Charles Curtis of Kansas, a descendant of the Kaw Indians, served as Herbert Hoover's vice president but is little remembered. One biography was published during the 1928 campaign—Don C. Seitz's *From Kaw Teepee to Capitol: The Life Story of Charles Curtis, Indian, Who Has Risen to High Estate* (New York: Frederick A. Stokes, 1928)—but is difficult to find these days. Better known, and more widely available, is Dolly Gann, *Dolly Gann's Book* (New York: Doubleday, Doran, 1928), a memoir of social events during the Hoover administration by the vice president's half sister. Also see Marvin Ewy, *Charles Curtis of Kansas* (Emporia: Kansas State Teachers College, 1961).

For historical assessments of the Hoover administration that mention Curtis in passing, see David Burner, *Herbert Hoover: A Public Life* (New York: Alfred A. Knopf, 1978); Gene Smith, *The Shattered Dream: Herbert Hoover and the Great Depression* (New York: William Morrow, 1970); Joan Hoff Wilson, *Herbert Hoover: Forgotten Progressive* (Boston: Little, Brown, 1975); Donald J. Lisio, *Hoover, Blacks, and Lily-Whites* (Chapel Hill: University of North Carolina Press, 1985); and Louis W. Liebovich, *Bylines in Despair: Herbert Hoover, the Great Depression, and the U.S. News Media* (Westport, Conn.: Greenwood Press, 1994).

The election of Franklin D. Roosevelt brought an end to the Republican ascendancy, but not an end to the frustration faced by the vice presidents. Roosevelt's first vice president was the Speaker of the House of Representatives, John Nance Garner of Texas. Known informally as Cactus Jack, Garner is best known for assessing the vice presidency as not being worth "a pitcher of warm spit." The last word had, in fact, been *piss,* but the newspapers would not print it. Garner's disdain for his new job was evident. After he took office Garner used more polite terms to describe "This Job of Mine," in *American Magazine* for July 1934. Garner burned all of his papers, and the two available biographies are credible but sketchy: Marquis James, *Mr. Garner of Texas* (Indianapolis: Bobbs-Merrill, 1939), and Bascom N. Timmons, *Garner of Texas: A Personal History* (New York: Harper and Brothers, 1948).

Henry A. Wallace, Roosevelt's second vice president, has fared much better than Garner and, for that matter, all of his twentieth-century counterparts. Wallace's career, including his vice presidency, has been the subject of important studies, all of which add valuable elements to the story of a complex man.

Any study of the Wallace vice presidency should begin with his diary for those years as edited by John Morton Blum. From 1942 to 1946, Wallace kept a detailed record of his thoughts and activities, and it is an extraordinary look into both the presidency and the vice presidency: *The Price of Vision: The Diary of Henry A. Wallace, 1942–1946* (Boston: Houghton Mifflin, 1973).

One of the first assessments of the Wallace vice presidency came in Russell Lord's *The Wallaces of Iowa* (Boston: Houghton Mifflin, 1947), a study of the three generations of Henry Wallaces and their collective influence on twentieth-century American agriculture, journalism, and politics. The last section in the book focuses on the Wallace vice presidency.

Two studies appeared in the early 1970s, beginning with the second volume of Edward Schapsmeier and Frederick Schapsmeier's two-volume study of Wallace's life. About half of this volume, *Prophet in Politics: Henry A. Wallace and the War Years, 1940–1965* (Ames: Iowa State University Press, 1970), is devoted to the Wallace vice presidency. Another study was Norman D. Markowitz's *The Rise and Fall of the People's Century: Henry A. Wallace and American Liberalism, 1941–1948* (New York: Free Press, 1973), which includes two long chapters on the vice presidency. See also J. Samuel Walker's *Henry A. Wallace and American Foreign Policy* (Westport, Conn.: Greenwood Press, 1976), which has two good chapters on Wallace's vice presidential role in U.S. foreign policy, and Robert L. Messer's *The End of an Alliance: James F. Byrnes, Roosevelt, Truman, and the Origins of the Cold War* (Chapel Hill: University of North Carolina Press, 1982). Graham White and John Maze recently produced *Henry A. Wallace: His Search for a New World Order* (Chapel Hill: University of North Carolina Press, 1995).

It is hard to know where to begin in discussing Harry S. Truman's brief and momentous vice presidency. Truman's life and times has been analyzed in detail, most recently by David McCullough, Robert H. Ferrell, and Alonzo L. Hamby. All three men have published major—some might say massive—biographies on this plainspoken man from Independence, Missouri. The vice presidency is discussed and analyzed in detail in these biographies and should be consulted first: see McCullough, *Truman* (New York: Simon and Schuster, 1992); Ferrell, *Harry S. Truman: A Life* (Columbia: University of Missouri Press, 1994); and Hamby, *Man of the People: A Life of Harry S. Truman* (New York: Oxford University Press, 1995).

Also of value is the first volume of Truman's *Memoirs: Year of Decisions* (Garden City, N.Y.: Doubleday, 1955). Other works with valuable insights are Margaret Truman's *Harry S. Truman* (New York: William Morrow, 1972), Robert H. Ferrell's *Choosing Truman: The Democratic Convention of 1944* (Columbia: University of Missouri Press, 1994), Richard L. Miller's *Truman: The Rise to Power* (New York: McGraw-Hill, 1986), and Robert Donovan's *Conflict and Crisis: The Presidency of Harry S. Truman, 1945–1948* (New York: W. W. Norton, 1977).

In truth, the list above barely skims the surface of the growing volume of literature on Harry S. Truman. Truman's vice president, the affable Alben Barkley, left his ghostwritten memoir, which is unfortunately long on anecdote and short on documentation. *That Reminds Me* (Garden City, N.Y.: Doubleday, 1954) does give a sense of Barkley's personality if not the substance of his vice presidency. Barkley's wife, Jane, added interesting anecdotes in *I Married the Veep* (New York: Vanguard, 1958). Barkley is mentioned briefly in many of the biographies of Truman and his presidency. In addition to those cited above, also consult Donald R. McCoy, *The Presidency of Harry S. Truman* (Lawrence: University Press of Kansas, 1984).

The vice presidency of Richard M. Nixon was controversial if only because he previously had been a controversial member of Congress. His vice presidency has been the subject of important biographical studies with several more to come. Even the smallest aspects of Nixon's life—his youth in California, his career in Congress, his nomination as the vice presidential candidate on the 1952 Republican ticket, his service in that office, and his candidacy for the presidency in 1960—have come in for intense scrutiny.

Certainly, the foremost study of the Nixon vice presidency is Stephen E. Ambrose, *Nixon: The Education of a Politician, 1913–1962* (New York: Simon and Schuster, 1987), a book that provides a lengthy analysis of Nixon's two terms. Ambrose's book will likely be superseded by the second volume of Roger Morris's massive biography of Nixon. Ambrose also offers a substantial analysis and information in his masterful *Eisenhower: The President* (New York: Simon and Schuster, 1984). Also see James Keogh, *This Is Nixon* (New York: G. P. Putnam's Sons, 1956), and Earl Mazo and Stephen Hess, *Nixon: A Political Portrait* (New York: Harper and Row, 1968).

Of the many studies and memoirs of the Eisenhower presidency that also include information on the Nixon vice presidency, see Sherman

Adams, *First Hand Report: The Story of the Eisenhower Administration* (New York: Harper and Brothers, 1961); Charles C. Alexander, *Holding the Line: The Eisenhower Era, 1952–1961* (Bloomington: Indiana University Press, 1975); Robert Branyan and Lawrence H. Larsen, eds., *The Eisenhower Administration, 1953–1961,* 2 vols. (New York: Random House, 1971); Dwight D. Eisenhower, *The White House Years,* 2 vols. (Garden City, N.Y.: Doubleday, 1965); Emmet J. Hughes, *The Ordeal of Power: A Political Memoir of the Eisenhower Years* (New York: Atheneum, 1963); Robert J. Donovan, *Eisenhower: The Inside Story* (New York: Harper and Brothers, 1956); Chester J. Pach and Elmo Richardson, *The Presidency of Dwight D. Eisenhower,* rev. ed. (Lawrence: University Press of Kansas, 1991); and Herbert S. Parmet, *Eisenhower and the American Crusades* (New York: Macmillan, 1972).

Nixon compiled a collection of vice presidential speeches and two volumes of memoirs that provide information on his vice presidency: *The Challenges We Face* (New York: McGraw-Hill, 1960), *Six Crises* (New York: Doubleday, 1962), and *RN: A Memoir* (New York: Grosset and Dunlap, 1978).

As colorful as was Lyndon Johnson, it is surprising that the volume of studies and memoirs on his vice presidency is so limited. Journalists offered their assessments, and of particular value are Rowland Evans and Robert D. Novak's *Lyndon B. Johnson: The Exercise of Power* (New York: New American Library, 1966), Leonard Baker's *The Johnson Eclipse: A President's Vice Presidency* (New York: Macmillan, 1966), and Doris Kearns's *Lyndon Johnson and the American Dream* (New York: Harper and Row, 1976). Also of value is Eric F. Goldman's *The Tragedy of Lyndon Johnson* (New York: Alfred A. Knopf, 1969), Sam Houston Johnson's *My Brother Lyndon* (New York: Cowles Book Company, 1969), Richard Reeves's *President Kennedy: Profile of Power* (New York: Simon and Schuster, 1993), Arthur M. Schlesinger Jr.'s *A Thousand Days: John F. Kennedy in the White House* (Boston: Houghton Mifflin, 1965), and William S. White's *The Professional: Lyndon B. Johnson* (Boston: Houghton Mifflin, 1964).

Few individuals were more qualified to serve as vice president than Hubert Humphrey, yet his term was the most frustrating period of his life. Humphrey's views can be found in *The Education of a Public Man* (Garden City, N.Y.: Doubleday, 1976); "On the Threshold of the White House," *Atlantic Monthly* 234 (1974); and "Changes in the Vice Presidency," *Current History* 67 (1974).

Journalists also have offered their assessments of the Humphrey vice presidency: Allan H. Ryskind, *Hubert* (New Rochelle, N.Y.: Arlington House, 1968); Robert Sherrill and Harry W. Ernst, *The Drugstore Liberal* (New York: Grossman, 1968); Theodore H. White, *The Making of the President, 1964* (New York: Atheneum, 1965); Winthrop Griffith, *Humphrey: A Candid Biography* (New York: William Morrow, 1965); Albert Eisele, *Almost to the Presidency* (Blue Earth, Minn.: Piper, 1972); and the best of the lot, Carl Solberg, *Hubert Humphrey: A Biography* (New York: W. W. Norton, 1984).

Also of value are memoirs by Johnson administration aides. See Joseph H. Califano Jr., *The Triumph and Tragedy of Lyndon Johnson* (New York: Simon and Schuster, 1991); George Christian, *The President Steps Down* (New York: Macmillan, 1970); George Reedy, *The Twilight of the Presidency* (New York: World, 1970); Harry McPherson, *A Political Education* (Boston: Little, Brown, 1972); Eric F. Goldman, *The Tragedy of Lyndon Johnson;* and Clark Clifford, *Counsel to the President* (New York: Random House, 1991).

Another colorful vice president with an interesting list of publications is Spiro T. Agnew. See Joseph Allbright, *What Makes Spiro Run* (New York: Dodd Mead, 1972); Rowland Evans and Robert D. Novak, *Nixon in the White House* (New York: Random House, 1971); Theo Lippman Jr., *Spiro Agnew's America* (New York: W. W. Norton, 1972); Robert Marsh, *Agnew: The Unexamined Man* (New York: M. Evans, 1971); and Jules Witcover, *White Knight: The Rise of Spiro Agnew* (New York: Random House, 1972). Agnew himself weighed in with a memoir with a dramatic title, *Go Quietly . . . Or Else* (New York: William Morrow, 1980). Perhaps the most damning critique is Richard M. Cohen and Jules Witcover, *A Heartbeat Away: The Investigation and Resignation of Vice President Spiro T. Agnew* (New York: Viking Press, 1974). Also see William Safire, *Before the Fall: An Inside View of the Pre-Watergate White House* (Garden City, N.Y.: Doubleday, 1975).

Gerald R. Ford's vice presidency is seen as a prelude to his presidency. Most accounts of those months focus on the tension that Ford and his staff lived through as the impeachment or resignation of Nixon became more likely. Two excellent overviews of Ford's vice presidency can be found in James Cannon's *Time and Chance: Gerald R. Ford's Appointment with History* (New York: Harper Collins, 1994) and John Robert Greene's *The Presidency of Gerald R. Ford* (Lawrence: University Press of Kansas, 1995). Also see Ford's own memoirs, *A Time to Heal: The Autobiography of Gerald R. Ford* (New York: Harper and Row, 1979).

Other accounts of value are Robert T. Hartmann's *Palace Politics: An Inside Account of the Ford Years* (New York: McGraw-Hill, 1980), Elizabeth Drew's *Washington Journal: The Events of 1973–1974* (New York: Random House, 1975), and Richard Reeves's *A Ford, Not a Lincoln* (New York: Harcourt Brace Jovanovich, 1975).

Nelson A. Rockefeller once said that he did not want to be vice president of anything, but he accepted Ford's invitation nonetheless. Always active, Rockefeller left a substantial body of vice presidential papers—more than 450 cubic feet—but the only book on his vice presidency is Michael Turner's *The Vice President as Policy Maker: Rockefeller in the Ford White House* (Westport, Conn.: Greenwood Press, 1982).

Also of value are Joseph Persico's *The Imperial Rockefeller: A Biography of Nelson A. Rockefeller* (New York: Simon and Schuster, 1982) and Michael Kramer and Sam Roberts's *"I Never Wanted to be Vice President of Anything!": An Investigative Biography of Nelson Rockefeller* (New York: Basic Books, 1976). Readers should not overlook the useful information on Rockefeller that can be found in the works by James Cannon and Robert Greene cited above. More substantive word on the Rockefeller vice presidency will no doubt be found in a future volume of Cary Reich's multivolume study, *The Life of Nelson A. Rockefeller*. The first volume—taking Rockefeller up to 1958—was published in 1996.

The nation's most recent four vice presidents—Walter Mondale, George Bush, Dan Quayle, and Albert Gore—have yet to receive much attention, if only because of the unavailability of their papers. The best account of Mondale and his vice presidency is Steven M. Gillon's *The Democrats' Dilemma: Walter F. Mondale and the Liberal Legacy* (New York: Columbia University Press, 1992). Bush, with assistance from Vic Gold, wrote *Looking Forward: An Autobiography* (Garden City, N.Y.: Doubleday, 1987), a book that offers some glimpses into the Bush vice presidential years. Quayle has had the first word on his vice presidency in his best-selling book, *Standing Firm: A Vice Presidential Memoir* (New York: Harper Collins/Zondervan, 1994). Two journalistic assessments of Gore are Ann Devroy and Stephen Barr's "Gore Bucks Tradition in Vice President's Role," *Washington Post* (February 18, 1995), and Elaine Sciolino and Todd S. Purdum's "Gore Is No Typical Vice President in the Shadows," *New York Times* (February 19, 1995).

The future of the vice presidency has been discussed in a range of reports and legal-journal articles. The best reports are Allan P. Sindler,

Unchosen Presidents: The Vice President and Other Frustrations of Presidential Succession (Berkeley and Los Angeles: University of California Press, 1976); [Twentieth Century Fund], *A Heartbeat Away: Report of the Twentieth Century Fund Task Force on the Vice Presidency* (New York: Twentieth Century Fund, 1988); and [White Burkett Miller Center], *Choosing and Using Vice Presidents: A Report of the Sixth Miller Center Commission* (Charlottesville, Va.: White Burkett Miller Center for Public Affairs, 1992).

Among the best journal articles are: Paul T. David, "The Vice Presidency: Its Institutional Evolution and Contemporary Status," *Journal of Politics* 29 (1967): 721–48; "Symposium on the Vice Presidency," *Fordham Law Review* 45 (1977): 707–804; Richard D. Friedman, "Some Modest Proposals on the Vice Presidency," *Michigan Law Review* 86 (1988); Akhil Reed Amar and Vik Amar, "President Quayle?" *Virginia Law Review* 78 (1992); and Joel K. Goldstein, "The New Constitutional Vice Presidency," *Wake Forest Law Review* 30 (1995): 505–61.

Notes on Sources

The essays in this volume were based on the authors' extensive research on the vice presidents and the vice presidency over many years. In lieu of footnotes, the contributors provided the following commentaries on the source materials that they believed to be most useful in writing their essays.

I. THE FIFTH WHEEL, 1905–1933

Theodore Roosevelt: The sources and literature on the first four vice presidents of the twentieth century are not large. Theodore Roosevelt offers a partial exception, with his voluminous published and unpublished papers and many biographies, but few of those give much attention to his brief vice presidency. A few of his letters from those months are reprinted in Elting E. Morison, ed., *The Letters of Theodore Roosevelt,* 8 vols. (Cambridge: Harvard University Press, 1951–1954); and a brief treatment can be found in John Milton Cooper Jr., *The Warrior and the Priest: Woodrow Wilson and Theodore Roosevelt* (Cambridge: Harvard University Press, 1983).

Charles W. Fairbanks: The only treatment of Fairbanks's vice presidential term is in John D. Hicks, "Fairbanks, Charles Warren," in vol. 3 of *Dictionary of American Biography* (New York: Scribners, 1932). The campaign biography by William Henry Smith, *The Life and Speeches of Hon. Charles Warren Fairbanks* (Indianapolis: Bobbs-Merrill, 1904), was published before Fairbanks's election.

James S. Sherman: Likewise, the only treatment of Sherman's single term is in Edward Conrad Smith, "Sherman, James Schoolcraft," in vol. 9 of *Dictionary of American Biography* (New York: Scribners, 1935).

Thomas Riley Marshall: Marshall is the best documented vice president of the four. In addition to John D. Hicks, "Marshall, Thomas Riley," in vol. 6 of *Dictionary of American Biography* (New York: Scribners, 1933), there is a full and informative biography by Charles M. Thomas, *Thomas Riley Marshall: Hoosier Statesman* (Oxford, Ohio: Mississippi Valley Press, 1939). His own memoir, *The Recollections of Thomas Riley Marshall, A Hoosier Salad* (Indianapolis: Bobbs-Merrill, 1925), resembles the man himself in being self-depreciating and chatty but contains some revealing comments. For Marshall's selection as vice president in 1912, see Arthur S. Link, *Wilson: The Road to the White House* (Princeton: Princeton University Press, 1947). For the attempt to dump Marshall in 1916, see Edward M. House Diary, May 24, 1916, in Arthur S. Link, ed., *The Papers of Woodrow Wilson*, vol. 37 (Princeton: Princeton University Press, 1981). There is no adequate treatment of Marshall's role during Wilson's illness, but see John Milton Cooper Jr., "Disability in the White House: The Case of Woodrow Wilson," in *The White House: The First Two Hundred Years*, ed. Frank Freidel and William Pencak (Boston: Northeastern University Press, 1994).

Calvin Coolidge: The three leading biographies are William Allen White, *A Puritan in Babylon: The Story of Calvin Coolidge* (New York: Macmillan, 1938); Claude M. Fuess, *Calvin Coolidge: The Man from Vermont* (Boston: Little, Brown, 1940); and Donald R. McCoy, *Calvin Coolidge: The Quiet President* (1967; reprint, Lawrence: University Press of Kansas, 1988). White's book has some correspondence with people who knew Coolidge, and White himself met him, but it is overwritten and on occasion imaginative. Fuess, an Amherst College graduate who actually interviewed Coolidge, has close analysis of Massachusetts events in his book, all of which helps. McCoy's book is incomparably the best of the three. There is no published account of Coolidge's vice presidency.

The Coolidge Papers are in the Library of Congress, except for a collection discovered in the attic of the house in Plymouth Notch and given to Forbes Library in Northampton by the president's son John in 1983 and 1984; some of these more personal papers, as compared with the routine correspondence now in the Library of Congress, are quite valuable. A recently opened collection of papers, those of the assistant White House physician in the 1920s, Joel T. Boone, in the Library of Congress, is immensely helpful in revealing Coolidge's private side.

Charles G. Dawes: This notable figure in American history frequently kept a diary, and as the years passed he published sections in books. Unfortunately, his *Notes as Vice President, 1928–1929* (Boston: Little, Brown, 1935) covers only fifteen months; apparently his diary for the vice presidency did not start until then. Dawes's papers are at Northwestern University.

They include manuscripts of his diaries, and the manuscripts show that almost all of the diaries went into publication—he did not write indiscreet commentaries. His correspondence is more interesting, although it tended to be open, ebullient, and somehow unrevealing. Paul R. Leach, *That Man Dawes* (Chicago: Reilly and Lee, 1930), enjoyed some cooperation from its subject, and is pro-Dawes all the way. Dawes made fun of the Progressive Party candidates of 1924 and described them as peewits, that is, tiny birds. Leach was a member of the Peewit Club, Nest No. 1. Bascom N. Timmons, *Portrait of an American: Charles G. Dawes* (New York: Henry Holt, 1953), borrows from Leach's book and quotes Dawes's speeches and published diary.

Charles Curtis: Curtis was one of the least conspicuous vice presidents of the present century, and perhaps for that reason there is very little historical literature pertaining to his life and works. James C. Malin's biographical sketch in *Dictionary of American Biography, Supplement 2* (New York: Scribners, 1958) is fair and reliable. Don C. Seitz, *From Kaw Teepee to Capitol: The Life Story of Charles Curtis, Indian, Who Has Risen to High Estate* (New York: Frederick A. Stokes, 1928), is nought but a campaign biography. *Dolly Gann's Book* (Garden City, N.Y.: Doubleday, Doran, 1928), by Curtis's half sister, is a detailed account of her campaign, for such it was, to obtain precedence at social functions for herself, as her half brother's hostess, vis-à-vis Alice Roosevelt Longworth, wife of the Speaker of the House of Representatives, Nicholas Longworth. The peculiar way in which Curtis received the vice presidential nomination in 1928 appears in the unpublished diary of Sen. Reed Smoot of Utah, who arranged the nomination.

II. NEW DEAL, OLD DUTIES, 1933–1953

John Nance Garner: Source materials on Garner's life are slim, in large part because he destroyed his personal papers. Researchers must, therefore, depend on comments in the papers of Garner's contemporaries. For example, James A. Farley's papers, which are in the Manuscript Division of the Library of Congress, offer insight into Garner. Garner's correspondence also can be found in several manuscript collections at the Franklin D. Roosevelt Library in Hyde Park, New York; in the Lewis W. Douglas Papers at the University of Arizona in Tucson; and in the Raymond Moley Papers at the Hoover Institution in Palo Alto, California.

There are no adequate biographies of Garner. For brief synopses of
Garner's career, see Donald R. McCoy, "Garner, John Nance," in *Dictionary
of American Biography, Supplement 8* (New York: Scribners, 1988), and the
obituary by Alden Whitman in the *New York Times* (November 8, 1967). For
a broader view, see James T. Patterson, *Congressional Conservatism and the
New Deal* (Lexington: University Press of Kentucky, 1967), and Michael J.
Romano, "The Emergence of John Nance Garner as a Figure in American
National Politics," Ph.D. diss., St. Johns University, 1974.

The standard biography, authored by a newspaperman-friend, is Bascom N. Timmons, *Garner of Texas: A Personal History* (New York: Harper
and Brothers, 1948). Less flattering is John Franklin Carter and others, *The
New Dealers* (New York: Simon and Schuster, 1934), which judged Garner's
career as founded "on the obituary column and the power of inertia." Also
critical are portraits by Otis L. Graham Jr., in Otis L. Graham and Meghan
Robinson Wander, eds., *Franklin D. Roosevelt: His Life and Times* (Boston:
G. K. Hall, 1985); Stanley High, "Whose Party Is It?" *Saturday Evening Post*
(February 6, 1937), which stresses Garner's presumptive leadership of
"old order" Democrats; and Ulric Bell, "Little Jack Garner," *The American
Mercury* (May 1939).

Henry A. Wallace: Wallace's own papers, divided among three locations—
the University of Iowa, the Franklin D. Roosevelt Library, and the Library
of Congress—and drawn together in a microfilm edition, are the best
source. Researchers interested in Wallace's correspondence with specific
individuals will want to consult Earl M. Rogers, ed., *The Wallace Papers:
An Index,* 2 vols. (Iowa City: University of Iowa Libraries, 1975).

Wallace's vice presidential papers fill 40 linear feet at the Roosevelt
Library and include a wide range of documents concerning Wallace's
service as vice president of the United States and as chairman of the Board
of Economic Warfare from 1941 to 1945.

Of particular value is a superb diary, much of it published by John Blum,
supplemented by a rich memoir developed by the Columbia University
Oral History Project. The records of the secretary of agriculture on his rise
to the vice presidency are useful; they are housed in the National Archives
with the records of the Board of Economic Warfare.

The papers of Franklin and Eleanor Roosevelt at the Roosevelt Library
contribute much, as do those of Jesse Jones at the Library of Congress. On
Wallace's relations with labor and liberals, see the papers of C. B. Baldwin
at the University of Iowa, the papers of Jim Patton at the University of

Colorado, the papers of Hubert Humphrey at the Minnesota Historical Society, and the papers of Raymond Clapper at the Library of Congress. For the "Guru letters," consult the papers of Samuel Rosenman at the Roosevelt Library and the papers of Westbrook Pegler at the Herbert Hoover Library. On the dumping of Wallace, consult the Robert Hannegan and Edwin Pauley Papers in the Truman Library.

Harry S. Truman: For Truman there is an embarrassment of riches. The first resort should be the biographies by David McCullough, *Truman* (New York: Simon and Schuster, 1992); Alonzo L. Hamby, *Man of the People: A Life of Harry S. Truman* (New York: Oxford University Press, 1995); and Robert H. Ferrell, *Harry S. Truman: A Life* (Columbia: University of Missouri Press, 1994). See also Truman's *Memoirs: Year of Decisions* (Garden City, N.Y.: Doubleday, 1955); within this first volume is a considerable account of the vice presidency. For the 1944 convention, see Ferrell's *Choosing Truman: The Democratic Convention of 1944* (Columbia: University of Missouri Press, 1994).

The Truman Papers at the Harry S. Truman Library in Independence are of course of considerable value, for the soon-to-be president wrote excellent letters and generally apprised correspondents of what he was up to. His papers include about 10 linear feet on the period from his selection as the Democratic vice presidential candidate in July 1944 to his accession to the presidency in April 1945. Truman's secretary did not open new files when Truman became vice president; instead, she continued using the senatorial files.

Also of value is the General and Personal File of the President Truman's Secretary's Files, which includes material relating to the 1944 Democratic convention, and the Longhand Notes File, which contains correspondence between President Roosevelt and Vice President Truman.

Roosevelt's choice of Truman as his running mate and the machinations of the 1944 Democratic National Convention are discussed in detail in several Truman Library collections. Among those worthy of special attention are the Robert E. Hannegan Papers, the Harry Easley Papers, and the Sam Wear Papers.

Alben W. Barkley: Alben W. Barkley was an indefatigable politician but not a writer of letters showing personal flair, nor did he ever manage a diary. His papers are at the University of Kentucky in Lexington. After retirement from the vice presidency, he published *That Reminds Me* (Garden City, N.Y.: Doubleday, 1954) with the assistance of Sidney Shalett.

In preparation for the book, Barkley and Shalett made massive tape recordings that contain utterances that did not make it into the biography. The tapes are at Lexington, together with a transcription. In addition, see Polly Ann Davis, *Alben W. Barkley: Senate Majority Leader and Vice President* (New York: Garland, 1979). James K. Libbey, *Dear Alben: Mr. Barkley of Kentucky* (Lexington: University Press of Kentucky, 1979), is a graceful, short biography. For the personal side, see Jane Barkley, *I Married the Veep* (New York: Vanguard, 1958).

Barkley's papers—senatorial as well as vice presidential—are housed in the Special Collections Department at the University of Kentucky. The papers have been processed, and a guide is available; the papers are open to research. The sixty-five thousand items and one hundred scrapbooks cover the years from 1900 to 1956 and include correspondence, speeches, political papers, news clippings, and photographs. The vice presidential materials are commingled with the entire collection.

III. THE SPRINGBOARD, 1953–1963

Richard M. Nixon: The vice presidential files of Richard M. Nixon are divided between the Pacific Southwest Regional Archives of the National Archives and Records Administration in Laguna Niguel, California, and the Richard Nixon Library and Birthplace in Yorba Linda, California. From 1978 to 1992 all of the vice presidential files were held in the regional archives branch, pending the establishment of the Nixon complex at Yorba Linda.

Most of the files held at the regional archives were never deeded to the federal government by Mr. Nixon; those materials were transferred to the Nixon Library in 1992. Those files that had been deeded to the federal government were retained by the regional archives.

The regional branch holds approximately 670 feet of pre-presidential materials with the largest series, Pre-presidential General Correspondence File, consisting of some 400 cubic feet. The files consist of correspondence between the vice president and a wide range of notable individuals. Also at Laguna Niguel are the Vice Presidential Trip Files (70 cubic feet), the Appearances [Speaking] Files (100 cubic feet), and Other Files and Materials (100 cubic feet). The vast majority of these materials are open to research, and indexes to the materials are available.

The pre-presidential materials held at the Richard Nixon Library are vast and diverse. These materials, which include a substantial portion covering the years between 1960 and 1968, are estimated at about 2,300 linear feet. The series titles indicate that the topics covered in the vice presidential files include election campaigns, press coverage, audiovisual materials, public appearances, correspondence, and family matters. Some of these materials are available for research, but all potential researchers are urged to contact the Nixon Library in advance of their first visit.

Lyndon B. Johnson: There is little serious study of Lyndon Johnson's vice presidency. The second volume of Robert Dallek's two-volume study of Johnson, *Splendid Misery: Lyndon Johnson and His Times, 1961–1973* (New York: Oxford University Press, in press), includes a lengthy opening chapter on Johnson's vice presidency.

Lyndon Johnson's vice presidential papers are located with other Johnson materials at the Lyndon B. Johnson Presidential Library on the campus of the University of Texas in Austin. Various components of the vice presidential papers are open to research, including correspondence between Johnson and President Kennedy; files relating to foreign affairs, the space program, education, and civil rights; and other materials, such as Johnson's daily diaries. All of these papers are open to research; the remaining papers are expected to be opened soon.

IV. TRAGEDY AND CRISIS, 1965–1973

Hubert H. Humphrey: Although no full-length book examines the Humphrey vice presidency, a number of works accord it shorter treatment. Of the principal works on the vice presidency, the following discuss Humphrey's experiences to some extent: Joel Goldstein, *The American Vice Presidency: The Transformation of a Political Institution* (Princeton: Princeton University Press 1982); Marie D. Natoli, *American Prince, American Pauper: The Contemporary Vice Presidency in Perspective* (Westport, Conn.: Greenwood Press, 1985); Donald T. Young, *American Roulette: The History and Dilemma of the Vice Presidency* (New York: Holt, Rinehart, and Winston, 1972); and Jules Witcover, *Crapshoot: Rolling the Dice on the Vice Presidency* (New York: Crown, 1994). Humphrey's memoir, *The Education of a Public Man* (Garden City, N.Y.: Doubleday, 1976), is quite useful and revealing.

Biographies of Humphrey include Allan H. Ryskind, *Hubert* (New Rochelle, N.Y.: Arlington House, 1968); Robert Sherrill and Harry W. Ernst, *The Drugstore Liberal* (New York: Grossman, 1968); Winthrop Griffith, *Humphrey: A Candid Biography* (New York: William Morrow, 1965); and

Albert Eisele, *Almost to the Presidency* (Blue Earth, Minn.: Piper, 1972). Of these, Eisele's book is the most interesting. The most thorough study is Carl Solberg, *Hubert Humphrey: A Biography* (New York: W. W. Norton, 1984).

Memoirs by various government personnel contain some interesting accounts and observations of Humphrey, especially Edmund Muskie, *Journeys* (Garden City, N.Y.: Doubleday, 1972); Joseph H. Califano Jr., *The Triumph and Tragedy of Lyndon Johnson* (New York: Simon and Schuster, 1991); Eric F. Goldman, *The Tragedy of Lyndon Johnson* (New York: Alfred A. Knopf, 1969); and George W. Ball, *The Past Has Another Pattern* (New York: W. W. Norton, 1982). See, too, Lawrence F. O'Brien, *No Final Victories* (Garden City, N.Y.: Doubleday, 1974); George Christian, *The President Steps Down* (New York: Macmillan, 1970); George Reedy, *The Twilight of the Presidency* (New York: World, 1970); Harry McPherson, *A Political Education* (Boston: Little, Brown, 1972); and Clark Clifford, *Counsel to the President* (New York: Random House, 1991).

The selection of Humphrey as Johnson's running mate is well discussed in Gerald Pomper, "The Nomination of Hubert Humphrey for Vice President," in *Journal of Politics* 28 (1966): 639. Other extended discussions of that subject occur in Rowland Evans and Robert Novak, *Lyndon B. Johnson: The Exercise of Power* (New York: New American Library, 1966), and Theodore H. White, *The Making of the President, 1964* (New York: Atheneum, 1965). Humphrey's 1968 campaign is also discussed in White's *The Making of the President, 1968* (New York: Atheneum, 1969).

Entries relating to Humphrey or the vice presidency in *The Public Papers of the Presidents: Lyndon B. Johnson 1963–1969* (Washington, D.C.: U.S. Government Printing Office, 1965–1970) provide interesting primary materials in many cases.

The Vice Presidential Files of Hubert H. Humphrey are held by the Minnesota Historical Society in St. Paul, Minnesota. The main set of files (around 400 cubic feet) are concerned with activities, agencies, and programs with which the vice president's office was formally connected or in which Humphrey had a personal or official interest. They are especially full for such programs as civil rights (through the President's Council on Equal Opportunity), health and sports (through the President's Committee on Physical Fitness), outer space (through the National Aeronautics and Space Administration), and poverty and youth (through the Youth Opportunity Campaign, summer employment programs, Volunteers in

Service to America, the Job Corps, and many other War on Poverty programs). There is also considerable material on foreign affairs, with emphasis on Vietnam, Latin America, and disarmament.

Supplementing the vice presidential office files are sets of speeches, speaking engagement files, articles, and newspaper clippings. Those for the vice presidential period total about 75 cubic feet. Also present are 122 cubic feet of Humphrey's 1968 presidential campaign files.

There are finding aids, in varying degrees of detail, for all of the materials. There are no access or use restrictions (other than standard provisions concerning copyright, fair use, and attribution). However, numerous security-classified documents have been removed from the files and sent to the National Archives pending declassification review.

Spiro T. Agnew: Agnew was an intensely private person who had little to say about his vice presidential years other than what was published in his memoirs, *Go Quietly . . . Or Else* (New York: William Morrow, 1980).

Agnew donated his papers to the Special Collections Department of the University of Maryland Libraries in 1974. Although not fully processed, significant portions of the papers totaling 180 linear feet have been opened for research. Among the materials that are open are correspondence files, speech files, campaign materials, and publication files by and about Agnew as vice president. The opened materials constitute about one-third of the total volume in the collection. A research guide to the opened materials is available, and a preliminary inventory of the other papers in the collection is under way.

V. RECOVERY AND REFLECTION, 1973–1981

Gerald R. Ford: The memoir of Vice President Ford is based on James Cannon, *Time and Chance: Gerald R. Ford's Appointment with History* (New York: Harper Collins, 1994). The president's own memoir, *A Time to Heal: The Autobiography of Gerald R. Ford* (New York: Harper and Row, 1979), is also very useful as is John Robert Greene, *The Presidency of Gerald R. Ford* (Lawrence: University Press of Kansas, 1995).

The Gerald R. Ford Vice Presidential Papers are in the Gerald R. Ford Library on the campus of the University of Michigan. The papers begin October 12, 1973, when President Richard Nixon nominated Ford for the vice presidency upon Spiro Agnew's resignation in disgrace. The papers end with Nixon's own resignation on August 9, 1974. The collection includes extensive material from Ford's congressional career, gathered for use in confirmation hearings as provided for under the Twenty-fifth Amendment.

The files of various staff compose most of the 105-cubic-foot collection. Prominent topics include speech writing, scheduling, travel, press relations and coverage, domestic and some foreign policy issues, and the House and Senate hearings on Ford's nomination. The collection is relatively silent on the Watergate revelations and impeachment hearings that ended the Nixon presidency, but elsewhere the library holds the papers of House Judiciary Committee member Edward Hutchinson. Material on the actual Nixon-Ford transition is highly fragmentary and widely scattered.
Nelson A. Rockefeller: The essay on Nelson Rockefeller's vice presidency is based on James Cannon's memories of working with him. Unfortunately, there are few studies of Rockefeller worth consulting, except for those listed in the guide at the end of this volume. Of particular value are Joseph Persico, *The Imperial Rockefeller: A Biography of Nelson A. Rockefeller* (New York: Simon and Schuster, 1982), Cannon's own book *Time and Chance,* and John Robert Greene, *Presidency of Gerald R. Ford,* cited fully in the paragraphs above and in the guide to reading. Cary Reich is at work on a multivolume work titled *The Life of Nelson A. Rockefeller.* The first volume, which takes Rockefeller up to 1958, was published by Doubleday in 1996.

The main repository for Nelson Rockefeller's vice presidential papers is the Rockefeller Archives Center in Pocantico Hills, New York. Presently, there are five series of records open for research: the Central Files (200 cubic feet), the Files of the National Commission on Water Quality (59 cubic feet), the Files of the New York Office (15 cubic feet), the Press Files (27 cubic feet), and the Speech Files (23 cubic feet).

The Ford Library also has significant material on Rockefeller's vice presidency. For example, Ford's controversial decision to nominate Rockefeller and the confirmation hearings that followed are richly documented in two collections from senior White House adviser Robert Hartmann. The vice president's attempts at policy making are revealed, especially in two collections from James Cannon, a close Rockefeller associate who became Ford's chief assistant for domestic affairs. Materials in many collections show conservative opposition, which was ultimately successful, to any renomination of Rockefeller for the 1976 Republican ticket. Finally, the library holds the complete records of the so-called Rockefeller Commission, the President's Commission on CIA Activities within the United States.

Walter Mondale: Mondale has been the subject of only one serious study: Steven M. Gillon, *The Democrats' Dilemma: Walter F. Mondale and the Liberal Legacy* (New York: Columbia University Press, 1992).

Mondale's vice presidential papers are on deposit at the Minnesota Historical Society along with the rest of his papers. His vice presidential files total approximately 300 cubic feet of material and focus on the vice presidential office's interactions with the office of the president, federal agencies, the general public, members of various interest groups, and other constituencies on a wide range of governmental matters and public policy issues. No strong topical focus is apparent.

About half of the files have been processed to some degree and are available for use under donor restrictions. These include the vice presidential office central files (128 cubic feet), trip files (19 cubic feet), press release/speech/appearance files (14 cubic feet), and several smaller series. The two components of the central files, one organized by correspondents' names and one by office-of-the-president file code, have not been closely analyzed for topical content. The unprocessed materials consist largely of staff, background, office administration, and political files.

There are finding aids, in varying degrees of detail, for the processed materials. Until April 2006, access to and use of these files requires written permission from Mondale or his representative. Mondale's foreign affairs files, which include numerous security-classified documents, remain in the custody of the National Archives' Office of Presidential Libraries.

VI. AT THE PRESIDENT'S SIDE, 1981–1993

George Bush: The essay in this volume was based on Chase Untermeyer's recollections of his term of service with Vice President Bush as well as two published memoirs: George Bush with Vic Gold, *Looking Forward: An Autobiography* (Garden City, N.Y.: Doubleday, 1987), and Helene von Damm, *At Reagan's Side* (Garden City, N.Y.: Doubleday, 1989).

Scholarly research on the Bush vice presidency is in its earliest stages, and the source materials for this research can be found at the George Bush Historical Materials Project located in College Station, Texas. There are approximately 1,500 cubic feet of Bush vice presidential records that include correspondence, memoranda, speeches, press releases, briefing material, notes, audiovisual material, clippings, and miscellaneous printed material covering the years 1981 to 1989. The records include alphabetical and subject files as well as files produced by the vice president's press office, counsel's office, chief of staff, the Task Force on Regulatory Relief, and other staff units. Under the terms of the 1978 Presidential Records Act, Bush vice presidential records became available for Freedom of Information Act requests on January 20, 1994.

Notes on the Contributors

R. W. APPLE JR. is Chief Washington Correspondent and Washington Bureau Chief for the *New York Times*. Since joining the *Times* in 1963, he has reported from more than one hundred countries. Apple is well known for his appearance on national television programs, including NBC's *Meet the Press* and PBS's *McNeill/Lehrer News Hour*. The author of a number of books and magazine articles, he is the recipient of many honors, including a George Polk Award, an Overseas Press Club Award, and three honorary doctorates.

JAMES CANNON has been a writer and political adviser for more than twenty-five years. Formerly the National Affairs Editor at *Newsweek*, Cannon left journalism to become a political adviser to Gov. Nelson Rockefeller of New York. He also served as Domestic Policy Adviser to President Gerald Ford and as Chief of Staff to Senate Majority Leader Howard Baker. In recent years Cannon has been the Executive Director of American Agenda and Director of the Eisenhower Centennial Foundation. He is the author of the widely heralded *Time and Chance: Gerald Ford's Appointment with History* (New York: Harper Collins, 1994).

JOHN MILTON COOPER JR. is the William Francis Allen Professor of History at the University of Wisconsin. Cooper is the winner of numerous prizes, including a Gugenheim Fellowship and a Fulbright professorship. He is the author of several works of history, including *The Warrior and the Priest: Woodrow Wilson and Theodore Roosevelt* (Cambridge: Harvard University Press, 1983) and *Pivotal Decades: The United States, 1900–1920* (New York: W. W. Norton, 1990).

ROBERT DALLEK is Professor of History at Boston University. Dallek, who is highly regarded for his many books on the history of American foreign policy, is currently writing a two-volume biography of Lyndon Johnson. The first volume, *Lone Star Rising,* was published in 1991, and the second volume is in press (both from Oxford University Press). Dallek has won many awards, including the Bancroft Prize.

ROBERT H. FERRELL is Distinguished Professor of History Emeritus at Indiana University in Bloomington and the author or editor of more than thirty-five books. He is well known for his books on a range of twentieth-century presidents, including Woodrow Wilson, Calvin Coolidge, and Harry S. Truman. His recent biography *Harry S. Truman: A Life* (Columbia: University of Missouri Press, 1994) received outstanding reviews.

STEVEN M. GILLON is University Lecturer in Modern History at Oxford University. Educated at Brown University, Gillon taught at Brown and at Yale University before his move to Oxford. He is the winner of a host of honors, awards, and research grants, and he is the author of several books, including *The Democrats' Dilemma: Walter F. Mondale and the Liberal Legacy* (New York: Columbia University Press, 1992). In addition to his writing, Gillon is a consultant to the History Channel of the Arts and Entertainment Cable Television Network.

JOEL K. GOLDSTEIN is an Assistant Professor in the School of Law at St. Louis University. Educated at Princeton University, Oxford University, and Harvard University, he practiced law at the St. Louis firm of Goldstein and Price before assuming his present position. He is the author of *The Modern American Vice Presidency: The Transformation of a Political Institution* (Princeton: Princeton University Press, 1982) and other works on American government and law.

JOHN ROBERT GREENE is Distinguished Professor of History and Communications at Cazenovia College in Cazenovia, New York. Educated at St. Bonaventure University and Syracuse University, Greene is the author of six books, including *The Limits of Power: The Nixon and Ford Years* (Bloomington: Indiana University Press, 1992) and, most recently, *The Presidency of Gerald R. Ford* (Lawrence: University Press of Kansas, 1995).

RICHARD S. KIRKENDALL is Bullitt Professor of American History at the University of Washington in Seattle. Formerly a professor of history at

Iowa State University, Indiana University, and the University of Missouri, Kirkendall also served as Executive Secretary of the Organization of American Historians for eight years. He is at work on his twelfth book, a biography of Henry A. Wallace.

RICHARD E. NEUSTADT is Douglas Dillon Professor of Government Emeritus in the John F. Kennedy School of Government at Harvard University. Educated at the University of California at Berkeley and at Harvard, Neustadt has received many awards, honorary doctorates, and research fellowships in recognition of his work on the operations and policy of the federal government. He has served the government in a number of different capacities, including as a consultant to Presidents Kennedy and Johnson. Neustadt is best known for his scholarship, including his classic works *Presidential Power*, rev. ed. (New York: Free Press, 1990), and *Thinking in Time* (New York: Free Press, 1986).

DAN QUAYLE served as the Forty-fourth Vice President of the United States from 1989 until 1993. As vice president, he was one of President Bush's closest advisers and served as the president's representative on numerous commissions and committees. Prior to the vice presidency, Quayle served as U.S. Senator and U.S. Representative from Indiana. In Congress he coauthored the Joint Training Partnership Act, legislation that has helped millions of students and seniors acquire job skills for employment in today's global economy. After leaving office, Quayle wrote *Standing Firm: A Vice Presidential Memoir* (New York: Harper Collins/Zondervan, 1994), which became a national best-seller.

ELLIOT A. ROSEN is Professor of History Emeritus at Rutgers University in New Brunswick, New Jersey, where he taught for thirty-five years. Educated at New York University, Rosen has received many grants and awards and is the author of *The First New Deal* (coauthored with Raymond Moley) (New York: Harcourt Brace and World, 1966) and *Hoover, Roosevelt and the Brains Trust* (New York: Columbia University Press, 1977).

HUGH SIDEY is the Washington Contributing Editor for *Time* and has written about the American presidency for more than thirty years, longer than any other Washington journalist. Sidey is the son of a country editor, reared at the family's weekly newspaper in Greenfield, Iowa. After an education at Iowa State University, he began his journalistic career at papers throughout the Midwest. He joined *Life* in New York in 1955 and then moved to *Time*. He has written or contributed to five books on the presidency and has been a panelist on the nationally syndicated television show *Inside Washington* for more than twenty years.

RICHARD NORTON SMITH is the Director of the Gerald R. Ford Library and Museum. Smith previously served as Director of the Hoover Library and Museum, as Acting Director of the Eisenhower Library and Museum, and as Director of the Ronald Reagan Library and Museum. A prolific and popular author, Smith has written a number of presidential biographies, including *The Uncommon Man: The Triumph of Herbert Hoover* (New York: Simon and Schuster, 1984) and *Patriarch: George Washington and the New American Nation* (Boston: Houghton Mifflin, 1993).

CHASE UNTERMEYER served in a number of positions in the Reagan and Bush administrations, including Executive Assistant to Vice President Bush, Assistant Secretary of the Navy, Assistant to the President, and Director of the Voice of America. Before entering government service, Untermeyer was a political reporter for the *Houston Chronicle*, Assistant to the Chief Administrative Officer of Harris County, and a member of the Texas legislature. He is currently Director of Public Affairs for the Compaq Computer Corporation and Chairman of the Board of Visitors of the U.S. Naval Academy.

TIMOTHY WALCH is Director of the Herbert Hoover Library and Museum. Prior to moving to West Branch, he served in a variety of positions at the National Archives, including Editor of *Prologue: Quarterly of the National Archives*. Walch, who was educated at the University of Notre Dame and Northwestern University, is the author or editor of fourteen books, including *Herbert Hoover and Harry S. Truman: A Documentary History* (Worland, Wyo: High Plains Publishing, 1992).

Index

Aaron, David, 147
Adams, John, 1
Adams, Sherman, 80, 84
Admiral House, 185, 199
Agnew, Spiro T.: popular among
  Republican activists, 83; surprise
  selection as vice president, 124, 170;
  political career, 124–25; political
  rhetoric, 125–26; duties as vice
  president, 127, 129–30; speeches, 128–
  29; attacks on the media, 128–29; role
  in the 1972 election, 130; investigated
  by U.S. attorney, 130–32; plea bargain,
  132; resignation, 132; life after the vice
  presidency, 132; replacement as vice
  president, 135; secondary sources, 223;
  primary sources, 235
Albert, Carl, 131, 135, 199
American Bar Association, 176
Americans for Democratic Action, 82
Arnall, Ellis, 59
Arthur, Chester, 2
Asia, 112
Atwater, Lee, 158, 166, 167

Baker, James, 158, 160, 173
Baker, Newton, 17, 18, 20
Baldridge, Malcolm, 160
Ball, George, 108, 110, 116, 185
Baltimore County Zoning Board of
  Appeals, 124
Barkley, Alben: asks for vice presidential
  nomination, 4; as leader of the U.S.
  Senate, 51, 75; as a politician, 63; views
  of Henry Wallace, 69; political career,
  69–70; selection as vice president, 71;

and 1948 campaign, 71–72; duties as
  vice president, 72; marriage to Jane
  Hadley, 73; sense of humor, 73–74;
  desire to be president, 74; return to
  the Senate, 75; secondary sources, 221;
  primary sources, 231–32
Baruch, Bernard, 51
Bayh, Birch, 185, 194, 199
Bay of Pigs (Cuba), 142
Beall, George, 130
Bell, Griffin, 148
Bethesda Naval Hospital, 65
Bicentennial of the Declaration of
  Independence, 130
Blacks, 98, 106
Board of Economic Warfare (BEW), 55–58
Borah, William E., 32, 38, 39
Brannan, Charles F., 36
Brown, Edmund (Pat), 104
Bryan, William Jennings, 10, 11, 16, 31
Brzezinski, Zbigniew, 147
Buchanan, Patrick, 125, 128, 129
Budget issues, 147, 177
Burke, Edward R., 51
Burns, Arthur, 136
Burr, Aaron, 202
Bush, Barbara, 158, 166
Bush, George: selection as vice president,
  157; relations with Reagan, 158–59;
  distrusted by Reagan's staff, 159–60;
  and Reagan assassination attempt,
  160–62; and Alexander Haig, 160–61;
  duties as vice president, 162–65;
  relations with Congress, 163; and
  foreign affairs, 164–65; and Iran-
  Contra, 165; and the 1984 election,

165–66; preparation for the 1988
election, 166–67; selects Quayle as
vice president, 171; relations with
Quayle, 172–73; assignments to
Quayle, 173–74; loyalty of Quayle to
Bush, 178; vice presidential transition,
205–6; secondary sources, 224; primary
sources, 237–38
Butler, Nicholas Murray, 29
Butler, William M., 32, 38
Buzhardt, J. Fred, 131
Byrd, Harry, 58
Byrnes, James F., 51, 60–68

Cabinet meetings attended by vice
presidents, 29, 48, 51, 72, 91, 93, 146,
173, 186–87; vice presidential support,
72, 99, 111; moderator in absence of the
president, 84, 161
Calhoun, John C., 152
Califano, Joseph, 110, 111
Cambodia, 127
Camp David Accords, 147
Carp, Bert, 147
Carter, Jimmy: defeats Gerald Ford, 143;
vice presidential selection process,
144–45; relations with Mondale,
145–46, 148–50; gives Mondale office
in west wing of White House, 146–47,
159; appoints Mondale staffers, 147;
rewrote role of the vice presidency, 153
Central Intelligence Agency, 127, 137,
139, 163
Cheney, Richard, 173
Chicago, 25, 26, 31, 79
China, 81, 127, 164
Churchill, Winston, 107, 209
Civil rights, 92, 105
Clifford, Clark, 71
Clinton, Bill, 186, 189, 190, 191
Clinton, George, 202
Clinton, Hillary, 212, 213
Clinton administration, 177
Cohen, Wilbur, 99
Colfax, Schuyler, 203
Commerce Department, 160
Committee on Equal Employment
Opportunity: and LBJ, 92–93, 96–98;
and Hubert Humphrey, 110

Committee to Re-elect the President, 130
Commonwealth Club of California, 176
Congress: vice president as president of
the Senate, 34–35, 128; vice president
as administration spokesman, 114, 147,
173, 177, 206–7
Congress of American Soviet Friendship,
57
Congress of Industrial Organizations, 51,
59, 60, 61
Connally, John, 128, 130, 135, 138
Connelly, Matthew J., 71
Coolidge, Calvin: compared to Thomas
Marshall, 19; nomination as vice
president, 24–26; campaign of 1920,
27–28; and Harding's health, 28;
anonymity, 28–29; duties as vice
president, 29–30; relations with
Harding, 29; and Charles Curtis,
40; secondary sources, 218; primary
sources, 228
Copeland, Royal, 51
Corcoran, Thomas, 48
Council of Recreation and Natural
Beauty, 116
Council on Competitiveness, 175
Council on Foreign Relations, 158
Cox, Channing, 38
Cox, James, 46
Crisp, Charles, 47
Curtis, Charles: political career, 24, 41;
and Warren Harding, 32; general,
37–38; Indian heritage, 38; selection
as vice president, 38–39, 169; sister's
status as hostess, 39–40; service in
the Senate, 40; renomination as vice
president, 41–42; secondary sources,
219; primary sources, 229

Daniels, Josephus, 20
Davis, John W., 46
Dawes, Charles G.: deserved the
presidency, 30; background and
education, 30–31; Dawes Plan, 32;
nomination as vice president, 32;
speeches, 33–34; service in the Senate,
34–35; farm problem, 35–36; post–vice
presidential career, 36–37; secondary

sources, 218–19; primary sources, 228–29

Deaver, Michael, 162

Democrats, 105

DeMuth, Christopher, 162

Deng Xiaoping, 164

Depew, Chauncey M., 26

Detroit, 157, 158

Dewey, Thomas E.: as the 1944 presidential nominee, 64, 66; as the 1948 presidential nominee, 72; as adviser to Richard M. Nixon, 79, 80

Dieterich, William, 51

Discrimination, 98

Dodd, Thomas, 104

Dole, Robert, 143, 145, 167

Domestic Policy Council: and Nelson Rockefeller, 139, 140, 141, 185; and Walter Mondale, 146

Douglas, Lewis W., 47, 49

Douglas, William O., 67, 68, 71

Dukakis, Michael, 167

Dunne, Finley Peter, 1

Eagleton, Thomas, 144

Eccles, Marriner S., 52

Economic Policy Group, 146

Eisele, Albert, 110

Eisenhower, Dwight D.: as candidate in 1952, 79–80; relations with Nixon, 80–83, 85; makes Nixon a "hatchet man," 82–83; suffers heart attack, 83–84, 204–5; Nixon's views of Eisenhower, 84; fails to support Nixon in 1960, 86–87; values Nixon as a conservative spokesman, 125–26

Eisenhower, Mamie, 86

Eizenstadt, Stuart, 146, 150

Erhard, Ludwig, 88

Erlichman, John, 130, 131

Essary, J. Fred, 20

Europe, 115, 164

Fairbanks, Charles King, 9, 12–14, 16, 217, 227

Fair Labors Standards Act, 52

Farley, James A., 48, 51, 52

Federal Bureau of Investigation, 137

Ferraro, Geraldine, 165

Fillmore, Millard, 2

Finch, Robert, 124

First ladies, 212

Florida, 163, 166

Flynn, Edward J., 66

Ford, Betty, 136

Ford, Gerald R.: and Hubert Humphrey, 122; and Spiro T. Agnew, 129; as vice president, 135–37; and Nelson Rockefeller, 137–38; and Ronald Reagan, 157; secondary sources, 223–24; primary sources, 235–36

Fortas, Abe, 97, 99

France, 141

Funerals, 164, 208–9

Gann, Dolly, 39–40

Garner, John Nance: political background, 45–46; in House of Representatives, 46–47; accommodates Republicans, 47–48; selection as vice presidential candidate, 47; as vice president, 48–50; relations with FDR, 48–49; opposes New Deal, 49–50; on the Supreme Court, 50; opposes third term for FDR, 52–53; assessment of vice presidential service, 53; secondary sources, 219; primary sources, 229–30

Gates, Robert, 172

Gerry, Elbridge, 202

Glenn, John, 141

Goldin, Dan, 176

Goldwater, Barry M., 104, 105, 113, 126

Goodell, Charles, 129

Goodwin, Richard, 97

Gorbachev, Mikhail, 164, 165, 172

Gore, Albert, Jr.: personal convictions, 154, 213; selection as vice president, 171; and 1992 campaign, 177–78; relations with Clinton, 189–90; as potential chief of staff, 201; and state funerals, 209; secondary sources, 224

Gore, Albert, Sr., 90

Graham, Billy, 129

Gray, C. Boyden, 162

Grayson, Cary T., 20–21

"Great Society," 107, 109, 110, 114

"Guru letters," 54–55

Hadley, Jane Rucker, 73
Haggerty, James, 83, 198
Haig, Alexander: on Hubert Humphrey, 116; as chief of staff to Nixon, 131; relations with Nixon, 137; as secretary of state, 160–61, 164
Haldeman, H. R., 131, 137
Hall, Leonard, 84
Hamlin, Hannibal, 202–3
Hanna, Mark, 10, 13
Hannegan, Robert, 59, 60, 66, 69
Harding, Florence, 29
Harding, Warren, 19, 29, 32
Harris, Fred, 118
Harrison, Pat, 50–51
Hartmann, Robert, 136
Hays, Will, 11
Hearst, William R., 47
Henderson, Leon, 52
Hendricks, Thomas, 203
Hillman, Sidney, 60, 61
Hiss, Alger, 79
Hoover, Herbert, 33, 36, 37, 38, 50
Hopkins, Harry, 47
House, Edward M., 17, 18, 22
House of Representatives, 131, 139, 163
Hughes, Charles Evans, 11, 14
Hughes, Richard, 118
Hull, Cordell, 57
Humphrey, Hubert: and Henry Wallace, 59, 62; selection as vice president, 103–5; credentials to be vice president, 105; vice presidential duties, 105–7, 110–12, 116; relations with LBJ, 106–7, 117–18, 170, 210; and Vietnam, 108–10, 117, 118–19; foreign travel, 112–14; as a presidential candidate, 117–18; and Spiro T. Agnew, 126; and Nelson Rockefeller, 137; and Walter Mondale, 144–45; Salt Lake City speech, 210; secondary sources, 222–23; primary sources, 233–35

Ickes, Harold L., 67
Illinois, 17, 158
Indiana, 9, 12, 16, 18
Indian Revenue Sharing Program, 129
Iowa, 55, 158, 166
Iran-Contra Scandal, 164

Jackson, Andrew, 152
Japan, 81, 112
Jews, 106, 144
Johnson, Andrew, 2, 203
Johnson, Hiram, 25, 26, 34
Johnson, Lyndon B.: relations with John Nance Garner, 53; relations with JFK, 89–93, 170; desire to expand vice presidential responsibilities, 89–90; duties as assigned by JFK, 90–93; frustration with the job, 93; goodwill ambassador, 93–95; and U.S. space program, 95–96; on equal employment opportunities, 96–98; relations with Humphrey, 103–23; heart attack, 107; and Vietnam, 126; secondary sources, 222; primary sources, 233
Johnson, Richard M., 202
Jones, Jesse, 57, 61, 62
Jordan, Len, 128

Kaiser, Henry J., 68
Kefauver, Estes, 85
Kelly, Edward, 51, 66
Kennedy, Edward M., 130, 149, 152
Kennedy, Jacqueline, 79
Kennedy, John F., 85, 88–100
Kennedy, Robert, 104, 117
Kern, John W., 11, 16
Khrushchev, Nikita, 86
King, Martin Luther, 92, 125
King, William Rufus, 202
Kissinger, Henry: relations with Rockefeller, 127, 136, 138; on Agnew, 128, 132; relations with Ford, 136; relations with Reagan, 157
"Kitchen debate," 86
Kosygin, Aleksi, 108, 113

Labor unions, 106, 144
La Guardia, Fiorello, 47
Lansing, Robert, 20
Laos, 127
League of Nations, 19, 22, 28, 29
Legal reforms, 176
LeMay, Curtis, 126
Lemke, William, 49
Lenroot, Irvine, 25
Lewis, John L., 51

Liberals, 144, 148
Link, Arthur, 195, 203–4
Lodge, Henry Cabot, Jr., 170
Lodge, Henry Cabot, Sr., 11, 26, 37
Longworth, Alice, 39
Longworth, Nicholas, 39, 40, 46
Lowden, Frank, 25, 32, 36
Luce, Clare Boothe, 57
Luce, Henry, 56

Mansfield, Mike, 90, 104, 135
Marcantonio, Vito, 49
Marshall, Thomas R.: and Indiana, 9, 16; as vice presidential candidate, 16; second term in doubt, 17–18; self-depreciation, 19; and Wilson's incapacity, 20–22; secondary sources, 218; primary sources, 227–28
Martin, Joseph W., 25
Massachusetts, 25, 158
Mattingly, Thomas W., 204
Maverick, Maury, 49, 50
Mayaguez incident, 142
McCamant, Wallace, 25, 26
McCarthy, Eugene, 104, 117
McCarthy, Joseph, 82, 128
McGovern, George, 130, 144
McKinley, William, 9, 10
McNamara, Robert, 104
McNary-Haugen bills, 36, 40
McPherson, Harry, 99, 118
Mellon, Andrew, 38, 39
Miller, James, 162
Mills, Ogden, 47
Minow, Newton, 95–96
Mitchell, John, 125, 131
Mitterrand, François, 172
Moe, Richard, 147, 150, 205–6
Mondale, Walter: and Hubert Humphrey, 122; selection as vice presidential candidate, 144–45, 171; as candidate, 145; redefines the vice presidency, 146–48; relations with Carter, 146–47, 149; budget issues, 147–48; resented by Carter staff, 148; concerned about his future, 150–51; considers resignation, 151–53; friendship with Carter, 153; model vice presidency, 153–54, 172, 199; advises Bush, 162, 163; as

presidential nominee, 164–65; selects Ferraro as vice presidential candidate, 165; as potential chief of staff, 201; and transition with Bush, 205–6; secondary sources, 224; primary sources, 237
Morganthau, Henry, 17, 66
Morse, Wayne, 115
Moynihan, Daniel, 99, 127
Murphy, Daniel, 163
Murphy, Frank, 52
"Murphy Brown" speech, 176–77
Muskie, Edmund, 118, 119, 144

National Advisory Council of the Peace Corps, 107
National Aeronautics and Space Administration, 88, 175–76
National Aeronautics and Space Council: and LBJ, 92–93, 95–96, 185; and Agnew, 127; and Quayle, 175–76
National Association for the Advancement of Colored People, 59, 97
National Council on Indian Opportunity, 116, 129
National Farmers Union, 57
National Industrial Recovery Act, 48
National Security Act amendments of 1949, 185, 186
National Security Council: and Barkley, 72; and Nixon, 82, 84; and LBJ, 99; and Humphrey, 109, 116, 186; and Agnew, 127; and Rockefeller, 139; and Mondale, 146; and Bush, 160; and Quayle, 172; vice presidents as members, 185, 186, 188–89
National Security Reorganization Act, 146
Neustadt, Richard E.: and vice presidential power, 120, 208; and the Twenty-fifth Amendment, 196, 200; and the Constitution, 201; and the vice president's calendar, 208; and *Presidential Power*, 209
New Deal, 48, 88, 94, 95
"New Frontier," 89
New Hampshire, 84, 158, 166
New York Liberal Party, 126

New York State: and James Sherman, 9, 14; and Theodore Roosevelt, 9–10; and the vice presidency, 11–12; and Rockefeller, 138, 140, 142, 143
New York Times, 69, 91, 114, 154
Nixon, Richard M.: and the vice presidency, 4; and the vice presidential nomination, 79–80; relations with Eisenhower, 80–81; and foreign affairs, 81–82; and the 1954 election, 82; and Eisenhower's heart attack, 83; as a presidential candidate, 84–87, 119; and Humphrey, 106; and Agnew, 124–32; as vice president, 194; secondary sources, 221–22; primary sources, 232–33
Norris, George, 35
North Atlantic Treaty Organization, 164

O'Brien, Larry F., 116
O'Donnell, Kenneth, 91
Office of Intergovernmental Relations, 127
Ohio: as the home state of presidents, 12; and William H. Taft, 14; and vice presidents, 17; and Charles Dawes, 31; and Agnew, 128; presidential primary, 144
Old Executive Office Building, 159, 185
Oregon, 25, 26
Oval Office, 159, 161, 173
Overman, Lee, 34

Panama Canal treaties, 147
Parsons, Dick, 141
Patton, Jim, 59
Pauley, Edwin, 59, 60, 66
Peace Corps, 130
Pepper, Claude, 59
Percy, Charles, 141
Perkins, Frances, 51
Perkins, Milo, 55, 57
Perot, Ross, 191
Pershing, John J., 31
Petersen, Henry, 131
Platt, Thomas C., 10
Political campaigning, 174
Powell, Jody, 148
Presidential families, 198
Presidential health, 204–5, 213

President's Council on Equal Opportunity, 107, 110
President's Council on Physical Fitness and Sports, 116

Quayle, Dan: and predecessors, 169–72; on his selection by Bush to be vice president, 171; and national security issues, 172; and George Bush, 173–74; foreign travel, 173–74; and political campaigning, 174; develops model for the vice presidency, 175; on Council on Competitiveness, 175; on the National Aeronautics and Space Administration, 175–76; on legal reform, 176; on families, 176–77; on budgets, 177; on Congress, 177–78; on the 1992 campaign, 177–78; affection for George and Barbara Bush, 178–79; and regulatory review, 186; publicity, 189–90; as a potential chief of staff, 201; secondary sources, 224

Rand, John L., 26
Raskob, John J., 46
Ray, Dixie Lee, 136
Rayburn, Sam, 53, 68, 69, 89
Reagan, Nancy, 158, 161
Reagan, Ronald: as a potential vice presidential candidate, 124, 135; on CIA commission, 139; as a presidential candidate in 1976, 142; election as president, 152; and George Bush, 157–68, 171; assassination attempt, 161–62
Reconstruction Finance Corporation (RFC), 37, 57, 62
Reed, James A., 34, 35
Reed, Thomas B., 38
Republican Party, 24, 33, 36, 37, 38, 174
Richardson, Elliot, 131
Robinson, Joseph T., 34, 46, 50
Rockefeller, Nelson A.: and Humphrey, 118, 120; and Nixon, 124, 127; and Agnew, 125; and Kissinger, 127; lack of interest in the vice presidency, 137; accepts Ford's offer, 138–39; congressional hearings, 139; and the Domestic Council, 139–40; relations

with Ford, 140–42; and the campaign of 1976, 142–43; secondary sources, 224; primary sources, 236–37
Rockefeller family, 139
Roerich, Nicholas, 55
Rogers, Will, 250
Rogers, William, 83, 85
Roosevelt, Eleanor, 49, 60, 62
Roosevelt, Franklin D.: and Garner, 47, 49–53; and Wallace, 54–62; and Truman, 65–69; political shadow, 85; and LBJ, 88
Roosevelt, Theodore, 2, 10–12, 217, 227
Root, Elihu, 11
Rossiter, Clinton, 185, 194, 196, 204
Rowe, James, 105
Rumsfeld, Donald, 139
Rusk, Dean, 91, 117–18

Safire, William, 124
Salt Lake City, 119, 210
Schlesinger, Arthur, Jr., 145
Scowcroft, Brent, 136, 172, 173
Senate: and LBJ, 90; and Humphrey, 104; and Rockefeller, 139; and Quayle, 173, 174; and the vice president's offices, 206–7
Senegal, 94
Shepherd, Alan, 95
Sherman, James S., 14–15, 217, 227
Shriver, Sargent, 130
Six Crises (Nixon), 83, 84
Smathers, George, 93
Smith, Alfred E., 11, 46
Smith, Walter Bedell, 84
Smoot, Reed, 38–39
Southern Christian Leadership Conference, 92
South Korea, 81, 112
Soviet Union: and Garner, 49; and Wallace, 59; and LBJ, 95; and Humphrey, 113
State Department, 57
Statuary Hall, 132
Stearns, Frank W., 37
Stevenson, Adlai, 82
Stimson, Henry L., 11
Stoddard, Henry L., 26
Strategic Defense Initiative (SDI), 175

Sullivan, Mark, 29, 30
Sununu, John, 172, 173, 174
Swanson, Claude, 34

Taft, Robert A., 125
Taft, William H., 11, 14–15, 35
Task Force on Regulatory Relief, 162, 163, 208
Task Force on Youth Opportunity, 107
Teheran Conference, 65
Teller, Edward, 140
Texas: and Garner, 45–46, 48, 53; and LBJ, 88, 94–95, 99; and Bush, 158, 166
Thatcher, Margaret, 172
Time, 113, 114
Timmons, Bascom, 47, 52
Travel, 173–74
Trilateral Commission, 158
Truly, Richard, 175
Truman, Bess, 69
Truman, Harry S.: impact on the presidency, 3, 169–70; candidate for vice president, 61–62, 66–68; political background, 64; duties as vice president, 69; and Barkley, 69–75; secondary sources, 220–21; primary sources, 231
Tully, Grace, 68
Twenty-fifth Amendment: and Eisenhower, 86, 204–5; and JFK, 106; passage and ratification, 122–23; and Agnew, 128; and Ford, 135, 138; and Rockefeller, 137, 138; and Quayle, 169; modification, 194–96; value, 199–200; general information, 216
Tyler, John, 1

Underwood, Oscar, 35
United Nations, 81, 164

Valenti, Jack, 113
Vance, Cyrus, 147
Vandenberg, Arthur, 48
"Veep": origin of the term, 72–73
Vice presidency: ambiguity of the office, 178, 183–84
Vice presidents: selection process, 9–10, 211–12, 194; travel, 93–94, 173–74; as crisis managers, 161–62; as successors

to the presidency, 167; relations with
the presidents, 167, 173, 183, 185,
198–99, 206; daily briefings, 172; public
images, 184; schedules, 191, 208; press
coverage, 198–99, 210; relations with
Congress, 206–7
Vietnam: and Humphrey, 112–14, 117,
118, 119, 188; and Agnew, 126, 129; and
Rockefeller, 142
Von Damm, Helene, 162
"Voodoo economics," 159, 162

Wage Stabilization Board, 72
Wagner, Robert, 104
Wagner Act, 49
Walker, Frank C., 66
Wallace, George, 126
Wallace, Henry A.: political background,
54–55; political liabilities, 55; and
Board of Economic Warfare, 55–56,
57, 61; and speeches, 56–57; and
Reconstruction Finance Corporation,
57–58; and FDR, 58–59, 60, 61; and
liberals, 59–60; campaign against
Wallace, 59–60; and 1944 nomination,

60–61; and Democratic National
Convention, 60; becomes secretary
of commerce, 61; and Humphrey, 62;
secondary sources, 219–20; primary
sources, 230–31
Walsh, Lawrence, 165
Warren, Charles, 34
Warren, Earl, 71
Watergate, 132, 137
Watson, Edwin M., 66
White, Paul Dudley, 204
White House, 198–99; west wing, 146,
159, 172, 173; physician's office, 195,
204–5
Wickenden, Elizabeth, 99
Wilkens, Roy, 94, 97
Wilson, Edith, 21
Wilson, Woodrow: and Marshall, 16–22;
and the campaign of 1920, 28; and
Coolidge, 29
Wood, Leonard, 25
World War I, 18, 22, 32

Yalta Conference, 69